SCHIRMER
PRONOUNCING

Pocket Manual
OF
Musical Terms

SCHIRMER PRONOUNCING

POCKET MANUAL OF MUSICAL TERMS

FIFTH EDITION

∽

EDITED BY
THEODORE BAKER

FOURTH EDITION REVISED BY
NICOLAS SLONIMSKY

FIFTH EDITION REVISED BY
LAURA KUHN

SCHIRMER BOOKS
An Imprint of Simon & Schuster Macmillan
New York
Prentice Hall International
London   Mexico City   New Delhi   Singapore   Sydney   Toronto

SCHIRMER BOOKS
An Imprint of Simon & Schuster Macmillan
1633 Broadway
New York, NY 10019-6785

Library of Congress Catalog Card Number: 95-31766

ISBN: 0-02-874567-1

Printed in the United States of America

Printing Number
 5 6 7 8 9 10

Library of Congress Cataloging-in-Publication Data

Schirmer pronouncing pocket manual of muscial terms / edited by
   Theodore Baker ; 4th ed. revised by Nicolas Slonimsky. — 5th ed. /
   revised by Laura Kuhn.
      p.   cm.
      1905 and 1947 editions published under title: A pronouncing pocket
   -manual of musical terms.
      ISBN 0-02-874567-1 (pbk. : alk paper)
      1. Music—Terminology. I. Baker, Theodore, 1851–1934.
   II. Slonimsky, Nicolas, 1894–   . III. Kuhn, Laura Diane.
   ML109.S35 1995
   780′.3—dc20
                                                            95-31766
                                                              CIP
                                                              MN

This paper meets the requirements of ANSI/NISO Z39.48-1992.

Contents

Preface

Compiling a pocket dictionary of musical terms at the turn into the 21st century is a bit like engaging in time travel—the compiler, like the reader in turn, moves through literally centuries of terms, each with its own relevance and use. Slam dancing and classical ballet, heterophony and time-brackets, coloratura and circular breathing, crumhorns and synthesizers . . . With each turn of the page, the reader is struck by a virtual panoply of musical worlds, and by the specialized language each seems to require.

The situation is not entirely confounding, however, for although few speak all of these languages, all speak some. Terms from the so-called "common practice" period, used with reference to the overarching musical development spanning Bach to Brahms, are surely the best known. Rhythm, meter, melody, harmony, as musical "descriptors," derive from this era, and continue to function as the basis for comparative understanding of musics across time.

Terms particular to both earlier and later times are usually less familiar. Musics of the pre-Christian era, like those of the Middle Ages and of the Renaissance, are little understood without knowledge of the parallel worlds to which they are closely allied. Music in these periods is frequently tied to liturgy, to poetry, to period instruments, and to social practices, all of which show a fundamental integration of music in the lives of individuals contemporary with their times.

Terms of the present pose particular challenges, reflecting an overtly philosophical approach to the making of music: an almost self-conscious abandonment of history, of the tried-and-true practices of the past, in favor of experimentation with untried methods and means. The reader needs, if not prolonged exposure to these developments, a willingness to expand the definition of music itself. And with greater and greater reliance of composers and performers alike upon electronics and sophisticated recording techniques, the reader is asked, again, to make connections to parallel worlds, here, most especially, to mathematics and physics.

The present edition, fifth in a series launched in 1905 by Theodore Baker and revised in subsequent editions by the revered (and irreverent) Russian-born American lexicographer Nicolas Slonimsky, covers it all. There are literally hundreds of terms, including many new additions from so-called "non-Western" musics, each defined in clear, succinct language and cross-referenced throughout. There's also a greatly revised "Noteworthy Musicians" section, equally inclusive in its coverage of individuals representing such diverse musical genres as classical, rock, and jazz.

All of which conspires to make one thing clear to even the most cursory of readers: there is no *one* music. This is true not only because history persists, but because the infusion of media so characteristic of the modern world brings with it an inevitable awareness of the musics of what were once (and not so long ago) exotic lands—Africa, Australia, Indonesia, among countless others. Music today is pluralism evidenced—encompassing multiculturalism and multimedia, to be sure—which may be another way of saying it is rich, noisy, diverse, and profuse.

Laura Kuhn
1995

Introduction

Elements of Notation

Notation is a system of signs used in writing music. The written signs for the time value (length, duration) of musical tones are called *notes*; the written signs for pauses (intervals of silence) between the tones are called *rests*.

Notes and Rests

Whole note o	Half note 𝅗𝅥	Quarter note ♩
Whole rest ▬	Half rest ▬	Quarter rest 𝄽
Eighth note ♪	16th note ♬	32nd note 𝅘𝅥𝅰
	64th note 𝅘𝅥𝅱	
Eighth rest 𝄾	16th rest 𝄿	32nd rest 𝅀
	64th rest 𝅁	

Whole note o = 2 𝅗𝅥, or 4 ♩, or 8 ♪, or 16 ♬,

   or 32 𝅘𝅥𝅰, or 64 𝅘𝅥𝅱

Half note 𝅗𝅥 = 2 ♩, or 4 ♪, or 8 ♬, or 16 𝅘𝅥𝅰, or 32 𝅘𝅥𝅱

Quarter note ♩ = 2 ♪, or 4 ♬, or 8 𝅘𝅥𝅰, or 16 𝅘𝅥𝅱

Eighth note ♪ = 2 ♬, or 4 𝅘𝅥𝅰, or 8 𝅘𝅥𝅱

Sixteenth note ♬ = 2 𝅘𝅥𝅰, or 4 𝅘𝅥𝅱

Thirty-second note 𝅘𝅥𝅰 = 2 𝅘𝅥𝅱

The Staff

The *staff* consists of five parallel horizontal lines. Notes are written on the lines, or in the spaces between. For higher or lower tones, additional short lines are provided, called *leger lines*.

—
— Leger lines

5th line ——————————————
4th line —————————————— 4th space
3rd line —————————————— 3rd space
2nd line —————————————— 2nd space
1st line —————————————— 1st space

—
— Leger lines

The Clefs

A *clef* is a sign written at the head (beginning) of the staff to fix the position of one note. The most common clefs are

the *G* clef
(Treble Clef)

fixing the place of the note *g*¹

the *F* clef
(Bass Clef)

fixing the place of the note *f*; and

the *C* clef, which designates a line on the staff as c¹ (middle C); it acquires a different name according to the line used:

Tenor Clef Alto Clef Soprano Clef

See next entry, SCALES.

The Scales

The staff and clefs together fix the pitch of the notes, showing whether they are high or low. A series of eight successive notes on the staff forms what is called a *scale*. To name the notes of the scale, we use the first seven letters of the alphabet, *A B C D E F G*. Scales are named after the notes on which they begin, which is called the *keynote*. The scale of *C*, written in whole notes, in the bass and treble clefs, is as follows:

The *C* written on the leger line just below the treble staff and just above the bass staff, is called Middle C.

The notes in the same vertical line are of the same pitch and have the same name. For ordinary purposes, any note marked *C (c)* is called simply "C." But, in order to fix the place which any given note occupies among all the others (that is, to fix its "absolute pitch"), the whole range of musical tones is divided into sections of seven notes each, called "octaves," and lettered and named as shown in the Table on page **xii**.

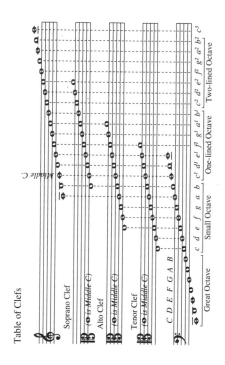

N.B.—The next octave below the Great Octave is the "Contra-octave": below that again is the "Double Contra-octave."

Chromatic Signs

The *chromatic signs* are set before notes to raise and lower their pitch.

The *sharp* ♯ raises its note a semitone;

The *flat* ♭ lowers its note a semitone;

The *natural* ♮ restores its note to the natural pitch on the staff (without chromatic signs);

The *double sharp* × raises its note two semitones;

The *double flat* ♭♭ lowers its note two semitones;

The sign ♮♯ restores a double sharped note to a sharped note;

The sign ♮♭ restores a double flatted note to a flatted note.

The Intervals

An *interval* is the difference in pitch between two notes. In measuring an interval, it is customary to take the lower note as the basis, and to measure up to the higher note. When the measurement is made downward, the interval is called "inverted."

Diatonic Intervals of the Major Scale

All Standard Intervals and Their Inversions

The Keys

A *key* is a scale employed harmonically, that is, employed to form chords and successions of chords. On the keynote *C*, or on any other note, two different species of scale or key may be built up:

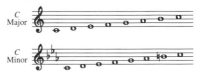

Such a key or scale is called *major* when its third and sixth are major intervals; it is *minor* when its third and sixth are minor intervals. The succession of intervals in every major key is the same as that in *C* major; in every minor key, as in *C* minor. To adjust the intervals properly, chromatic signs are employed.

Table of Major Keys

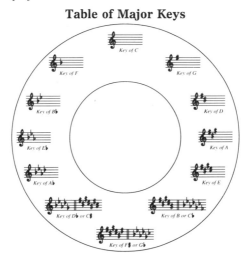

It will be seen, on passing around the circle in either direction, that the keynotes of the successive keys always follow each other at the interval of a perfect fifth; hence, this circle of keys, ending where it began, is called the *circle of fifths*.

Chords

A *chord* is formed by a succession of from three to five different tones, built up in intervals of diatonic thirds from a given tone, or *root*. A three-tone chord is a *triad*; a four-tone chord is a *seventh chord* (chord of the *seventh*); a five-tone chord is a *ninth chord* (chord of the *ninth*).

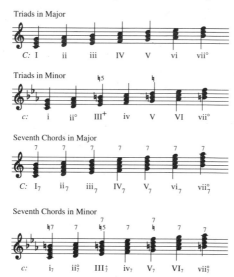

Ninth chords

When the root of the chord is the lowest tone, the chord is in the fundamental position; when some other tone is the lowest, the chord is inverted. Each triad has two inversions; each seventh chord has three.

Inversions of Triad   Inversions of Seventh Chord

The first inversion of a triad is called a 6 chord.

The second inversion of a triad is called a $^6_4$ chord.

The first inversion of a seventh chord is called a $^6_5$ chord.

The second inversion of a seventh chord is called a $^4_3$ chord.

The third inversion of a seventh chord is called a 2 chord.

Time Signatures

The *time signature* appears after the clef, at the beginning of the staff; the lower figure shows the *kind* of notes taken as the unit of measure, while the upper figure shows the number of these notes that can fit in a measure, and the groupings of beats.

For instance **3/4** (3/4 time) means "three quarter notes to the measure":

12/16 (12/16 time) means "twelve sixteenth notes to the measure":

Rules for Pronouncing
German, French, and Italian

VOWELS:

The vowels are often not pronounced as in English. The system of pronunciation employed in this manual is explained below.

ah is the broad *a* in *father*.

ăh is the same sound, only not dwelt upon; like *ah* in the college cheer "*rah! rah! rah!*" Never pronounce *ăh* like the short English *ă* in *bat*.

ă is the short English *a*, as in *bat*.

â is like *a* in *bare*.

ä is nearly like *â*, but closer. Short *ä* is nearly like *e* in *bet*, but more open.

ā is nearly like *a* in *bate*; only the long English *a* ends with a soft sound like short *ĭ*, called a "vanish," caused by slightly raising the root of the tongue (ā^{i}); whereas the long "Continental" *a* has no vanish.

ĕh is the short sound of long *a* (closer than *e* in *bet*).

ĕ is short *e*, as in *bet*.

ē is long *e*, like *ee* in *beet*.

ī is long *i*, as in *bite*.

ĭ is short *i*, as in *bit*, though sometimes shaded towards *ee*.

oh is like *o* in *bode*; only the long English *o* ends with a soft sound like *u* in *bull*, called a "vanish," caused by drawing the lips together (ō^{u}); whereas the long "Continental" *o* has no vanish.

ŏh is short *o*, like the first *o* in *opinion*. Never pronounce it like the short English *o* in *blot*.

ô is the so-called broad Italian *o*, pronounced like *aw* in *law*.

ö is a sound not found in English. To pronounce long *ö*, set the lips as if to say "oh," and then say "*ā*" (as in *bate*), keeping the lips fixed in the first position; for short *ö*, set the lips as before, but then say "*ĕ*" (as in *bet*), keeping the lips fixed in the first position.

oo is like long *oo* in *boot*.

oŏ is like short *oo* in *book*.

ŭ is short *u*, as in *but*.

ûh is like the *u* in *fur*.

ü is a sound not found in English. To prounounce long ü, set
the lips as if to say "oo" (as in *boot*), and then say "ee"
(as in *beet*), keeping the lips fixed in the first position; for
short ü, set the lips as before, but then say "ĭ" (as in *bit*),
keeping the lips fixed in the first position. (This ü, long or
short, is the so-called *French* u.)

DIPHTHONGS:

ahü represents the German *äu* or *eu*; pronounce as one syllable quickly drawn together, accent on the "ah" (ah͜'ü). It
is somewhat like the English *oi* in *boy* (aw͜'i).

wăh represents the French *oi*; pronounce as if written
o ăh, in one syllable quickly drawn together, accent on the
"ah" (o͜ ăh').

ow is like *ow* in *brow*.

CONSONANTS:

The consonants are usually pronounced as in English. The
following signs need explanation:

yh represents a sound not found in English, namely, the *soft*
German *ch*. Set the tongue as if to pronounce "ye," and
then breathe (whisper) "he" through the tongue and hard
palate (see ALLMÄHLICH).

h represents a sound not found in English, namely the *hard*
German *ch*. It is merely a rough breathing, as if one were
trying gently to clear one's throat. Never pronounce it like
k, unless explicitly so marked.

ngᵏ represents the sound *ng* at the end of German words,
which finish, after the usual *ng*-sound (*ng* as in *ring*), with
a light *k*-sound (see AUFSCHWUNG).

n represents a sound not found in English, namely, the French
nasal *n*. To get the correct nasal sound, the *n* must be
pronounced, not *after* the vowel, but *together with* the
vowel; that is, the vowel must be spoken through the nose,
thus becoming a nasal vowel. Never pronounce like "ang,"

"ong," etc., as the pronunciation is often printed; there is no *ng*-sound about the French nasal *n*. For example, to get the sound of *ain*, as in the French word *main* (mănn), first sound "n," setting the tongue firmly against the hard palate so that the vocal air (air vibrating with tone) passes through the nose instead of between the lips; then, letting the "n" still vibrate through the nose, drop the tongue and instantly blend the vowel "ă" (as in *bat*) with the "n." This *blending* of "ă" and "n" gives the exact sound desired, if cut off short like a staccato trumpet tone. To say "main," simply put an "m" before the nasal vowel "ănn." The nasal vowels "ähn" and "öhn" are obtained similarly.

r is to be pronounced with a roll, the tip of the tongue against the hard palate.

s must be pronounced *sharp*, wherever it occurs in the marked pronunciation; *soft* s is represented by z.

zh represents the z in *azure*.

The consonants *d* and *t* are usually formed, in the Continental languages, by touching the root of the upper front teeth with the tip of the tongue. To make this point clear, first pronounce the English word "dry" in the ordinary way, tip of tongue against the hard palate; then pronounce the German "drei," but taking the *dr* with tip of tongue against the root of the upper front teeth. Form *l* in the same manner.

The German *w* is a compound of the English *w* and *v*; i.e., to get it right, the lips must almost close and, *at the same time*, the lower lip must lightly touch the upper front teeth.

N.B.—All accents (vowel marks) found on the key words, such as à, ä, é, è, ê, ö, ü, etc., belong to the words as correctly written in their respective languages.

Comparative Table of Tempo Marks

CLASS I
INDICATING A STEADY RATE OF SPEED

Larghissimo, molto largo
Largo (broad, stately)
  Largamente
  Larghetto
Grave (heavy, dragging)
Lento (slow)
  Adagissimo
Adagio (slow, tranquil)
  Adagietto
  Andantino

> Group I.
> General
> signification
> of terms is
> SLOW.

Andante (moving, going along)
Moderato
  Allegretto
  Allegramente
Allegro (brisk, lively) [con moto,
vivace] [agitato, appassionato]
Presto (rapid) [con fuoco, veloce]
  Prestissimo

> Group II.
> General
> signification
> of terms is
> FAST.

CLASS II
INDICATING ACCELERATION

Accelerando	(with increasing rapidity)
Stringendo Affrettando Incalzando	(swiftly accelerating, usually with a *crescendo*)
Doppio movimento	(twice as fast)
Più mosso Più moto Veloce	(a steady rate of speed, *faster* than preceding movement)

CLASS III
INDICATING A SLACKENING IN SPEED

Rallentando
Ritardando
Allargando
Tardando   (gradually growing slower)
Slentando
Strascinando

Molto meno mosso ($\flat = \sigma$ del movimento precedente)
                    (half as fast)

Ritenuto
Meno mosso   (a steady rate of speed, *slower* than pre-
Meno moto   ceding movement)

Calando
Deficiendo
Mancando
Morendo   (growing slower and softer)
Sminuendo
Smorzando

Musical Terms

A

A. 1. (Ger. *A*; Fr. and It. *La*). The SIXTH TONE and DEGREE in the typical DIATONIC SCALE of *C* MAJOR. 2. In musical THEORY, capital *A* stands for the *A*-major TRIAD, small *a* for the *a*-MINOR triad. 3. In Italian, *a* (ăh), in French, *à* (ăh) signifies to, at, for, by, in, etc. 4. In this *Manual*, an *-a* following an Italian word means that in the feminine form of the word *a* takes the place of the masculine ending *o*.

Ab (Ger., ăhp). Off (in ORGAN music).

ABA. A symbolic representation for TERNARY FORM, in which the first statement (*A*) is repeated after the second (*B*). Most classical SONGS follow this formula. *ABA* is, therefore, also known as SONG FORM.

A ballata (It., ăh băhl-lah'tăh). In BALLAD style.

Abandon, avec (Fr., ăh-vek' ăh-băhn-dŏhn'). ABBANDONO, CON.

A battuta (It., ăh băht-too'tăh). "With the BEAT"; in strict TIME.

Abbandono, con (It., kŏhn ăhb-băn-doh'noh). Yielding wholly to emotion; with a burst of passion; carried away by feeling.

Abbandonare (It., ăhb-băhn-dŏh-nah'rĕh). To abandon, to quit. *Senza abbandonare la corda*, without quitting the STRING.

Abbellimenti (It., ăhb-bĕl-lē-men'tē). EMBELLISHMENTS.

Abendmusik (Ger., ăh'bend'moo-zĭk). Literally "evening music."

A bene placito (It., ăh bâ'nĕh plah'chē-tŏh). At pleasure; meaning that the TEMPO may be altered, GRACES or CADEN-

1

zas added, or that certain specified instruments may be
used, or not, at the performer's pleasure.

Aber (Ger., ah'behr). But.

Abgemessen (Ger., ăhp'gĕ-mes'sen). Measured; in strict TIME.

Abgestossen (Ger., ăhp'gĕ-shtoh'sen). "Struck off"; detached;
see STACCATO.

Ablösen (Ger., ahb'lö-zen). To loosen; to separate one NOTE
from another.

Abnehmend (Ger., ăhp'nā'ment). DIMINUENDO.

Abschnitt (Ger., ahb'shnitt). SECTION.

Abschwellen (Ger., ăhp'shvel'len). DECRESCENDO.

Absetzen (Ger., ahb'zet-zen). To separate; to detach.

Absolute music. Music without extramusical connotation.
See PROGRAM MUSIC.

Absolute pitch. The ability to name instantly and correctly
any NOTE struck on the PIANO KEYBOARD or played on an
instrument. This is an innate faculty, which appears in
a musical child at a very early age, distinct from RELATIVE
PITCH, common among all musicians, in which an INTER-
VAL is named in relation to a previously played note.
Absolute pitch is rare, even among professional musicians and is not a sure indication of great musical talent.
Also known as PERFECT PITCH.

Abstract music. See ABSOLUTE MUSIC; PROGRAM MUSIC.

Abwechseln (Ger., ăhp'vek'seln). To alternate. *Mit abwech-
selnden Manualen* (măh-noo-ah'len), with alternating
MANUALS.

A cappella (It., ăh căhp-pel'lăh). "As in chapel," that is, in
the church style; CHORAL singing without instrumental AC-
COMPANIMENT.

A capriccio (It., ăh căhp-prit'choh). "As a caprice"; according
to one's own fancy.

Accarezzevole (It., ăhk-kăh-**r**et-tsă'vŏh-lĕh). Caressingly, coaxingly.

Accelerando (It., ăht-cheh-lĕh-**r**ăhn'dŏh). "Accelerating," growing faster.

Accelerato (It., ăht-chĕh-lĕh-**r**ah'tŏh). "Accelerated," livelier, faster.

Accent. A stress, or added emphasis given to a NOTE.

Accento, con (It., kŏhn ăht-chen'tŏh). Accented, marked. *Accentate* (-tah'tĕh; plural form of *accentata*, or imperative), accent the NOTES.

Accentuando (It., ăht-chen-tŏŏ-ăhn'dŏh). Accenting.

Accentué (Fr., ăhk-sahnt-tyoo-a'). Accented.

Acciaccato,-a (It., ăht-chăh-kăh'tŏh,-tăh). Vehemently.

Acciaccatura (It., ăht-chăh-kăh-too'**r**ăh). 1. A short accented APPOGGIATURA. 2. A NOTE a SECOND above, and struck with, the PRINCIPAL note, and instantly released.

Acciaio (It., ăh-chăh'yo). "Steel." *Instrumento d'acciaio*, "instrument of steel," is Mozart's designation for the GLOCKENSPIEL part in *The Magic Flute*.

Accidental. Any CHROMATIC SIGN not found in the KEY SIGNATURE, occurring in the course of a PIECE.

Accompagnamento (It., ăhk-kohm-păhn-yăh'men'tŏh). ACCOMPANIMENT.

Accompagnato (It., ăhk-kohm-pahn-yah'tŏh). 1. Accompanied. 2. A RECITATIVE with ENSEMBLE ACCOMPANIMENT.

Accompagnement (Fr., ăh-kŏhm-păhn-yŭ-măhn'). ACCOMPANIMENT.

Accompanied fugue. A fugal form sometimes occurring in ORATORIOS, in which the CHORAL FUGUE is accompanied by instruments.

Accompaniment. Any PART or parts that complement the voices or instruments bearing the principal part or parts in a musical COMPOSITION. It is AD LIBITUM when the piece can be performed without it, and OBBLIGATO when it is necessary to the piece. *Additional accompaniments* are parts added to a composition by some other person than its original author. *Accompaniment of the scale* is a series of CHORDS used to harmonize the ascending or descending DIATONIC SCALE.

Accopiato (It., ăhk-kŏp-pē-ăh'tŏh). Tied, bound.

Accord (Fr., ah-kor'). CHORD.

Accordando (It., ăhk-kor-dăhn'dŏh). "Accordant," in tune. In comic stage scenes, it means that the tuning of an instrument is imitated by the orchestra.

Accordatura (It., ăhk-kor-dăh-too'răh). The "tuning," or series of tones according to which a stringed instrument is tuned; g-d^1-a^1-e^2 is the *accordatura* of the VIOLIN.

Accorder (Fr., ah-kor-day'). To TUNE.

Accordion. A FREE-REED instrument invented by Damian, of Vienna, in 1829. The elongated BODY serves as a bellows, to be drawn out and pushed together. Early *button accordions* featured two or three rows of buttons played by the right hand, featuring two or more SCALES (i.e., a b-c button accordion featured the B MAJOR and C MAJOR SCALES). On the other end of the instrument, two or more chord buttons provided appropriate harmonies. In the 1920s, the *piano accordion* was introduced, with a full CHROMATIC KEYBOARD arranged like that of a PIANO, played by the right hand, with buttons on the left to offer CHORD ACCOMPANIMENTS. Various STOPS were added for special effects and for doubling or tripling scale NOTES. See CONCERTINA; MELODEON.

Accordo (It., ăhk-kor'dŏh). CHORD.

Accoupler (Fr., ahk-koo-play'). "To couple," as in ORGAN playing.

Achtelnote (Ger., ah'-tel-no'tay). EIGHTH NOTE.

Acid rock. A 1960s version of loud, primarily instrumental ROCK music meant to simulate the experience of an LSD "trip." The spiritual grandfather of HEAVY METAL.

Acoustic (ăh-koo'stĭk) **color**. 1. The TIMBRE (character or quality) of a musical TONE. 2. Acoustic music generally refers to music produced by instruments which are not ELECTRONIC.

Acoustics. Musical acoustics is the science of musical tones, applicable to matters of auditory perception (psychoacoustics), sound sources, and rooms.

Action. In KEYBOARD instruments, the mechanism set in motion by the player's fingers (KEYS) or feet (ORGAN PEDALS). In the harp, the "action" (a set of pedals) does not directly produce the sound, but changes the instrument's tuning by shortening the strings by a SEMITONE or WHOLE TONE.

Action music. Music in which the actions of performers equal in importance the sounds they make.

Action song. A children's song in which bodily movements depict the action of the words, such as folding the hands and closing the eyes to represent sleep, fluttering of the fingers downward to represent rain, crossing the arms in a circular movement to represent the sun, flapping the hands to imitate a bird in flight, etc.

Act-tune. Music played between the acts of a drama. See ENTR'ACTE.

Acute. High in PITCH, sharp, shrill; opposed to GRAVE.

Adagietto (It., ăh-dăh-jet'tŏh). 1. A MOVEMENT slightly faster than ADAGIO. 2. A short ADAGIO.

Adagio (It., ăh-dăh'jŏh). Slow, leisurely; a slow MOVEMENT. *Adagio adagio, a. assai, a. molto,* very slow; *a. non molto* or *non tanto,* not too slow.

Adagissimo (It., ăh-dăh-jis'sē-mŏh). Extremely slow.

Adaptation. An ARRANGEMENT.

Added seventh. A MINOR or MAJOR SEVENTH added to the concluding MAJOR TRIAD. In JAZZ, the minor seventh (e.g., *C, E, G, B* flat) is one of the BLUE NOTES (along with the flatted third) and is characteristic of the BLUES. Much more dissonant is the major seventh in a TONIC major triad at the end of a piece, often played in TREMOLO by jazz pianists.

Added sixth. A SIXTH added to the MAJOR TONIC TRIAD, usually at the end of a PHRASE, and treated as a CONSONANCE. First used by Debussy and composers early in the 20th century, the added SIXTH CHORD (*C, E, G, A* in *C* major) became extremely popular in JAZZ PIANO playing.

Additional keys. Those above f^3 on the PIANO.

Addolorato (It., ăhd-dŏh-lŏh-rah'tŏh). Plaintive; in a style expressing grief.

Adel, mit (Ger., mit ah'del). "With nobility"; in a lofty style.

À demi-jeu (Fr., ăh dŭ-mē-zhö'). With half the power of the instrument.

À demi-voix (Fr., ăh dŭ-mē-vwăh'). MEZZA VOCE.

À deux (Fr., ăh dö'). For two; *à deux mains,* for two hands. See DUE.

Adjunct. Closely related, as one KEY or SCALE to another. *Adjunct note,* an unaccented AUXILIARY NOTE not essential to the HARMONY.

Ad libitum (L., ăhd lĭ'bĭ-tŭm, "at will"). A direction signifying that (1) performers may employ the TEMPO or expression that suits them; or (2) any vocal or instrumental PART so marked may be left out, if desired. *Cadenza ad libitum* means that a given CADENZA may be performed or not, or another substituted for it, at the performer's pleasure.

A due (It., ăh doo'ĕh). DUE.

A dur (Ger., ah door'). *A* major.

Aeolian harp or **lyre**. A STRINGED INSTRUMENT sounded by the wind. It is a narrow, oblong wooden box, with low BRIDGES at either end, across which are stretched a number of GUT STRINGS. The harp is placed in an open window, or some other aperture where a draft of air will sweep the strings.

Aeolian mode. A MODE corresponding to the progression from *a* to *a* on the white keys of the piano.

Aerophones. A class of musical instruments that produce their sound by the vibration of air, i.e., FLUTE, CLARINET.

Affabilmente (It., ăhf-făh-bĕl-men'tĕh). Sweetly and gracefully; suavely.

Affannato (It., ăhf-făh-nah'tŏh). Uneasily, distressfully.

Affannosamente (It., ăhf-făh-noh-săh-men'-tĕh). Anxiously, restlessly.

Affannoso (It., ăhf-făh-nŏh'sŏh). Anxious, restless.

Affettuoso (It., ăhf-fet-tŏŏ-oh'sŏh). With passion, emotion, feeling; very expressively; tenderly.

Affezione, con (It., kŏhn ăhf-fĕh-tsē-oh'nĕh). In a style expressive of tender emotion.

Afflitto (It., ăhf-flēt'tŏh). Melancholy, sad.

Afflizione, con (It., kŏhn ăhf-flē-tsē-oh'nĕh). Sorrowfully, mournfully.

Affrettando (It., ăhf-fret-tăhn'dŏh). Hurrying.

Affrettare (It., ăhf-fret-tah'rĕh). To hasten. *Senza affretare*, without hastening.

Affrettato (It., ăhf-fret-tah′tŏh). Hurried. *Tempo più affrettato*, at a swifter pace.

Affrettoso (It., ăhf-fret-toh′sŏh). Hurriedly.

A fior di labbra (It., ăh fē-or′dē lăhb′brăh). Very lightly and softly sung or spoken.

After beat. An ending to a TRILL, comprising two NOTES, the lower AUXILIARY and the PRINCIPAL.

After note. 1. Unaccented APPOGGIATURA. 2. The unaccented NOTE of a pair.

After-striking. An accompanying NOTE or CHORD, played in the BASS REGISTER, that comes after the MELODY NOTE. Opposite of ANTICIPATION.

Agevolmente (It., ăh-jā-vŏhl-men′tĕh). Easily, lightly.

Aggiustatamente (It., ăh-jŏŏs-tăh-tăh-men′-tĕh). Strictly in TIME.

Aggregate. 1. The collected NOTES in a SERIAL COMPOSITION representing one instance of a PITCH CLASS. 2. A collection of notes heard at the same time.

Agiatamente (It., ăh-jă-tăh-men′-teh). Easily, indolently.

Agilità (It., ăh-jē-lē-tah′); **Agilité** (Fr., ah-zhē-lē-tā′). Agility, sprightliness, vivacity. *Con agilità*, in a light and lively style.

Agilmente (It., ăh-jēl-men′tĕh). Lightly, vivaciously.

Agitamento (It., ăh-jē-tăh-men′tŏh). Agitation.

Agitatamente (It., ăh-jē-tăh-tăh-men′tĕh). Excitedly, agitatedly.

Agitato (It., ăh-jē-tah′tŏh). Agitated. *Agitato con passione*, passionately agitated.

Agitazione, con (It., kŏhn ăh-jē-tăh-tsē-oh′-nĕh). With agitation, agitatedly.

Agogic. From the Greek verb, "to lead"; applied musically, indicates slight deviations from the main RHYTHM.

Agraffe (ăh-grähf′). In the PIANO, a small metallic support of a string, between BRIDGE and PIN, serving to check vibration in that part.

Agréments (Fr., ah-grā-mahn′). Plural noun for ORNAMENTS and GRACE NOTES, as used in BAROQUE MUSIC.

Air (Fr., är). Air, MELODY, TUNE; also, a SONG. *Airs detachés*, single NUMBERS taken from OPERAS, etc.

Aïs (Ger., ah′iss). *A* sharp.

Aisis (Ger., ah′iss-iss). *A* double sharp.

À l'aise (Fr., ah lehz′). "At ease"; in a relaxed manner.

À la mesure (Fr., ăh lăh mŭ-zür′). In strict TIME.

Alberti bass. A BASS in BROKEN CHORDS, like

named after Domenico Alberti, who frequently used this effect.

Alborada (Sp., ăhl-bŏ-räh′-dăh). Type of Spanish music; originally a morning SERENADE. AUBADE.

Albumblatt (Ger., ăhl′-bŭm-blăht); **Album-leaf**. Title of a short and (usually) simple vocal or instrumental PIECE.

Alcuno,-a (It., ăhl-koo′noh,-năh). Some; certain. *Con alcuna licenza*, "with a certain freedom" (as regards TEMPO).

Aleatory. A modern word as applied to music, from the Latin *alea*, "a game of dice." In aleatory music, rhythmic values and even NOTES themselves are subject to multiple choices by the performer. Sometimes only DURATION is specified by the composer; in extreme cases, even the length of the piece itself is aleatory. Aleatory music is sometimes also called CHANCE MUSIC.

Aliquot strings. Additional strings placed above the regular strings of the PIANO and tuned according to SYMPATHETIC VIBRATIONS so as to reinforce the tone of the instrument.

Al fine (It., ăhl fē-něh). "To finish"; used in phrases like *Dal segno al fine*, "from the sign to the end marked *Fine*."

All', Alla (It., ăhl, ăhl'-läh). To the, in the, at the, etc.; in the style of, like.

Alla breve (It., brâ'věh). 𝄵 In modern music, a METER of 2/2, i.e. two BEATS per MEASURE with the HALF NOTE carrying the beat; also called CUT TIME. The implication is of a faster TEMPO than 4/4.

Alla caccia (It., căht'chäh). In the hunting style.

Alla camera (It., kah'měh-räh). In the style of CHAMBER MUSIC.

Alla marcia (It., mahr'chäh). In MARCH style.

Alla militare (It., mē-lē-tah-rěh). In military style.

Alla moderna (It., mŏh-dâr'näh). In modern style.

Allargando (It., ăhl-lar-gähn'dŏh). Growing slower.

Allagare, senza (It., sen'tsäh ăhl-lar-gah'rěh). Without slackening speed.

Allargate (It., -gah'těh). Go slower.

Alla russa (It., rŏŏs'säh). In the Russian style.

Alla scozzese (It., skŏht-tsä-zěh). In the Scottish style.

Alla siciliana (It., sē-chēl-yäh'näh). In the Sicilian style.

Alla stretta (It., strě'täh). 1. Growing faster and faster. 2. In the style of a STRETTA (or STRETTO).

Alla tromba (It., trôm'bäh). Like a TRUMPET.

Alla turca (It., toor'käh). In the Turkish style.

Alla veneziana (It., věh-něh-tsē-ah'näh). In the Venetian style (like a BARCAROLE).

Alla zingara (It., tsin'gäh-räh). In the style of Gypsy music.

Alla zoppa (It., tsôp'päh). Lamely, haltingly; in SYNCOPATED style.

Allegramente (It., ăhl-lĕh-grăh-men'tĕh). Nimbly, lightly, gaily, vivaciously.

Allegrettino (It., ăhl-lĕh-gret-tē'nŏh). 1. A short ALLEGRETTO MOVEMENT. 2. A TEMPO slower than ALLEGRETTO.

Allegretto (It., ăhl-lĕh-gret'tŏh). Quite lively; moderately fast (faster than ANDANTE, slower than ALLEGRO).

Allegria, con (It., kŏhn ăhl-lĕh-grē'äh). With liveliness, vivacity.

Allegrissimo (It., ăhl-lĕh-gris'sē-mŏh). Very rapidly.

Allegro (It., ăhl-lā'grŏh). Lively, brisk, rapid. An Allegro (MOVEMENT) is not quite as fast as a PRESTO. *Allegro assai, a. di molto,* very fast (usually faster than the foregoing movement); *a. di bravura,* a technically difficult PIECE or passage to be executed swiftly and boldly; *a. giusto,* a movement the rapidity of which is suited to its subject; *a. risoluto,* rapidly and energetically; *a. ma non troppo* (-măh nŏhn trŏp'pŏh), fast, but not too fast.

Allein (Ger., ăhl-līn'). Alone; only.

Alleluia. The Latin form of Hallelujah ("Praise the Lord!") as used in the Roman Catholic service.

Allemanda (It., ăhl-lĕh-măhn'däh); **Allemande** (Fr., ăhl-l'-mahn'd). 1. A German dance in 3/4 TIME, like the LÄNDLER. 2. A lively German dance in 2/4 time. 3. A MOVEMENT in the SUITE (either the first, or following the PRELUDE) in 4/4 time and moderate TEMPO (ANDANTINO).

Allentamento (It., ăhl-len-täh-men'tŏh). Slowness.

Allentato (It., ăhl-len-tah'tŏh). Slower.

All' espagnuola (It., ăhl ĕh-spăhn-yô'läh). In the Spanish style.

All' ingliese (It., ăhl in-glā'zĕh). In the English style.

All' italiana (It., ăhl ē-tăh-lē-ah'năh). In the Italian style.

All-interval set. A 12-NOTE SET in which every INTERVAL is represented.

Allmählich (Ger., ăhl-mä'līyh). Gradually, by degrees. Also spelled **allmählig, allmälig**.

Al loco (It., ăhl lô'kŏh). "To the place"; a direction following "*8va*," meaning "perform the music as written." Also directs a violinist to return to a former POSITION after a SHIFT.

Allongé (Fr., ăhl'lohn-zhā'). Prolonged stroke (of the BOW).

Allontanando(si) (It., ăhl-lōhn-tăh-năhn'dŏh[-sē]). Withdrawing; dying away.

All' ottava (It., ăhl ŏht-tah'văh). "At the OCTAVE"; meaning, "play the notes an octave higher than written." The sign *8va*--------------- or *8*----------------- is usually employed.

All'unisono (It., ăhl oo-nē'sŏh-nŏh). In UNISON (or OCTAVES).

Alma, con (It., kŏhn ăhl'măh). With soul, spirit; loftily; ardently.

Alphorn. A very long Swiss HORN used by shepherds in the Alps to call the sheep back home at sunset.

Al segno (It., ăhl sen'yoh). "To the sign," directing the performer to go on playing until the sign 𝄋.

Alt (from the It., *alto*). Notes "in alt" are those of the next OCTAVE above *f²*. NOTES in the OCTAVE higher than this are said to be "in ALTISSIMO."

Alt (Ger., ăhlt). ALTO (VOICE or PART).

Alt-clarinet. An alto CLARINET. See ALTO.

Altered chords. CHORDS containing CHROMATIC alterations of chords properly belonging to the TONALITY of the music; also called *chromatic chords*.

Alterezza (It., ăhl-tĕh-**ret**'săh). Pride, loftiness.

Alternando (It., ăhl-târ-nahn'dŏh). Alternating, alternatively.

Alternativo (It., ăhl-târ-năh-tē'vŏh). Alternative, or, rather, a contrasting section in dance FORMS, such as a TRIO in a MINUET.

Alt-horn. The ALTO SAXHORN.

Altieramente (It., ăhl-tē-ĕh-**r**ăh-men'tĕh). In a lofty, majestic style.

Altíssimo (It., ăhl-tis'sĕ-mŏh). Highest. See ALTO.

Alto (from the It., *alto*). 1. The deeper of the two main divisions of women's or boys' voices, the SOPRANO being the higher. Also called *contralto*. Ordinary COMPASS from *g* to *f²*; in voices of great range, down to *d* and up to *c²*, or even higher. 2. An instrument of similar compass; as the ALT-HORN. 3. The COUNTERTENOR voice. 4. The VIOLA, or TENOR VIOLIN.

Alto,-a (It., ăhl'tŏh,-tăh). High. *Alta viola*, tenor VIOLIN; *ottava alta*, an OCTAVE higher.

Alto clef. A *C*-CLEF on the third line of the STAFF.

Altro,-a (It., ăhl-**tr**ŏh,-**tr**ăh). Other; *altri, altre*, others.

Alzamento (It., ăhl-tsăh-men'tŏh). A raising or lifting.

Alzando (It., ăhl-tsăhn'dŏh). Raising. *Alzando un po' la voce*, raising the voice a little.

Amabile (It., ăh-mah'bē'lĕh). Sweet, tender, gentle.

Amabilità, con (It., kŏhn ăh-măh-bē-lē-tah'). With sweetness; tenderly.

Amarezza, con (It., kŏhn ăh-măh-**ret**'săh). Bitterly; mournfully, grievingly.

Amarissimo (It., ăh-măh-**ris**'sĕ-mŏh). Very bitterly, with great anguish.

Amaro (It., ăh-măh'-**r**ŏh). Grief, bitterness.

Amateur (Fr., ăh-măh-tör'). A "lover" of art, who, while possessing an understanding for and a certain practical knowledge of it, does not pursue it as a profession.

Ambitus. In the music of the Middle Ages, the range of SCALE DEGREES comprising a given MODE; also, the range of a voice, instrument, or PIECE.

Ambrosian chant. The system of liturgical singing connected with the practice established by St. Ambrose in the 4th century. Its structure is much freer than that of the GREGORIAN CHANT that followed two centuries later, and there are some "modern" applications (such as very long CADENZAS, wandering from one MODE to another, etc.) that are attractive to contemporary musicians.

Amen. "So be it"; the concluding word in a prayer. Sometimes an Amen section in an ORATORIO is extended so as to become a concluding CHORUS of considerable length.

American organ. REED ORGAN.

Ametric. Literally, without METER; lacking a regular, sustained PULSE.

A mezza aria (It., ăh-med'zăh ah're̅-ăh). Halfway between an ARIA and a RECITATIVE.

A mezza voce (It., voh'chĕh). With half the power of the voice (or instrument).

A moll (Ger., ah mŏhl'). *A* minor.

Amore, con (It., kŏhn ăh-moh're̅h). Amorously; lovingly, fondly, devotedly, tenderly.

Amoroso (It., ăh-mŏh-roh'sŏh). Amorous; loving, fond.

Amplifier. Electric device used in all reproducing sound systems to increase volume.

Amplitude. The widest disturbance in a VIBRATION; the scientific correlate to the sensation of loudness.

Amplitude modulation (AM). Change made to the AMPLITUDE of a sound wave enabling information transfer to an electromagnetic wave.

Anacrusis (Gk., ăn-ŭ-kroo'sĭs). Unaccented syllables beginning a verse of poetry. In music, the weak BEAT, or weak part of a MEASURE, with which a PIECE or PHRASE may begin. See AUFTAKT.

Analysis. The study of musical STRUCTURE and FORM.

Anapest. A metrical foot of three syllables, two short and one long: ⌣⌣–.

Ancor or **Ancora** (It., ăhn-kohr',-răh). Again, also, yet, still, ever. *Ancora più mosso*, still faster; *ancora piano*, continue singing (or playing) softly; *ancora più piano*, still more softly.

Andächtig (It., ăhn'děyh'tĭyh). With devotion; devoutly.

Andamento (It., ăhn-dăh-men'-tŏh). Literally, "going"; an energetic TEMPO.

Andando (It., ăhn-dăhn'dŏh). "Going on"; easy and flowing.

Andante (It., ăhn-dăhn'těh). "Going," "moving"; a TEMPO mark indicating a moderately slow, easily flowing movement between ADAGIO and ALLEGRETTO. *Andante affettuoso*, rather slowly and pathetic; *a. cantabile*, flowingly, in a singing style; *a. con moto, a. mosso, a. un poco allegretto*, a flowing and rather more animated movement; *a. non troppo*, easily flowing, but not too fast; *a. maestoso*, a flowing and stately movement; *a. pastorale*, flowing with tranquil simplicity; *a. sostenuto*, rather slow, flowing smoothly; *meno a.*, slower.

Andantamente (It., ăhn-dăhn-těh-men'těh). Smoothly and flowingly.

Andantino (It., ăhn-dăhn-tē'nŏh). A diminutive of ANDANTE, meaning, properly, a little slower than ANDANTE (but often used as if meaning a little faster).

Andare (It., ăhn-dah'rĕh). To move on. *Andare diritto*, go straight on; *a. in tempo*, keep strict TIME.

Anfang (Ger., ăhn'făhngᵏ). Beginning. *Vom Anfang*, same as DA CAPO.

Angemessen (Ger., ăhn'gĕ-mĕssen). Suitable, comfortable.

Angenehm (Ger., ăhn'gĕ-nāhm). Pleasing, agreeable.

Angklung. A Javanese rattle made of bamboo, and included in a GAMELAN, producing a pleasing sound in irregular RHYTHM.

Anglaise (Fr., ăhn-gläz'). The English COUNTRY DANCE.

Anglican chant. Liturgical singing generally adopted in the English-speaking Protestant liturgy; it is usually harmonized with simple CHORDS.

Angoscioso (It., ăhn-gŏh-shŏh'sŏh). With anguish, with agony of mind.

Ängstlich (Ger., engst'lĭyh). Anxiously, fearfully.

Anhang (Ger., ăhn'hăhngᵏ). CODA, CODETTA.

Anima, con (It., kŏhn ah'nē-măh). ANIMATO.

Animando (It., ăh-nē-măhn'dŏh). With increasing animation; growing livelier. *Animando e crescendo*, growing livelier and louder; *a. sempre (più)*, growing more and more animated; *a. un poco*, with somewhat more animation; *lo stesso tempo e a. sempre più*, the same rate of speed, with ever increasing animation (of expression).

Animato (It., ăh-nē-mah'tŏh). With spirit, spiritedly, vivaciously. *Animato di più*, with greater animation.

Animosissimo (It., ăh-nē-mŏh-sis'sē-mŏh). With utmost animation, spirit, boldness.

Animoso (It., ăh-nē-moh'sŏh). Animated, spirited.

Anlaufen (Ger., ăhn'low-fen). To increase in volume.

Anmut(h)ig (Ger., ăhn'moo'tĭyh). With grace, charm; gracefully, suavely.

Anomaly. Slight deviation from true PITCH caused by tempering INTERVALS on fixed-tone instruments; hence, an *anomalous chord* is one containing an interval rendered, by unequal tempering, extremely SHARP or FLAT.

Anschlag (Ger., ăhn'shlăh). 1. The touch in PIANO playing. 2. An APPOGGIATURA or ORNAMENT. 3. A stroke, or the striking of a CHORD.

Anschwellen (Ger., ăhn'shvel'len). To swell, increase in loudness.

Ansiosamente (It., ăhn-sē-ŏh-săh-men'tĕh). In a style expressive of anxiety or hesitation.

Anstimmen (Ger., ăhn'shtĭm-men). To TUNE, to begin to sing.

Anstimmung (Ger., ăhn'shtĭm-moong^k). TUNING, INTONATION.

Answer. In a FUGUE, the taking-up by the *second* PART (at a different PITCH) of the SUBJECT proposed by the *first* part.

Antecedent. The THEME or SUBJECT of a CANON or FUGUE, as proposed by the first PART; the LEADER. Also, any THEME or MOTIVE proposed for IMITATION, or imitated further on.

Anthem. A piece of sacred vocal music usually based on biblical words, with or without instrumental ACCOMPANIMENT, and of moderate length.

Anticipation. The advancing of one or more of the PARTS constituting a HARMONY before the rest; which part or parts would, if all the parts progressed together, enter later.

Antico (It., ăhn-tē'kŏh). Antique, ancient. *All' antico*, in the ancient style.

Antiphon(e). Originally, a responsive system of singing by two CHOIRS (or divided choir), an early feature in the Catholic service of SONG; later applied to responsive or alternate singing, CHANTING, or INTONATION in general, as practiced in the Greek, Roman, Anglican, and Lutheran churches. Also, a short sentence, generally from Holy Scripture, sung before and after the PSALMS for the day.

Antiphonal. 1. A book or collection of ANTIPHONS or ANTHEMS. 2. In the style of an antiphon; responsive, alternating.

Antiphony. Responsive singing by two CHOIRS (or divided choir) of alternate VERSES of a PSALM or ANTHEM; also, music composed for two or more groups of performers separated in space, often in a CALL AND RESPONSE manner.

Antique cymbal. A very small pair of brass CYMBALS, such as were used in accompanying dances in ancient Greece. They are sometimes used in modern scores for special effects.

Anvil. A metal bar used as a PERCUSSION instrument for special effects, as in the famous "Anvil Chorus" in Verdi's opera *Il Trovatore*.

Anwachsend (Ger., ăhn'văhk'sent). CRESCENDO.

Aperto (It., ăh-pâr'tŏh). Open, without a MUTE. *Allegro aperto,* an ALLEGRO with broad, clear phrasing.

Aphony. Loss of voice.

A piacere (It., ah pee-ah-cher'eh). "As you please"; that is, free in TEMPO and DYNAMICS.

Aplomb (Fr., ăh-plŏhn'). Coolness, self-possession, steadiness.

Appassionatamente (It., ăhp-păhs-sē-ŏh-năh-tăh-men'tĕh). Passionately, ardently; also **appassionato,-a** (It., ăh păhs-sē-ŏh-năh-tŏh).

Appena (It., ăhp-pā'năh). Hardly, very little. *Appena animando,* a trifle more animated; *a. meno,* a very little slower; *a. sensibile,* hardly audible.

Appenato (It., ăhp-pĕn-nah'tŏh). Distressed; in a style expressive of distress or suffering.

Appoggiando (It., ăhp-pŏhd-jăhn'doh). "Leaning on," "supported." Said of a TONE gliding over to the next without a break, like an APPOGGIATURA or the PORTAMENTO.

Appoggiato (It., ăhp-pŏhd-jah'tŏh). "Leaned against," "supported." Calls for same style of execution as APPOGGIANDO. In the example, it is equivalent to MEZZO LEGATO.

appoggiato e piano

Appoggiatura (It., ăhp-pŏhd-jăh-too'răh). An *accented appoggiatura* is a GRACE NOTE that takes the ACCENT and part of the TIME VALUE of the *following* PRINCIPAL NOTE. The *long appoggiatura*

performed

is seldom written now; the *short appoggiatura*

is performed

The *unaccented appoggiatura*,

is performed

taking its time value from the *preceding* principal note, to which it is smoothly bound.

A punta d'arco (It., ăh pŏŏn'tăh dar'kŏh). With the point of the BOW.

À quatre mains (Fr., ăh kăh'tr măn); **A quattro mani** (It., ăh kwăht'trŏh mah'nĕ). For four hands; DUETS on PIANO or ORGAN.

À quatre voix (Fr., ăh kăh'tr vwăh); **A quattro voci** (It., ăh kwăht-trŏh voh'chĕ). For four VOICES or PARTS.

Arabesque. A type of fanciful PIANO PIECE; ornamental PAS-SAGES accompanying or varying a THEME.

Arbitrio (It., ar-bē′trē-ŏh). Will, please. *A suo arbitrio*, at your pleasure.

Arcato (It., ar-kah′tŏh). With the BOW.

Arch- (Eng.), **Archi-** (L., ar′kē), **Arci-** (It., ar′chē). A prefix signifying "chief, preeminent," formerly applied to instruments in the sense of "largest," and to official titles in the sense of "head." *Archchanter*, precentor; *archlute* (Fr., *Archiluth* [ar-shē-lüt′]; It., *Arciliuto* [archē-lē-oo′-tŏh]), a large kind of BASS LUTE.

Arco (It., ar′kŏh). BOW. *Arco in giù* (joo′), DOWN-BOW; *arco in su* (soo′), UP-BOW.

Ardentemente (It., ar-den′tĕh-men′tĕh). Ardently, passionately.

Arditezza, con (It., kŏhn ar-dē-tet′săh). With boldness; boldly, spiritedly.

Ardito (It., ar-dē′tŏh). Bold, spirited.

Ardore, con (It., kŏhn ar-doh′rĕh). With ardor, warmth.

Aretinian syllables. The syllables *ut, re, mi, fa, sol, la*, first used to name the TONES of the HEXACHORD by Guido d'Arezzo (c. 991-c. 1033).

Arhythmic. Literally, without RHYTHM; lacking a regular, sustained BEAT or PULSE.

Aria (It., ah′rē-ăh; plural **Arie** [ah′rē-ĕh]). An AIR, SONG, TUNE, MELODY. The *grand* or *da-capo aria* (*aria grande* [grähn′-dĕh]) is in three divisions: 1) THEME, fully developed; 2) a more tranquil and richly harmonized second section; and 3) a repetition *da capo* of the first, with more florid ORNAMENTATION.

Aria buffa (It., bŏŏf′făh). A comic or BURLESQUE aria.

Aria concertante (It., kŏhn-châr-tähn'tĕh). An aria for concert singing, with OBBLIGATO instrumental ACCOMPANIMENT.

Aria da chiesa (It., dăh k'yâ'zäh). Church aria.

Aria da concerto (It., dăh kŏhn-châr'toh). An aria for concert singing.

Aria d'entrata (It., den-trah'täh). An aria sung by any character in an OPERA, on his or her first entrance.

Aria di bravura (It., dē brăh-voo-răh). An aria replete with ORNAMENTS and difficulties for showing off the singer's skill.

Aria di sortita (It., dē sohr-tē'täh). See SORTITA.

Arie (Ger., ah'rē-ĕ). ARIA.

Arietta (It., ahrē-et'täh); **Ariette** (Fr., ăh-rē-et'). A short AIR or SONG; a short ARIA.

Arioso (It., ăh-rē-oh'sŏh). In vocal music, a style between ARIA and RECITATIVE; or, a short, melodious strain interrupting or ending a recitative. Also, an impressive, dramatic style suitable for the *aria grande*; hence, a vocal PIECE in that style. In instrumental music, the same as CANTABILE.

Armoniosamente (It., ăr-mŏh-nē-ŏh-săh-men'tĕh). Harmoniously.

Arpa (It., ar'-pah). HARP.

Arpeggiando (It., ar-ped-jähn'dŏh). Playing in HARP-style; sounding BROKEN CHORDS.

Arpeggiato (It., ar-ped-jah'tŏh). Arpeggiated.

Arpeggio (It., ar-ped'jŏh; plural **Arpeggi** [ar-pĕd'jē]). Playing the TONES of a CHORD in rapid, even succession; playing BROKEN CHORDS. Hence, a chord so played; a broken or spread chord, or chord passage.

Arrangement. The adaptation of a COMPOSITION for performance on an instrument, or by any vocal or instrumental combination, for which it was not originally written. Hence, any composition so adapted or arranged.

Ars antiqua (L., ahrz ăn-tē′kwŭ). A CONTRAPUNTAL, sometimes DISSONANT style of 12th-13th century France.

Arsin et thesin, per. Imitation of a weak PART (arsis) by a strong BEAT (thesis) in a CANON. Also, IMITATION by INVERSION.

Arsis and thesis (Gk., ahr′sēs, thēs′ēs). UPBEAT and DOWNBEAT.

Ars nova (L. ahrz nō′vŭ, "new art"). The period of 14th century music that contrasted with the ARS ANTIQUA by its more complex COUNTERPOINT.

Articolato (It., ar-tē-kŏh-lah′tŏh). "Articulated." *Ben articolato*, clearly and neatly pronounced and phrased.

Articulation. The manner in which NOTES are joined one to another by the performer; a principal component of PHRASING.

Artificial harmonics. HARMONICS produced on a STOPPED STRING rather than on an OPEN STRING (as on the VIOLIN).

Artiglich (Ger., ar′tiyh-līyh). Prettily, neatly, gracefully.

As (Ger., ăhss). A♭ (A flat).

Asas, Ases (Ger., ăhss′ăhss, ăhss′ess). A double flat.

As dur (Ger., dōōr). A♭ major.

Asprezza, con (It., kŏhn ăh-spret′săh). With harshness; harshly, roughly.

Assai (It., ăhs-sah′ē). Very. *Allegro assai*, very fast; *adagio a.*, very slow; *a. moderato*, very moderate.

Assez (Fr., ăhss-sā′). Enough; rather.

Assottigliando (It., ăh-sŏh-tē-l′yăhn′dŏh). Diminishing, softening.

A suo arbitrio (It., ăh soo'ŏh ar-bē'trē-ŏh); **A suo bene placito** (It., bâ'nĕh plah'chē-tŏh); **A suo comodo** (It., kôh'mŏh-dŏh). At the pleasure or discretion of the singer or player.

Atempause (Ger., ah'tŭm-powze). Literally, ''breath-pause''; a slight break to catch the breath before a strong BEAT.

A tempo (It., ăh tem'pŏh). In TIME; at the preceding rate of speed.

Athematic. Literally, without THEME; lacking a discernible theme or MELODY.

At(h)emlos (Ger., ah'tem-lohs). Breathlessly.

Atonality. The absence of TONALITY. A type of modern music in which the traditional tonal structures are abandoned, and the KEY SIGNATURE is absent.

Attacca, -o (It., ăht-tăhk'kăh). ''ATTACK,'' or begin what follows without pausing, or with a very short pause. *Attacca* (or *attaccate* [ăht-tăhk-kah'tĕh]) *subito*, attack instantly. Also, stroke of the glottis.

Attack. The act (or style) of beginning a PHRASE, PASSAGE, or PIECE.

Attendant keys. Of a given KEY are its RELATIVE MAJOR or MINOR, together with the keys of the DOMINANT and SUBDOMINANT and their relative major or minor keys. For instance, the attendant keys of *C* major are *a* minor, *G* major, *F* major, *e* minor, and *d* minor.

Attenzione, con (It., kŏhn ăht-ten-tsē-oh'nĕh). ''With attention''; in a marked style; significantly.

Aubade (Fr., ōh-băhd). Morning or dawn music.

Audacia, con (It., kŏhn ăh-oo-dah'chah). With boldness.

Aufführung (Ger., owf'füh-rŏŏng^k). Performance.

Aufgeregt (Ger., owf'gĕ-ra**yh**t'). Agitated, excited.

Aufhalten (Ger., owf'hăl-ten). To stop or retard.

Aufschwung (Ger., owf′shvŏŏng^k). Lofty flight, soaring impetuousity. *Mit Aufschwung*, in a lofty, impetuous, impassioned manner.

Aufstrich (Ger., owf′strĭyh). An UP-BOW.

Auftakt (Ger., owf′tăhkt). UPBEAT, ANACRUSIS; a fractional MEASURE beginning a MOVEMENT, PIECE, or THEME.

Auftritt (Ger., owf′trĭtt). A scene of an OPERA.

Aufzug (Ger., owf′zŭg). An act of an OPERA.

Augmentation. Doubling (or increasing) the TIME value of the NOTES of a THEME or MOTIVE, often in IMITATIVE COUNTERPOINT.

Augmented fourth. The INTERVAL a SEMITONE larger than the perfect FOURTH, as from *C* to *F* SHARP.

Augmented second. The INTERVAL a SEMITONE larger than a MAJOR SECOND. It is used between the SIXTH and the SEVENTH DEGREES of the MINOR HARMONIC SCALE, as between *F* and *G* SHARP in the *a* minor scale. It is characteristic of oriental melodies.

Augmented sixth. The INTERVAL a SEMITONE larger than a MAJOR SIXTH, as from *C* to *A* SHARP. It is the basic interval of the so-called FRENCH SIXTH, GERMAN SIXTH, and ITALIAN SIXTH.

Augmented triad. A TRIAD consisting of two MAJOR THIRDS, as in *C*, *E*, *G* sharp.

Aulos. An ancient Greek WIND INSTRUMENT resembling an OBOE. It usually had two connected PIPES, blown simultaneously.

Ausdruck (Ger., ows'drŏŏk). Expression. *Mit innigem Ausdruck*, with heartfelt expression.

Ausgabe (Ger., ows'gäbe). Edition.

Ausgelassen (Ger., ows'gĕ-lässen). Boisterous, exuberant.

Auszug (Ger., ows'tsŭh). ARRANGEMENT or REDUCTION, as in *Klavierauszug*, a PIANO reduction from a full SCORE.

Authentic melody. One whose range covers all, or nearly all, the OCTAVE SCALE above its TONIC or FINAL; opposed to PLAGAL MODE.

Authentic mode. One in which the KEYNOTE is the lowest TONE; in a PLAGAL MODE, the keynote is a FOURTH above the lowest tone.

Authentic part of the scale. That part lying between the KEYNOTE and its *higher* DOMINANT; the part between keynote and *lower* dominant being called PLAGAL MODE.

Autoharp. Invented by Charles Zimmerman in the late 19th century, a ZITHER-like instrument equipped with CHORD bars that automatically dampen certain NOTES, allowing the player to easily play CHORDS. In the Southern Appalachians, a unique style of "picking" melodies was developed.

Auxiliary note. A note not essential to the HARMONY or MELODY; particularly, a GRACE NOTE a SECOND above or below a given melody note.

Auxiliary scales. Those of ATTENDANT KEYS.

Avant-garde (Fr. for "vanguard" or "in advance"). Usually denoting the musical ideas and practices of such European masters as Boulez, Stockhausen, or Berio, as distinct from those of the American experimental school, i.e., Cage, Feldman, or Wolff. See also EXPERIMENTAL MUSIC.

Avec (Fr., ăh-vĕk'). With. *Avec âme* (ahm), the same as CON ANIMA; *a. le chant* (shăhn), the same as COL CANTO.

À volonté (Fr., ăh vŏh-lŏhn-tā'). At pleasure.

Ayre. An English court SONG of the 16th and 17th century, usually accompanied on the LUTE. The word is an old English spelling of AIR.

B

B. 1. (Ger. *H*; Fr. and It. *si*.) The SEVENTH TONE and DEGREE in the DIATONIC SCALE of *C* MAJOR. 2. In musical THEORY, capital *B* designates the *B*-MAJOR TRIAD, small *b*, the *b*-MINOR TRIAD. 3. In German, *B* stands for *B♭* 4. *B*. is also an abbreviation for BASS or BASSO (*c. B.* = COL BASSO; *B. C.* = BASSO CONTINUO).

Baby grand. The smallest size of the GRAND PIANO.

B-A-C-H. The letters of Bach's name, which represent in German nomenclature the NOTES *B* flat, *A*, *C*, and *B* natural. Bach used this chromatically sounding THEME in the unfinished last FUGUE of his *The Art of the Fugue*, and many composers since then have paid tribute to him by writing pieces based on the same four notes.

Bachelor of Music (B.M.). In the U.S., the lowest of the academic musical degrees, Master of Music (M.M.) being the higher, and Doctor of Music (D.M., or Ph.D., Doctor of Philosophy [in Music]) the highest.

Backturn. A melodic ORNAMENT that begins on a lower NOTE; if *C* is followed by an INVERTED TURN, the ornament will be *C, B, C, D, C*.

Badinerie (Fr., bah-dee-neh-ree'). "Teasing"; occasionally used in BAROQUE music as the title of a quick MOVEMENT in 2/4 TIME.

Bagatelle. A trifle; usually, a short, fairly easy PIECE.

Bagpipe. A very ancient WIND INSTRUMENT of Eastern origin, still popular in Great Britain. The commonest form, the Scottish bagpipe, has four PIPES, three DRONES (single-REED pipes tuned to a given TONE, its FIFTH and its OCTAVE, respectively, and sounding on continuously), and one chanter or melody-pipe (a double-reed pipe with six or eight holes), on which the TUNE is played. The "bag" is a leather sack, filled with wind either from the mouth or from small bellows worked by the player's arm; the pipes are inserted in and receive wind from the bag.

Baguette (Fr., bah-get'). Conductor's BATON; also, a drum-stick.

Baile (Sp., bi'-leh). A general term for a wide variety of dances.

Balalaika (Russian, băl-a-lī'kăh). Popular three-stringed Russian instrument of the LUTE family with a distinctive triangular BODY.

Ballabile (It., băhl-lah'bē-lĕh). 1. A piece of dance music. 2. BALLET music. 3. In the style of, or suitable for, dance music.

Ballad. Originally, a SONG intended for a dance ACCOMPANI-MENT; hence, the AIR of such a song. In modern usage, a ballad is a simple narrative poem, generally meant to be sung. As a purely musical term, it was originally applied to a short, simple vocal MELODY, set to one or more STANZAS, with a slight instrumental accompaniment. It now includes instrumental melodies of a similar character; also, COMPOSITIONS for single instruments, or for OR-CHESTRA, supposed to embody the idea of a narrative.

Ballade (Ger., băhl-lah'dĕ); **Ballade** (Fr., băhl-lähd'). A BAL-LAD-like ART SONG, or an instrumental solo PIECE.

Balladenmässig (Ger., băhl-lah'd'n-mä'sĭyh). In BALLAD style.

Ballad opera. An OPERA chiefly made up of BALLADS and FOLK SONGS.

Ballata (It., băhl-lah'tăh). A BALLAD. *A ballata*, in ballad style.

Ballet (băl-lay', or băl-let; Fr., băl-lay'). 1. In Western tradition, professional theatrical dancing emerging from France in the early 18th century and reaching its classical culmination in Russia at the turn into the 20th century; thus, any work comprised thereof. 2. A spectacular dance introduced in an OPERA or other stage work. 3. A PANTOMIME, with music and dances, setting forth the thread of the story. *Also* **Ballett** (Ger., băhl-let').

Balletto (It., băhl-let'tŏh). 1. A BALLET. 2. The title of an ALLEGRETTO by Bach, in common (4/4) TIME.

Ballo (It., băhl'lŏh). A dance; a BALLET. *Balli inglesi*, English dances; *B. ungaresi*, Hungarian dances; *da b.*, in dance style, light and spirited.

Band. 1. A company of musicians playing martial music (brass-band, military band). 2. An ORCHESTRA. 3. A section of the orchestra playing instruments of the same class (BRASS band, STRING band, wind band, wood band).

Banda (It., băhn'dăh). 1. A military BAND. 2. The BRASS and PERCUSSION instruments in the Italian OPERA ORCHESTRA. 3. An orchestra playing on the stage.

Bandmaster. Conductor of a military BAND.

Bandola (Sp., băhn-doh'lăh). Instruments of the LUTE family, with a greater or smaller number of steel or GUT STRINGS, and played with a PLECTRUM ("pick"); very similar to the MANDOLIN. Also the *Bandolon, Bandora, Bandura*.

Banjo. American folk instrument, developed around 1850 by minstrel musician Joel Sweeney. Originally, with four to ten MELODY STRINGS, and an additional, shorter DRONE string. In the minstrel style, the banjo was either "frailed" (the player sweeping the back of the hand across the strings) or "picked." By the 1880s, most banjos had five strings (four melody and one drone). In the 1910s, a new type of banjo called variously *tenor, tango,* or *plectrum* was developed, having four strings, and chorded like a guitar which was popular in JAZZ bands. In the 1950s, the five-string variety gained renewed popularity, played either in the old frailing style or picked with metal picks, as pioneered by BLUEGRASS player Earl Scruggs.

Bar. 1. A vertical line dividing MEASURES on the STAFF, and indicating, unless otherwise noted, that the strong BEAT falls on the NOTE just after it. 2. The popular name for measure (the notes and RESTS contained between two bars).

Barbaro (It., bar'băh-rŏh). FEROCE.

Barbershop harmony. The type of close, four-part HARMONY, often with CHROMATIC passing notes, which was popular in America at the turn of the century.

Barcarole (Ger., bar-kăh-roh'lĕ); **Barcarolle** (Fr., bar-kăh-rŏhl'); **Barcaruola** (It., bar-kăh-rŏŏ-ô'lăh). 1. A GONDOLIERA; SONG of the Venetian gondoliers. 2. A vocal or instrumental solo, or concerted PIECE, imitating the Venetian boat-songs, and usually in 6/8 TIME (however, Chopin's, for piano, is in 12/8). Also *Barcarola.*

Bariolage (Fr., băh-rē-ŏh-lăh'zh). 1. A MEDLEY. 2. A group of several NOTES played in the same position on two, three, or four STRINGS on the VIOLIN.

Baritone. 1. The male voice between BASS and TENOR, and more or less similar in quality to both. Compass from G to f^1. Also, a singer having such a voice. 2. A bowed instrument taking the baritone part in a COMPOSITION, like the VIOLA DA GAMBA. 3. The EUPHONIUM (BASS SAXHORN).

Baritone clef. The obsolete *F* CLEF on the *third* line of the STAFF:

Baroque music. The type of music developed within the historical period of about 1600–1750, lorded over by Bach and Handel, highlighted by the institution of even TEMPERAMENT and a pervasive use of THOROUGHBASS, the culmination of POLYPHONY and the rise of HOMOPHONY, the birth of OPERA, the rise of instrumental music, and the establishment of certain fixed forms, including, early on, the TRIO SONATA and DA CAPO ARIA, and, later, the ARIA and RECITATIVE, CONCERTO, and SONATA. Although little agreement has been reached regarding the etymology of the term applied to music, it has acquired the connotation of dignity, elegant elaboration, and precise craftsmanship.

Baroque organ. A highly developed Gothic ORGAN with several MANUALS and a variety of STOPS, such as was used by Bach.

Baroque suite. CLASSICAL SUITE.

Barocco (It., băh-rôhk′kŏh). Eccentric, strange, odd, whimsical.

Barré (Fr., bar-rā′). In LUTE or GUITAR playing, the stopping of several or all the strings with the left-hand forefinger. *Grand* (grähn) *barré*, a stop of more than three strings.

Barrel organ. A mechanical ORGAN, which originally used a rotating "barrel" with projecting pins (much like a music box) to activate its pipes. By the mid-nineteenth century, paper rolls replaced the barrel, and the pipes were generally supplanted by reeds such as those found in REED ORGANS. The most elaborate is the ORCHESTRION.

Bass. 1. The lowest TONE in a CHORD, or the lowest PART in a COMPOSITION. 2. The lowest male voice; ordinary

COMPASS from *F* to *c*¹ (or *d*¹); extreme compass from *C* to *e*¹. 3. A singer having such a voice.

Bass (Ger., băhs). Besides the three English meanings above, *bass* denotes (*a*) an old bowed instrument between the VIOLONCELLO and DOUBLE BASS, with five or six STRINGS; (*b*) the same as *Kontrabass* (double bass); (*c*) when appended to the name of an ORGAN-STOP, it means that the STOP is on the PEDAL (i.e., *Gemshornbass*).

Bass-bar. In VIOLINS, etc., a long narrow strip of wood glued to the inner surface of the BELLY parallel with and just beneath the *G*-string, put in to strengthen the belly and to equalize vibration.

Bass clarinet. A popular instrument among 20th-century orchestral composers; in B-flat, sounding an OCTAVE below the CLARINET.

Bass clef. *F* CLEF on the *fourth* line of the STAFF:

Bass drum. The biggest and lowest pitched DRUM. It does not, however, produce a definite PITCH.

Bass fiddle. A colloquial name for the DOUBLE BASS.

Bass guitar. Common name for the ELECTRIC BASS GUITAR, with a solid BODY, and held like the ELECTRIC GUITAR.

Basse (Fr., băhs). BASS.

Basse danse (Fr., băhs dăhns). A medieval French dance, characterized by feet shuffling across the floor.

Basset horn. A TENOR CLARINET of mellow, though somber, timbre, with a COMPASS from *F* to *c*³.

Basso (It., băhs'soh). BASS; also, the DOUBLE BASS.

Basso buffo (It., bŏŏf'fŏh). A comic BASS.

Basso cantante (It., kăhn-tăhn'tĕh). A BASS-BARITONE.

Basso continuo (It., kŏhn-tē'nŏŏ-ŏh). FIGURED BASS.

Basso giusto (It., jŏŏ'stŏh). A BASSO CANTANTE.

Basso obbligato (It., ŏhb-blē-gah'tŏh). An indispensable BASS PART or ACCOMPANIMENT.

Bassoon. A WOODWIND INSTRUMENT of the OBOE family with a long, curving, metallic MOUTHPIECE with double REED. Its COMPASS is from Bb_1 to c^2, or even to f^2, and its tone is soft and mellow.

Basso ostinato (It., oh-stē-nah'toh). See GROUND BASS.

Basso profondo (It., prō-fōhn'dŏh). Literally, "profound bass"; the lowest BASS voice.

Baton. A conductor's stick.

Battery (also Fr., **batterie**). 1. The group of PERCUSSION INSTRUMENTS. 2. A DRUM roll. 3. An 18th-century term for BROKEN CHORD figures.

Battuta (It., băht-tŏŏ'tăh). BEAT; DOWNBEAT; MEASURE. *A battuta*, in strict TIME.

B dur (Ger., bā door). *B* flat major.

Be (Ger., bā). The flat sign (♭).

Beam. Horizontal lines connecting adjacent NOTES.

Beat. 1. A movement of the hand in marking ("beating") TIME. 2. A division of a MEASURE marked by a BEAT. 3. In a TRILL, the pulsation of two consecutive TONES. 4. An APPOGGIATURA. 5. A throbbing caused by the interfering sine waves of two tones of different PITCH.

Bebop. A type of JAZZ that emerged in America in the 1940s characterized by rapid, complex improvised melodies, unusual CHORD changes, and energetic drumming; often associated with Charlie Parker and Dizzy Gillespie.

Bebung (Ger., beh'boong). Literally, "trembling"; a VIBRATO effect on STRINGED INSTRUMENTS or on a CLAVICHORD.

Bécarre (Fr., beh-car'). Natural sign (♮).

Becken (Ger., bek'en). CYMBAL (singular); cymbals (plural).

Bedeutungsvoll (Ger., bĕ-dahü'tŏŏngs-fŏhl'). Full of meaning; significantly.

Bedrohlich (Ger., bĕ-drŏh'lῐyh). Menacing.

Begeisterung, mit (Ger., mit bĕ-gῑ'stĕ-rŏŏng^k). With enthusiasm, spirit.

Begleitung (Ger., be-glῑ'toong^k). ACCOMPANIMENT.

Beguine. A Latin American dance in a lively SYNCOPATED RHYTHM, popularized in the playfully named Cole Porter song, "Begin the Beguine."

Behaglich (Ger., be-hahg'liyh). Easily, comfortably; COMODO.

Bel canto (It., bel kähn'tŏh). The art of beautiful SONG, as exemplified by the finest Italian singers of the 18th and 19th centuries. Opposed to RECITATIVE, and to the "declamatory" style of singing brought into prominence by Richard Wagner.

Belebt (Ge., bĕ·lāpt'). Animated, brisk.

Bell. 1. A hollow metallic PERCUSSION INSTRUMENT, sounded by a clapper hanging inside, or a hammer outside, of its BODY. 2. The flaring end of various WIND INSTRUMENTS.

Bellezza, con (It., kŏhn bel-let'säh). With beauty; gracefully, suavely.

Bell harp. A kind of DULCIMER used in the 18th century in England.

Bellicoso (It., bel-lē-kŏh'sŏh). In a martial, warlike manner.

Bell metronome. A METRONOME with a bell attachment that may be set to strike with every second, third, fourth, or sixth BEAT of the pendulum.

Belly. The face (upper side) of the SOUNDBOX of the VIOLIN, etc. Also, the SOUNDBOARD of the PIANO.

Bémol (Fr., bā-mŏl). The flat sign (♭).

Bene (It., bâ′nĕh; abbrev., *ben*). Well. *Ben marcato*, well marked; *a bene placito*, at pleasure; *ben ritmato*, with careful and precise observance of the RHYTHM; *ben sostenuto*, *ben tenuto*, well-sustained.

Benedictus. In Latin, "blessed"; the concluding portion of the Sanctus in the Roman Catholic MASS.

Bequem (Ger., bĕ-kvām′). Easily, comfortably.

Berceuse (Fr., bâr-söz′). A cradle SONG; lullaby.

Bergamask. A clownish dance like that of the peasants of Bergamasca, Italy.

Bergerette (Fr., bâr-zhâr-et′). A pastoral or rustic SONG; also a type of 18th-century French lyrical poetry.

Beruhigend (Ger., bĕ-roo′-īyhent). Becoming calm.

Beschleunigen (Ger., bĕ-shlähü′nī-gen). To hasten.

Beschwingt (Ger., bĕ-shvingt′). Winged. *Leicht beschwingt*, lightly and swiftly; VOLANTE.

Beseelt (Ger., bĕ-zält′). "Soulfully"; animated.

Bestimmt (Ger., bĕ-shtimt′). With decision, energy.

Betont (Ger., bĕ-tohnt′). Accented, marked.

Betonung, mit (Ger., mit bĕ-toh′nŏŏng^k). With emphasis.

Betrübt (Ger., bĕ-trü′bt). Grieved, afflicted.

Bewegt (Ger., bĕ-vāyht′). Moved, agitated.

Bewegter (Ger., bĕ-vāyh′ter). Faster; PIÙ MOSSO.

Bewegung (Ger., bĕ-vā′gŏŏng^k). Movement; agitation.

Bichord. Having two STRINGS. A bichord instrument is one (like the MANDOLIN, LUTE, and certain PIANOS) having a pair of strings, tuned in UNISON, for each TONE.

Bicinium. A SONG for two VOICES.

Bien (Fr., b'yĕn). Well. *Bien chanté*, same as MOLTO CANTABILE; *b. rhythmé*, same as BEN RITMATO.

Binary. Dual; two-part. *Binary form*, a form of MOVEMENT founded on two principal THEMES (see SONATA), or divided into two distinct or contrasted SECTIONS; *b. measure*, that of common TIME, the first of every two members taking the ACCENT (regular and equal alternation between DOWNBEAT and UPBEAT).

Bind. 1. A TIE. 2. A BRACE.

Bis. "Twice"; commonly used in Europe to request an ENCORE. Also used in printed music to indicate that a PASSAGE is to be repeated.

Biscroma. In Italian, a THIRTY-SECOND NOTE.

Bisogna (It., bē-zŏhn'yăh). Is necessary, must. *Si bisogna da capo al segno*, must be repeated from the beginning to the sign.

Bitonality. HARMONY in two different TONALITIES, as *C* major and *F* sharp major, played simultaneously. Bitonality is often used in modern compositions.

Biwa. A Japanese plucked LUTE, related to the Chinese PIPA.

Bizzarria, con (It., kŏhn bid-zar-rē'ăh). In a bizarre, whimsical, fantastic, extravagant style.

Black bottom. A rapid ballroom dance of the roaring twenties characterized by sinuous hip movements.

Blasinstrumente (Ger., blaz'in-stru-men-teh). WIND INSTRUMENTS.

Blech (Ger., bleh). BRASS. *Blechmusik*, brass music.

Block. 1. In VIOLINS, etc., small pieces of wood within the BODY, glued vertically to the ribs between BELLY and back to strengthen the instrument. A HAMMER in the PIANO *"blocks"* when it remains against the string after striking, instead of recoiling, thus *"blocking"* (deadening) the TONE. 2. A self-sufficient portion of a COMPOSITION.

Blockflöte, Blochflöte (Ger., blŏhk'flŏ'tĕ, blŏh'flŏ'tĕ). 1. An old kind of RECORDER. 2. An ORGAN STOP having pyramid-shaped flue PIPES of 2', 4', 8', or 16' PITCH, and sometimes stopped.

Bluegrass. A musical style pioneered by Kentucky-born mandolinist Bill Monroe, c. 1946, with his band, The Blue Grass Boys. Characterized by brisk TEMPOS, high-pitched lead vocals, and elaborate vocal HARMONIES; common bluegrass BANDS feature GUITAR, MANDOLIN, FIDDLE, BANJO (played in a three-finger picked style), and BASS.

Blue note. The lowered THIRD and SEVENTH DEGREES in a MAJOR SCALE, as *B* flat and *E* flat in the key of *C* major; the blue note is characteristic in African-American music, such as BLUES and JAZZ.

Blues. An African-American SONG style characterized by "sad" or "blue" contents and the use of BLUE NOTES. *12-bar blues,* a common blues FORM featuring a repeating 12-bar CHORD pattern; *country b.,* older blues styles, dating from the late 19th century, often free-form and featuring a vocalist accompanied by a single ACOUSTIC GUITAR; *city* or *urban b.,* a post-World War II style, originating in Chicago, featuring a vocalist accompanied by ELECTRIC GUITAR, BASS, HARMONICA, and DRUMS.

B moll (Ger., bā mŏhl'). *B* flat MINOR.

Boat song. BARCAROLE; GONDOLIERA.

Bob. A term in CHANGE-RINGING applied to the various sets of changes which may be rung on six (bob minor), eight (bob major), ten (bob royal), or 12 (bob maximus) BELLS.

Bocca (It., bŏhk'kăh). Mouth. *(Con) bocca chiusa* (kew'-săh), with closed mouth; humming. See BRUMMSTIMMEN.

Bocedisation. A medieval system of SOLMISATION, with the NOTES of the SCALE named *bo-ce-di*, etc., instead of *do-re-mi*, etc.

Body. 1. The SOUNDBOX of a STRINGED INSTRUMENT. 2. That part of a WIND INSTRUMENT remaining when MOUTHPIECE, CROOKS, and BELL are removed. 3. The tube of an ORGAN PIPE above its mouth. 4. A TONE is said to have "body" when it is full and sonorous; the RESONANCE of a tone is also called the "body."

Boehm system. A system of constructing a FLUTE with KEYS, replacing the holes in the older instruments, making it more convenient to play. Named after the 19th-century German inventor, Theobald Boehm. Also applied to other WOODWINDS.

Bogen (Ger., boh'gen). 1. A BOW. 2. A SLUR or TIE.

Bois (Fr., bwăh). "Wood"; the WOODWINDS.

Bolero (Sp., bŏh-leh'rŏh). 1. A Spanish national dance in 3/4 TIME and lively TEMPO (ALLEGRETTO), the dancer accompanying his or her steps with CASTANETS. 2. A COMPOSITION in bolero style.

Bombard. 1. A large kind of OBOE, or SHAWM, popular in 14th and 15th century France, now obsolete. *Also* **Bombarde** (Fr., bŏhn-bar'd). *See also* POSAUNE. 2. A 16′ REED STOP in the ORGAN.

Bombardon. A large bass TRUMPET; also a BASS SAXHORN. Also, a deep-toned ORGAN STOP.

Bones. A RHYTHM instrument consisting of two bones or wooden bone-shaped clappers clicked together by the fingers.

Bongos. Paired, hand-held Cuban DRUMS, struck by the fingertips.

Boogie-woogie. Type of JAZZ, popularized in the 1930s by pianists like Meade Lux Lewis, characterized by OSTINATO BASS FIGURES.

Bop. Shortened name for BEBOP.

Bore. The diameter of a PIPE. Used to describe the shape of the bodies of WOODWIND and BRASS instruments.

Boston. A form of slow WALTZ; also called the "hesitation waltz," popular in the 1910s and 1920s.

Bossa nova. Popular Brazilian dance music influenced by American JAZZ. The name means "new voice" in Portuguese.

Bouche (Fr., boosh). Mouth. *À bouche fermée*, same as BOCCA CHIUSA.

Bouffe (Fr., boof). BUFFO.

Bourdon (Fr., boor-dŏhn'). 1. A low-pitched DRONE or PEDAL POINT. 2. An ORGAN STOP of 16' or 32' pitch, having stopped wooden PIPES, sometimes with metallic tops; French organs also have open bourdons of 8' and 4' pitch. 3. A great BELL, as the bourdon of Notre-Dame. 4. The lowest string of the VIOLONCELLO and DOUBLE BASS.

Bourée (Fr., boo-rā'). 1. A dance of French or Spanish origin, in rapid TEMPO, having two sections of eight MEASURES each, in 2/4 or 4/4 TIME. 2. An optional MOVEMENT in the CLASSICAL SUITE, in ALLA BREVE TIME.

Boutade (Fr., boo-tăhd'). 1. A short, impromptu BALLET. 2. An instrumental IMPROMPTU or FANTASIA.

Bouts. The incurvations on either side of the VIOLIN, etc., which form the "waist."

Bow. 1. The implement used in playing instruments of the VIOLIN type. The *hair* is attached to the *stick* by a bent *point* or *head*, and drawn into proper tension by the sliding NUT, which is worked by the *screw*. *Bow-arm* or

-hand, the right arm or hand; *B.-guitar*, a kind of violin with a GUITAR-shaped body; *B.-instrument*, one played with a BOW; *B.-zither*, see ZITHER. 2. To execute with a bow; also to mark a piece with signs indicating the bowing.

Bowing. The art of handling the BOW; a player's method or style; also, the signs for, and manner of, executing any given passage.

Braccio (It., brah'cho). "Arm"; instruments held in the arms were designated *da braccio*, "of the arm."

Brace. 1. The character { that connects two or more staves indicating that the parts on these staves are to be played simultaneously. 2. The group of staves so connected, as the *upper brace*.

Branle, Bransle (Fr., brahn'l'). An old French dance in 4/4 TIME, in which several persons joined hands and took the lead in turn. The English commonly called this dance form *Brangles* or *Brawls*.

Brass band. Differs from a full military BAND by the omission of REED instruments.

Brass instruments. The HORNS (TRUMPET, TROMBONE, FRENCH HORN, TUBA, etc.).

Bratsche (Ger., brah'che). The VIOLA.

Brautlied (Ger., browt'-lēt). Bridal or wedding SONG.

Bravo,-a. A shout of acclaim for the performer.

Bravour (Ger., brăh-voor). BRAVURA. *Bravourarie*, same as ARIA DI BRAVURA; *Bravourstück*, a vocal or instrumental PIECE of a brilliant and difficult character.

Bravoure (Fr., brăh-voor). BRAVURA. *Valse de bravoure*, an instrumental WALTZ in brilliant, showy style.

Bravura (It., brăh-voo'răh). Boldness, spirit, dash, brilliancy. *Aria di bravura*, a vocal solo consisting of difficult runs and passages, designed to show off the singer's voice or skill; *con b.*, with boldness.

Break. 1. The point where one REGISTER of a voice or instrument passes over into another; in the voice, the junction of the head and chest registers; in the CLARINET, between

the NOTES . *Breaking of the voice*, see

MUTATION. 2. A false or imperfect TONE produced by incorrect lipping of a HORN or TRUMPET; or by some difficulty with the REED of the clarinet (this "break" is called "the goose"); or, in singing, by some defect in the vocal organs. 3. In an ORGAN STOP, when playing up the SCALE, the sudden return to the lower OCTAVE (caused by an incomplete set of PIPES); also, in compound stops, any point in their scale where the relative PITCH of the pipes changes.

Breathing mark. A sign inserted in a vocal part to show that the singer may (or must) take a breath at that point; written variously (', *, ♩, v, ").

Breit (Ger., brit). Broadly.

Breve (brēv). A NOTE equal to two WHOLE NOTES or SEMIBREVES; the longest used in modern NOTATION, written:

Breve (It., brā'vĕh). Short.

Bridge. In bowed instruments and many LUTES, a thin, arching piece of wood set upright on the BELLY to raise and stretch the STRINGS above the SOUNDBOX, to which the BRIDGE communicates the vibrations of the strings. In the PIANO, a rail of wood or steel over which the strings are stretched.

Brillante (It., brēl-lähn'teh). Brilliant, showy, sparkling.

Brindisi (It., brēn-dē'-zē). A drinking SONG.

Brio, con (It., kŏhn brē′ŏh). "With noise" and gusto; spiritedly.

Brisé (Fr., brē-zā′, "broken"). In VIOLIN playing, short, detached strokes of the BOW.

Broken chords. CHORDS whose TONES are sounded in succession instead of together. See ARPEGGIO.

Broken octaves, series of OC-TAVES in which the higher tones alternate with the lower:

Broken consort. A term common in the Renaissance to describe a consort having both stringed and wind instruments; contrasted in Shakespeare with WHOLE CONSORT, where all the instruments were of the same kind.

Bruitism (from the Fr. *bruitisme* [*bruit* = "noise"]). A term denoting the use of noise as a compositional element.

Brummstimmen (Ger., brŏŏm′shtim′men). "Humming voices"; production of the TONE without words, through the nose, with closed mouth (BOCCA CHIUSA).

Bruscamente (It., brŏŏ-skäh-men′tĕh). Brusquely or forcibly accented.

Buffo,-a (It., bŏŏf-fŏh,-fäh). Comic, burlesque. *Buffo, buffo-singer*, a comic actor (singer) in an OPERA; *aria buffa*, comic AIR or ARIA; *opera buffa*, comic or burlesque opera.

Bugle. 1. A WIND INSTRUMENT of brass or copper, with cupped MOUTHPIECE, used for infantry calls and signals. 2. The key-bugle, with six KEYS, and a COMPASS of over two OC-TAVES. 3. The VALVE-bugle. See SAXHORN.

Bühne (Ger., bü′-ne). Stage.

Bühnenfestspiel (Ger., bü′-nen-fĕst-spēl). Stage festival play.

Bühnenmusik (Ger., bü′-nen-moo-zĭk′). INCIDENTAL MUSIC for plays or music performed on the stage.

Bullroarer. A common instrument found in world musical cultures by a variety of names. The bullroarer consists of a long whip topped by a small, often arrow-shaped piece of bone, wood, metal, or other material. When the whip is spun around the head, the air is set into VIBRATION, creating a mysterious whirring sound.

Burden. 1. A CHORUS or REFRAIN repeated after each STANZA of a SONG. 2. The DRONE of a BAGPIPE. 3. The BASS PART. 4. A dance ACCOMPANIMENT sung without instruments.

Burlando (It., bŏŏr-lăhn'dŏh). Joking, jesting, romping.

Burlescamente (It., bŏŏr-lĕ-skăh-men'tĕh). In burlesque style.

Burlesque (bur-lesk'). A dramatic extravaganza, or farcical travesty of some serious subject, featuring more or less music. *Also* **Burletta**.

C

C. 1. (Ger. *C*; Fr. *ut*; It. *do*). The first TONE and DEGREE in the typical DIATONIC SCALE of *C* MAJOR. 2. In music THEORY, capital *C* designates the *C*-major TRIAD small *c* the *c*-MINOR triad.

3. Middle-*C* is the note *c*¹ on the PIANO KEYBOARD:

TENOR-*C* is the lowest note in the tenor voice, *c*:

Cabaletta (It., kăh-băh-let'tah). In late Italian OPERA, the concluding section of an ARIA, forming a summary in rapid TEMPO.

Cabaret. A form of nightclub entertainment dating from c. 1880–1930s, especially popular in Paris and Berlin.

Caccia (It., căht'chăh). Chase or hunt. *Alla caccia*, in hunting style, that is, accompanied by HORNS.

Cachucha (Sp., căh-choo'chăh). A dance much like the BOLERO.

Cacophony. A raucous conglomeration of sound.

Cadence. 1. A CADENZA. 2. The closing strains of a MELODY or harmonized MOVEMENT, the close or ending of a PHRASE, SECTION, or movement. *Amen cadence*, a popular term for *plagal c.* (to which the word "Amen" is often sung); *authentic c.*, a cadence in which the penultimate CHORD is the DOMINANT, and the final chord is the TONIC; *avoided, broken, deceptive, evaded*, or *false c.*, a cadence that settles on an unexpected chord; *full c.*, a perfect cadence; *half c.* (half close), or *imperfect c.*, a cadence on any chord other than the tonic; *interrupted* or *irregular c.*, an unexpected progression avoiding some regular cadence; *mixed c.*, an authentic c. with dominant, SUBDOMINANT, dominant, and tonic chords in succession; *perfect c.*, an authentic c. in which both dominant and tonic chords are in ROOT POSITION, and the last chord has the root in the highest voice as well as in the lowest; the "authentic c." of the church MODES; *plagal c.*, the subdominant chord followed by the tonic; *radical c.*, a close, either partial or complete, formed with two FUNDAMENTAL chords; *surprise c.*, an interrupted c.; *whole c.*, a perfect c. Many of these categories overlap.

Perfect
Authentic   Plagal   Interrupted, Deceptive, etc.

Cadenza (It., kăh-den'dzăh). 1. In a vocal solo, a brilliant PASSAGE, usually performed at the end. 2. An elaborate passage or FANTASIA at the end of the first or last MOVEMENT of a CONCERTO, and played by the solo instrument.

Cæsura. CESURA.

Caisse (Fr., kāss). DRUM. *Caisse claire* (kāss klâr), snare drum; *c., grosse* (grōs kāss), bass drum; *c. roulante* (kāss roo-lähn't), side drum; *c. sourde* (kāss soord'), tenor drum.

Cakewalk. An African-American folk dance in RAGTIME RHYTHM, popular from the 1890s to the 1910s.

Calando (It., kăh-lähn'dŏh). "Decreasing"; growing softer and (usually) slower.

Calcando (It., kăhl-kăn'dŏh). "Pressing"; hastening the TEMPO.

Call and Response. ANTIPHONY.

Calliope (cal-li'o-pe). A steam ORGAN; a pipe organ whose harsh tone is produced by steam instead of wind, under pressure.

Callithumpian concert. A boisterous SERENADE given to some person who has become an object of popular hostility or ridicule; characterized by the blowing of HORNS, beating on tin pans, derisive cries, hoots, groans, catcalls, etc.

Calma, con (It., kŏhn kăhl'măh). With calm; calmly, tranquilly.

Calmando(si) (It., kăhl-măhn'dŏh[-sē]). Growing calm, becoming tranquil.

Caloroso (It., kăh-lŏh-**r**oh'sŏh). With warmth, passion; passionately.

Calypso. Popular music of the West Indies, much influenced by American JAZZ, with lyrics often reflecting topical subjects. A short calypso fad swept the American pop-music charts in the late 1950s and early 1960s.

Cambiata (It., kăhm-byăh'tah). "Changed." *Nota cambiata*, a CHANGING NOTE.

Camera (It., kah'mĕh-**r**ăh). Chamber, room, small hall. *Alla camera*, in the style of CHAMBER MUSIC; *musica da c.*, chamber music.

Camminando (It., kăhm-mē-năhn'dŏh). "Walking"; a flowing movement, like ANDANTE.

Campagnuolo,-a (It., kăhm-păhn-yô'lŏh,-lăh). Pastoral, idyllic; rustic.

Campana (It., kăhm-pah'năh). A BELL.

Campanello (It., -nel'lŏh). A small BELL.

Campestre (It., kăhm-pĕ'strĕh). Pastoral, rural, idyllic.

Canarie. A French dance in TRIPLE TIME, popular in the 17th century and supposedly imitating the RHYTHMS of the native music of the Canary Islands.

Cancan. A fast French VAUDEVILLE dance in 2/4 TIME, once regarded as naughty.

Cancel. The natural sign, ♮.

Canción (Sp., kăhn-thē-ŏn). SONG.

Cancrizans (Latin). Retrogressive; moving-backward.

Canon. The strictest form of musical IMITATION, in which two or more PARTS take up, in succession, the given SUBJECT note for note. See also FUGUE.

Canonical Hours. Established times for daily prayer within the Roman Catholic Church: *matins* (including *nocturns* and *lauds*), *prime, terce, sext, nones, vespers,* and *complin*.

Canonic imitation. Strict IMITATION of one PART by another.

Cantabile (It., kăhn-tah′bē-lĕh). "Singable"; in a singing or vocal style.

Cantando or **Cantante** (It., kăhn-tăhn′dŏh or kăhn-tăhn′teh). Singing; smooth and flowing.

Cantata (It., kăhn-tah′tăh). A vocal work with instrumental ACCOMPANIMENT, consisting of CHORUSES and SOLOS, RECITATIVES, DUETS, etc.; may be sacred or secular.

Canterellando (or **Canticchiando**) (It., kăhn-tĕh-rel-lăhn′dŏh [kăhn-tik-yăhn′dŏh]). Singing softly; humming.

Canticle. One of the nonmetrical HYMNS of praise and jubilation in the Bible; or a sacred CHANT similar to it.

Cantillation. CHANTING in a simple manner without ACCOMPANIMENT; usually applied to Jewish liturgy.

Cantilena (It., kăhn-tē-lâ′năh); **Cantilene** (Ger., kăhn-tē-lä′nĕ); **Cantilène** (Fr., kăhn-tē-län′). "A little SONG"; a BALLAD or light popular song; a flowing, songlike PASSAGE on an instrument.

Canto (It., kăhn′tŏh). A MELODY, SONG, CHANT; the SOPRANO (highest vocal or instrumental PART). *Col canto*, "with the melody," a direction to accompanists to follow the SOLO PART in TEMPO and expression; *c. fermo*, a CANTUS FIRMUS.

Cantor. The leading singer in German Protestant church services or in Jewish synagogues.

Cantus firmus (Latin). A fixed or given MELODY: (*a*) PLAINSONG; (*b*) in COUNTERPOINT, a given melody, like a PLAINSONG TUNE, to which other parts are to be set according to rule.

Canzone (It., kăhn-tsoh′neh). A SONG, FOLK SONG; also, a PARTSONG in MADRIGAL style.

Canzonet. A little AIR or SONG; a short PART SONG; a MADRIGAL.

Capo (It., kah'pŏh). Head, beginning. *Da capo*, from the beginning; *da c. al segno*, from the beginning to the sign (𝄋 or ⊕). 2. See also CAPOTASTO, 2.

Capo d'astro. (An English corruption of *capotasto*). The "capo d'astro bar" in the PIANO is a metallic bar fixed across the STRINGS near the wrestplank, bearing down on the three highest OCTAVES (more or less).

Capotasto (It., kah-pŏh-tăh'stŏh). 1. The NUT of stringed instruments having a FINGERBOARD. 2. A piece of wood, ivory, or a rubber bar or clamp that can be set across a fretted fingerboard to raise the PITCH of all the STRINGS at once.

Cappella (It., kăhp-pel'lăh). A CHOIR; an ORCHESTRA; both together. *A* (or *alla*) *cappella*, vocal CHORUS without instrumental ACCOMPANIMENT.

Capriccio (It., kăh-prit'chŏh). An instrumental piece free in-FORM, distinguished by originality in HARMONY and RHYTHM; a caprice. *A capriccio*, at pleasure.

Capriccioso (It., kăh-prit-chŏh'sŏh). In a capricious, fanciful, fantastic style.

Caressant (Fr., kăh-rĕs-sähn'); **Carezzevole** (It., kăh-ret-sā'-vŏh-lĕh). Caressingly, soothingly.

Carillon (Fr., kăh-rē-yŏhn'). 1. A GLOCKENSPIEL, or set of fixed BELLS played from a KEYBOARD or by a barrel-mechanism; also a TUNE played on these bells, or an instrumental PIECE imitating their effect. 2. A PIANO with bells instead of STRINGS. 3. A mixture STOP in the ORGAN.

Carità, con (It., kŏhn kăh-rē-tah'). With tender expression.

Carol. To sing joyously; hence, a joyous Christmas SONG of praise.

Cassa (It., kăh'săh). DRUM. *Cassa, gran* (grähn kăh'săh), bass drum.

Cassation. An 18th-century instrumental SUITE, similar to the DIVERTIMENTO and SERENADE.

Castanets. A pair of small concave pieces of wood or ivory, attached by a cord to a dancer's thumb and forefinger, and struck together in time with the music. Commonly used in Spanish dance music.

Castrato (It., kăh-strah'tŏh). A castrated adult male singer with SOPRANO or ALTO voice.

Catch. A ROUND or CANON for three or more voices, each singer having to "catch" or take up his PART at the right instant. Catches are generally humorous.

Catgut. Popular name for GUT STRINGS.

Cavallina (It., kăh-văhl-lē'năh). A forced, jerky delivery (COL-ORATURA).

Cavatina (It., kăh-vă'htē'năh). A SONG; particularly, a short ARIA without a second SECTION or DA CAPO.

C clef. A CLEF, variously written 𝄡 𝄡 𝄡 𝄡 etc.

CD. COMPACT DISC.

CD-ROM (COMPACT DISC-Read Only Memory). A late 20th-century means of data storage that allows for massive amounts of information, including music, text, and images (still and moving), to be stored on a single CD-sized disc. CD-ROM players are usually sold as an adjunct to a personal COMPUTER, but may also be connected to a home SYNTHESIZER or SAMPLER, in order to access large numbers of prerecorded sounds.

C dur (Ger., tsā door'). *C* major.

Cedendo (It., chā-den'dŏh). Growing slower.

Cédez (Fr., sā-dā'). Go slower.

Celere (It., chĕh-lĕh-rĕh). Rapid, swift.

Celerità, con (It., kŏhn chĕh-lĕh-rē-tah′). With celerity, rapidity.

Celesta. PERCUSSION instrument invented by Mustel in Paris, 1886, consisting of tuned steel bars connected to a KEYBOARD. Tchaikovsky's "Dance of the Sugar Plum Fairies" from his *Nutcracker Suite* is one of the best-known works featuring this instrument.

Céleste (Fr., sā-lest′). Celestial.

Cell. A modern term generally denoting a small group of NOTES, indicative of PITCH and/or RHYTHM, which serve as an organizing device in the composition of music.

'Cello (It., chel′lŏh). Third instrument in the VIOLIN family, played in an upright position, with the instrument resting on the floor and poised between the player's knees, producing a sweet, singing tone. *'Cello* is actually a nickname, shortened from VIOLONCELLO; in written usage, the initial apostrophe is generally dropped.

Cembalo (It., chĕm′băh-lŏh). HARPSICHORD, PIANOFORTE; in olden times, a DULCIMER. *A cembalo*, for PIANO (or harpsichord).

Cencerros. Cuban cowbells, heard often in Latin American dance music.

Ces (Ger., tsĕss). *C* flat.

Ceses (Ger., tsĕss′ĕss). *C* double flat.

Cesura, Cæsura. The dividing line between two melodic and rhythmical PHRASES.

Cha-cha. Latin American dance in an insistent BINARY RHYTHM; sometimes called more emphatically Cha-cha-cha.

Chaconne (Fr., shäh-kŏhn′). 1. A Spanish dance. 2. An instrumental PIECE consisting of a series of VARIATIONS above a GROUND BASS not over eight MEASURES in length, in a slow 3/4 TEMPO.

Chalumeau (Fr., shăl-u-moh). 1. An 18th-century forebearer of the CLARINET, popular in Germany. 2. Chanter of the BAGPIPE. 3. The lowest OCTAVE played on the modern clarinet.

Chamber music. Vocal or instrumental music suitable for performance in a room or small hall; especially, quartets and similar concerted PIECES for solo instruments.

Chamber orchestra. A small ORCHESTRA.

Chamber opera. An OPERA suitable for performance in a small hall, with a limited number of performers and accompanied by a CHAMBER ORCHESTRA.

Chamber symphony. A SYMPHONY for CHAMBER ORCHESTRA.

Chance music. See CHANCE OPERATIONS; ALEATORY.

Chance operations. The practice, highly developed by the American composer John Cage (1912–1992), of composing music via chance means (throwing dice, consulting the *I Ching*, making use of random-number generators, etc.), resulting in works devoid of a composer's taste or intentions.

Change. 1. In HARMONY, MODULATION. 2. In the voice, MUTATION. 3. Any MELODIC PHRASE or FIGURE played on a chime of BELLS.

Change-ringing. The art and practice of ringing a peal of BELLS in varying and systematic order.

Changing note. A DISSONANT TONE entering on the strong BEAT, and passing by a STEP to a CONSONANCE, or by a SKIP to a CHORD tone belonging to another chord.

Chanson (Fr., shăhn-sŏhn'). A SONG.

Chansonette (Fr., shăhn-sŏhn-net'). A short song of a light nature.

Chant. A short, sacred SONG, usually unharmonized, and characterized by a free, unmetered MELODY. 1. The Anglican chant, adapted to the CANTICLES and PSALMS, consists of seven MEASURES, harmonized, the TIME-VALUE of the single NOTE constituting the first and fourth measures being lengthened or shortened to fit the words, whereas the others are sung in strict time. Each of its two divisions (of three and four measures, respectively) begins on a RECITING-NOTE and ends with a CADENCE. 2. The GREGORIAN CHANT, established by Pope Gregory I (d. 604), is a Gregorian melody repeated with the several verses of biblical prose text; it has five divisions: (1) the intonation, (2) the first dominant, or reciting-note, (3) the mediation, (4) the second dominant, or reciting-note, and (5) the cadence.

Chant (Fr., shähn). SONG; singing; MELODY; TUNE. Also, voice (the vocal PART as distinguished from the ACCOMPANIMENT).

Chanter. The melody-pipe of the BAGPIPE.

Chanterelle (Fr., shăn-t'-rel'). The highest STRING on a VIOLIN, LUTE, etc.

Chapel. A company of musicians attached to the establishment, frequently a private church, of any distinguished personage.

Character piece. One depicting a definite mood, impression, scene, or event.

Characteristic tone. 1. The leading TONE. See APPOGGIATURA. 2. That tone in any KEY that specially distinguishes it from nearly related KEYS, i.e., the $F\sharp$ in G major, distinguishing it from C major.

Charme, avec (Fr., ăh-vek' sharm). With charm; gracefully.

Chef d'orchestre (Fr., shef dor-kes'tr). CONDUCTOR of an ORCHESTRA.

Chest of viols. Old English description of a set of STRINGED INSTRUMENTS of various sizes, in olden times kept in a specially constructed chest.

Chest register. The lower REGISTER of the male or female voice, the TONES of which produce SYMPATHETIC VIBRATION in the chest.

Chest voice (or **tone**). Vocal quality of the CHEST REGISTER.

Chiarezza, con (It., kōhn k'yäh-ret'säh). Clearly, distinctly, limpidly.

Chiesa (It., kee-eh'sah). Church. *Sonata da chiesa*, a SONATA suitable for church performance.

Chime. 1. A set of from five to twelve BELLS tuned to the SCALE, and played by swinging either the bells themselves or clappers hung within them. Also, a TUNE so played. 2. A set of bells and HAMMERS played by a KEYBOARD; a CARILLON.

Chinese blocks. Resonant WOODBLOCKS struck with a drumstick or mallet.

Chin rest. An oval plate of ebony attached to the edge of the VIOLIN to the left of the TAILPIECE.

Chitarra (It., kē-tar'räh). A GUITAR.

Chitarrone (It., kē-tar-roh'nĕh). A large LUTE.

Chitarrata (It., kē-tar-rah'täh). A PIANO piece imitating the GUITAR.

Chiuso,-a (It., kew'soh,-säh). Closed. *A bocca chiusa*, with closed mouth; humming.

Choeur (Fr., kühr). CHORUS.

Choir. 1. A company of singers, especially in a church. 2. A choral society. 3. In the Anglican Church, the singers of the daily choral service, who sit divided on the *decani* and *cantoris* sides of the chancel. 4. A subdivision of a chorus; for example, the first and second choirs in eight-part music.

Choirmaster. Leader of a CHOIR.

Choral. Relating or pertaining to a CHORUS, or to vocal concerted music. *Choral notes*, the square NOTES used for writing PLAINSONG; *c. service*, a church service with music by the CHOIR.

Chorale (kŏh-rahl'). A HYMN TUNE of the German Protestant Church, or one similar in style.

Chorale prelude. An instrumental composition based on a CHORALE or HYMN TUNE, often played before the chorale proper.

Choralmässig (Ger., kŏh-rahl'mä'sĭyh). In the style of a CHORALE.

Chord. 1. A HARMONY of two or more TONES. 2. A harmony of from three to five tones, forming an ascending series of DIATONIC THIRDS (see "Chords," pp. xvi–xvii). 3. A *flat* or *solid* chord is one whose tones are produced simultaneously, as opposed to *broken*. 4. A STRING.

Chordophones. A class of musical instruments that produce their sound by means of vibrating STRINGS stretched between fixed points, i.e., GUITAR, VIOLIN, etc.

Choreography. The dancing scenario in a stage work.

Chôros. A Brazilian folk dance, or a work written in a Brazilian folk style.

Chorus. A company of singers; hence, a COMPOSITION, often in four PARTS, each sung by several or many singers; a double chorus has eight parts. Also, the REFRAIN or BURDEN of a SONG.

Chorus master. A CHOIRMASTER.

Christe eleison (Gk., crēs'tä ā-lā'ē-sohn, "Christ, have mercy"). Part of the KYRIE. See MASS.

Chromatic. Relating to TONES foreign to a given KEY (SCALE) or CHORD; opposed to DIATONIC. *Chromatic signs*: the sharp (♯), flat (♭), natural (♮), double sharp (×), and double flat (♭♭).

Church modes. The OCTAVE SCALES employed in medieval church music.

Ciaccona (It., chăhk-koh'năh). A CHACONNE.

Cimbalo (It., chĭm'băh-lŏh). 1. A CYMBAL; a TAMBOURINE. 2. Also, used occasionally in Renaissance or Baroque periods to describe a HARPSICHORD.

Cimbalom. A large DULCIMER, typical of Hungarian Gypsy bands; played with mallets and having a CHROMATIC SCALE of four OCTAVES (from E to e^3.

Cinelli (It., chĭn-nĕl'lē). CYMBALS.

Cinque-pace (sink'pās). An old dance, probably French, with a five-step movement.

Cipher. 1. A TONE is said to "cipher" on the ORGAN when, owing to some derangement of the action, it persists in sounding. 2. The practice of basing a COMPOSITION on musical tones that are tonal equivalents to letters of the alphabet.

Circle of Fifths. A series of FIFTHS tuned (as on the PIANO) in equal TEMPERAMENT, so that the *twelfth* fifth in the series has the same letter name as the first TONE. See "The Keys," p. xv.

Circular breathing. A modern technique, primarily among vocalists and flutists, wherein the performer inhales breath through the nose while simultaneously exhaling breath through the mouth, thus sustaining sound for an indefinite length of time.

Circular canon. A CANON closing in the KEY a SEMITONE above that in which it begins; twelve repetitions would thus carry it through the "circle" of twelve keys.

Circus music. A type of BAND music associated with circuses; early on with FIDDLES and DRUMS, later with bands of up to thirty-six players, mostly BRASS and TIMPANI. The repertoire, like early extemporized ACCOMPANIMENT to silent film, is determined by the character of the acts being supported.

Cis (Ger., tsiss). *C* sharp.

Cis dur (Ger., tsiss door). *C* sharp major.

Cis moll (Ger., mohl). *C* sharp minor.

Cisis (Ger., tsiss'iss). *C* double sharp.

Cither (sith'er), **Cithern**, **Cittern** (sit'-). A kind of LUTE or GUITAR, strung with wire and played with a PICK; used in the 16th and 17th centuries.

Civetteria, con (It., kŏhn chē-vet-tĕh-**rē**'ăh). With coquetry; in a coquettish, trifling style.

Clang (Ger., *Klang*). A FUNDAMENTAL TONE with its HARMONICS; *Clang-color*, *Clang-tint*, "tone color," TIMBRE.

Claque. Hired groups of people paid to applaud an opera singer or some other performer.

Clarinet. A TRANSPOSING SINGLE-REED WIND INSTRUMENT derived from the CHALUMEAU. It has a cylindrical wooden tube pierced by eighteen holes, thirteen being closed by KEYS, yielding a CHROMATIC series of nineteen prime tones (*e* to *B*♭¹). Its COMPASS comprises three OCTAVES in four different REGISTERS: the Low ("chalumeau"), Medium, High ("clarinetto"), and Super-acute.

Clarinet stop. An ORGAN STOP imitating the sound of the CLARINET.

Clarinetto (It., klăh-rē-net'tŏh). CLARINET.

Clarion. 1. A small, shrill-toned TRUMPET. 2. In the ORGAN, a 4' REED STOP of shrill, piercing tone.

Classical music. Colloquially, any serious, "art" music, as opposed to POPULAR or FOLK MUSIC.

Classical suite. An instrumental SUITE of stylized dance forms, also called the *Baroque Suite*. It has four principal movements: ALLEMANDE, COURANTE, SARABANDE, and GIGUE, in that order. Lighter dance movements, such as the MINUET, BOURRÉE, and GAVOTTE, are often interpolated between the SARABANDE and the closing GIGUE.

Clavecin (Fr., klăh-v'-săn'); **Clavicembalo** (It., klăh-vē-chem'-băh-lŏh). A HARPSICHORD.

Claves. Hardwood sticks used in Latin American rhythm bands, which produce a sharp sound when clicked together.

Clavichord. A precursor of the PIANOFORTE, differing in action from the latter in having, instead of hammers, upright metal wedges called TANGENTS on the rear end of the KEYS; on pressing a key, the tangent strikes the wire string and remains pressed against it until the finger is lifted, causing only one section of the string to vibrate.

Clavier (Fr., klăh-v'yā'). A KEYBOARD; a MANUAL. *Clavier de récit*, swell manual.

Clef. A character set at the head of the STAFF to fix the PITCH or position of one NOTE, and thus of the rest. See "The Clefs," p. x.

Cloches (Fr., klōsh). CHIMES.

Close (klōz). A CADENCE ending a SECTION, MOVEMENT, or PIECE.

Close harmony. In regular four-voice settings, the three upper voices placed within an OCTAVE.

Cluster. See TONE CLUSTER.

C moll (Ger., bă mohl). *C minor.*

Coda (It., kŏh'dăh). A "tail"; hence, a PASSAGE ending a MOVEMENT.

Codetta (It., kŏh-det'tăh). A short CODA.

Collage. 1. As in the visual arts, heterogeneous compositions in which unexpected or inharmonious elements are juxtaposed, frequently with reference to other, earlier musics. 2. The practice of assembling bits of musical material to make a new COMPOSITION, as in the tape collages of MUSIQUE CONCRÈTE.

Color. 1. TIMBRE. 2. In 14th and 15th century ISORHYTHMIC music, a repeated PITCH pattern.

Coloratura (It., kŏh-lŏh-rǎh-too'rǎh). Vocal RUNS, PASSAGES, TRILLS, etc., enhancing the brilliancy of a COMPOSITION and displaying the singer's skill (also used for instrumental ORNAMENTS).

Coloris (Fr., kŏh-lŏh-rē'). The changes in vocal or instrumental "tone color," or in the INSTRUMENTATION or REGISTRATION, employed for obtaining special effects; the "color-scheme" of a COMPOSITION.

Colpo (It., kŏhl'pŏh). A blow. *Di colpo*, suddenly.

Combination pedal. A metal foot-lever above the ORGAN PEDALS; the *forte pedal* draws all the STOPS of its KEYBOARD; the *mezzo pedal*, the chief 8' and 4' stops of its keyboard; the *piano pedal* pushes in all but a few of the softest stops.

Combinatoriality. A characteristic of a SET that its elements can be found in combination in other segments of the same, generating 12-NOTE ROW.

Combo. A JAZZ ENSEMBLE; the word is short for combination.

Come (It., kô'měh). As, like.

Come prima (It., kô'měh prē'mǎh). As before, as at first (that is, "resume the previous tempo").

Come retro (It., kô'měh rǎ'trŏh). As before.

Come sopra (It., kô'měh soh'prǎh). As above.

Come sta (It., kô'měh stah). As it stands, as written.

Comes (L., coh'mās). Answer to the SUBJECT in a FUGUE. Literally, "companion."

Comic opera. OPERA with a comic subject; in French *Opéra Comique*, opera that includes spoken dialogue.

Comma. The Greek term for the minute INTERVAL that represents the difference between a PERFECT FIFTH in TEMPERED PITCH and the pure interval formed in the natural HARMONIC SERIES.

Commodo (It.). COMODO.

Common chord. A MAJOR or MINOR TRIAD. *Common hallelujah metre,* or *c. long metre,* see METRE; *c. measure,* common TIME; *c. metre, double c. metre, c. particular metre,* see METRE; *c. time,* a MEASURE containing two (or four) half notes, or four QUARTER NOTES, with two or four beats, respectively; DUPLE or QUADRUPLE time. (Ordinarily, common time is understood to mean four quarter notes, and as many beats, to the measure.)

Comodo (It., kô'mŏh-dŏh). Easy, leisurely, at a convenient pace.

Comp. In *Bebop,* short for "accompany," referring to a style of PIANO ACCOMPANIMENT in which the pianist plays partial BLOCK CHORDS in the right hand, spread sporadically throughout the music, rather than as a regular "oom-pah" beat.

Compact disc (**CD**; see-dee). A revolutionary, noninteractive, digital recording; also called simply *disc.*

Compass. The range of a voice or instrument; the SCALE of all the TONES it can produce, from the lowest to the highest.

Complacevolmente (It., kŏhm-p'yăh-chā-vohl-men'tĕh). Pleasing(ly), charming(ly).

Complement, Complementary interval. An INTERVAL that, added to any given interval not wider than an OCTAVE, completes the octave; a FOURTH is the complement of a FIFTH, a MINOR THIRD the complement of a MAJOR SIXTH, etc.

Complin(e). A short evening service, completing the seven Canonical Hours.

Composer. A person who writes music.

Composition. The broadest term for writing music, or for music so written, in any form for any instruments or voices.

Composition pedal. In the ORGAN, a PEDAL that draws out or pushes in several STOPS at once.

Compound interval. An interval greater than an octave, i.e., one formed by adding any simple interval (one less than an octave) to an octave. See TENTH, TWELFTH, FIFTEENTH.

Compound meter or **time**. 1. A MEASURE with a number of BEATS composed of two or more different SIMPLE meters, such as 5/4 (2/4 + 3/4) or 7/4 (4/4 + 3/4). 2. A meter with a TRIPLE PULSE within each of its beats, i.e., 6/8 as a compound of 2/4, 12/8 of 4/4 etc. Double compound meters are also possible, although rare.

Computers. Digital machines used by COMPOSERS to (1) calculate details of COMPOSITIONS; (2) store information for subsequent use; and/or (3) generate new and/or transform existing sound(s).

Con (It., kŏhn). With; in a style expressive of. (*N.B.* For definitions of phrases beginning with "con," see the second word in the given phrase.)

Concentrando (It., kŏhn-chen-trähn'dŏh). "Concentrating"; an EXPRESSION MARK in vocal music calling for an intensified effect of TONE.

Concert. A musical performance on the concert stage.

Concertante (It., kŏhn-chăr-tähn'tĕh). 1. A concert piece. 2. A COMPOSITION for two or more solo voices or instruments with ACCOMPANIMENT by ORCHESTRA or ORGAN, in which each solo PART is in turn brought into prominence. 3. A composition for two or more unaccompanied solo instruments in orchestral music. *Concertante style*, a style of composition admitting of a brilliant display of skill on the soloist's part.

Concerted music. Music written in PARTS for several instruments or voices, i.e., TRIOS, QUARTETS, etc.

Concertina. A family of FREE-REED, bellows-driven instruments, sometimes confused with the ACCORDION. The *English concertina* was invented by Charles Wheatstone in 1844, and has four rows of buttons, the two inner rows activating the natural NOTES, the outer two the ACCIDENTALS. The *treble c.* (with the range of a VIOLIN) is the most common; the English system plays the same note on the press or draw of the bellows. The *Anglo c.* plays a different note on the press or draw; common, inexpensive instruments feature only two rows of buttons, and play in the KEYS of *C* and *G*. There are other less-common types, including the *Duet system*, popularized by the Salvation Army.

Concert grand. The largest GRAND or full-size PIANO, which, like grand pianos of any size, features the STRINGS placed on a horizontal frame or harp.

Concertino. 1. A small CONCERTO, scored for a small ensemble. 2. The group of soloists in a CONCERTO GROSSO.

Concertmaster. The leader of the first VIOLIN section in the ORCHESTRA.

Concerto (It., kŏhn-châr'tŏh). An extended COMPOSITION for a solo instrument and ORCHESTRA, frequently in a (modified) SONATA form.

Concerto grosso (It., kŏhn-châr'tŏh' grô'sŏh). An instrumental COMPOSITION employing a small group of solo instruments (see CONCERTINO 2) against a larger group or full orchestra (see RIPIENO 4).

Concerto for orchestra. A symphonic work in which the orchestral instruments play the role of soloists.

Concert overture. An OVERTURE for full ORCHESTRA, performed as an independent COMPOSITION at a SYMPHONY concert.

Concert pitch. 1. The actual sound produced by an instrument, as distinct from a written NOTE in TRANSPOSING INSTRUMENTS, i.e., the *B*-flat CLARINET, wherein the written note *C* sounds *B*-flat. 2. The standard TUNING of the *A* above middle *C* to equal 440 vibratory cycles per second so as to facilitate the tuning of orchestral or small ensembles.

Concertstück (Ger., kŏhn-tsârt′shtük). Concert-piece; CONCERTO.

Concitato (It., kŏhn-chē-tah′tŏh). Moved, excited, agitated.

Concord. Euphony; HARMONY; CONSONANCE.

Concrete music. MUSIQUE CONCRÈTE.

Conductor. Director of an ORCHESTRA or CHORUS.

Conductus. A CONTRAPUNTAL PART combined with a given original MELODY in POLYPHONIC music of the Middle Ages.

Conical mouthpiece. See CUPPED MOUTHPIECE. *Conical tube,* one tapering very gradually; a *cylindrical tube* does not taper.

Conjunct degree. The nearest DEGREE in the SCALE (CHROMATIC or DIATONIC) to the given degree. *Conjunct motion,* PROGRESSION by conjunct degrees or INTERVALS.

Consecutive intervals. INTERVALS of the same kind following each other in immediate succession; ''consecutives'' are progressions of PARALLEL FIFTHS or OCTAVES, forbidden in strict, common practice HARMONY.

Consequent. In a CANON, the follower; the PART imitating the ANTECEDENT or LEADER.

Conservatoire (Fr., kŏhn-sâr-văh-twar'); **Conservatorium** (L.); **Conservatory**. A public or private institution for providing practical and theoretical instruction in music.

Consolante (It., kŏhn-sŏh-lähn'tĕh). Consoling, soothing.

Console. The KEYBOARD, STOPS, and PEDALS of the ORGAN.

Consonance. A combination of two or more TONES, harmonious and pleasing in itself, and requiring no further PROGRESSION. *Consonant intervals*, consonances of two tones; *imperfect consonances*, the MAJOR and MINOR THIRDS and SIXTHS; *perfect consonances*, the OCTAVE, FIFTH, and FOURTH.

Consonant chord. One containing no DISSONANT INTERVAL(S).

Consort. An old English term for an instrumental ENSEMBLE; see WHOLE CONSORT and BROKEN CONSORT.

Constructivism. As in the visual arts, compositions that exhibit a high degree of evident structure.

Contano (It., kŏhn'tăh-nŏh). "They count"; in a score, PARTS so marked are to pause.

Continuo (It., kŏhn-tē'nŏŏ'ŏh). FIGURED BASS.

Contra (L.; It.). "Against"; prefixed to names of instruments, it means "an OCTAVE below."

Contrabass; **Contrabasso** (It., kŏhn-trăhb-băhs'sŏh). DOUBLE BASS.

Contradanza (It., kŏhn-trăh-dahn'tzăh). English COUNTRY DANCE.

Contrafagotto (It., kŏhn-trăhf-făh-gŏht'tŏh). 1. DOUBLE-BASSOON. 2. A REED STOP in the ORGAN.

Contraltino (It., kŏhn-trăhl-tē'nŏh). A high, light TENOR voice of fluent delivery.

Contralto (It., kŏhn-trăhl'tŏh). ALTO 1.

Contra-octave. The OCTAVE below the GREAT OCTAVE.

Contrapuntal. Pertaining to the art or practice of COUN-TERPOINT.

Contrapuntist. One versed in the theory and practice of COUN-TERPOINT.

Contrary motion. PARTS are said to progress in CONTRARY MO-TION when one moves up while the other moves down.

Contre (Fr., kŏhn'tr). "Against"; also contra-, counter-.

Contredanse (Fr., kŏhn'truh-dahns'). COUNTRY DANCE.

Cool. An American JAZZ style of the 1950s, characterized by a less frenetic ("hot") atmosphere than earlier styles, use of atypical instruments (FLUTE, FRENCH HORN), and adoption of "classical" compositional techniques (i.e., FUGUE).

Coperto (It., kŏh-pâr'tŏh). Covered, muffled.

Cor (Fr., kor). A HORN. *Cor anglais* (ăhn-glä'), the ENGLISH HORN.

Coranto (It., kŏh-răhn'tŏh). 1. COURANTE. 2. COUNTRY DANCE.

Corda (It., kôr'dăh). A STRING. (Plural: *corde* [kôr'-dĕh].) *Sopra una corda*, play "on the string"; *una corda*, or *U.C.*, engage soft PEDAL of PIANO; *due corde* (piano), release soft pedal, or, when the soft pedal shifts the KEYBOARD, "play with soft pedal pressed halfway down"; *due corde* (stringed instruments), "play the note on two strings"; *tutte (le) corde*, "all the strings", that is, "release the soft pedal"; *corda vuoto*, open string.

Cornemuse (Fr., kôr-ne-müz). BAGPIPE.

Cornet. 1. A TRANSPOSING BRASS INSTRUMENT of the TRUMPET family (*cornet à pistons*), with conical tube and cupped MOUTHPIECE; improved from the old post horn by the addition of three valves; medium COMPASS two OCTAVES and three TONES, this being for the ordinary cornet in B♭. The old cornet was a wooden instrument with finger holes. 2. On the ORGAN, there are various cornet STOPS.

Corno (It., kôr'nŏh). A HORN (plural *corni*).

Cornon (Fr., kôr-nŏh n'). 1. A CORNET STOP on the ORGAN. 2. A BRASS INSTRUMENT, invented in 1844.

Cornopean (kor-nŏ'pe-an). 1. *Cornet à pistons.* 2. An ORGAN STOP on the swell MANUAL.

Corrente (It., kŏhr-ren'tĕh). COURANTE.

Corto,-a (It., kohr'tŏh,-tăh). Short. *La cadenza sia corta,* let the CADENZA be short.

Cotillion (Fr., *cotillon* [kŏh-tē-yŏhn']). A French dance, popular in the 19th century. Usually performed at the end of a formal dance, the *cotillion* can feature a variety of steps, performed by a lead couple and then imitated by the others.

Cottage organ. A portable REED ORGAN.

Coulé (Fr., koo-lā'). LEGATO, slurred; also, a HARPSICHORD GRACE NOTE.

Count. An ACCENT, BEAT, or PULSE of a MEASURE.

Counter. Any vocal PART set to contrast in some manner with the PRINCIPAL part or MELODY, i.e *bass counter,* a second BASS part, or COUNTERTENOR. Also, *counter-exposition,* re-entrance of a FUGUE-SUBJECT; *c.-subject,* a fugal THEME following the subject in the same part; *c.-tenor clef,* the C-CLEF on the *second* line of the STAFF (now obsolete).

Counterpoint. 1. The art of POLYPHONIC COMPOSITION. 2. Composition with two or more simultaneous MELODIES. *Double counterpoint* is written so that the upper PART can become the lower part, and vice versa; in *triple* and *quadruple c.,* three and four parts are written so that they can be mutually exchanged.

Countertenor. The Anglicized term for the Latin contratenor.
1. A contratenor line (on the STAFF), lying just above that
of the tenor, in RENAISSANCE POLYPHONY. 2. A male singer,
usually a falsettist, with an unusually high TESSITURA; a
male ALTO, COMPASS from *g* to *c*♭.

Country dance. A dance in 2/4 or 3/4 TIME in which the part-
ners form two opposing lines, which advance and retreat,
the couples also dancing down the lines and returning
to their places.

Country-Western. A term that covers a variety of American
rural and cowboy SONG styles.

Coup de glotte (Fr., koo dŭh glaht, "stroke of the glottis").
A highly dramatic way of interrupted breath in singing
that was very popular among Italian singers, but is now
regarded as somewhat exaggerated.

Coupler. A mechanical ORGAN STOP acting to connect two
MANUALS, or PEDAL with manual, so that when one is
played on, the other is combined with it. A *Coupler-pedal*
is a coupler worked by the foot.

Couplet. 1. Two successive lines forming a pair, usually
rhymed. 2. In triple TIME, two equal NOTES occupying the
time of three such notes in the established RHYTHM, thus:

Also called a DUPLET.

Courante (Fr., koo'rähn't). A Courant, or old French dance
in 3/2 TIME; hence, the instrumental PIECE so called.

Covered. See OCTAVE. *Covered strings*, strings of silk, wire, or
GUT, covered with spiral turns of fine silver or copper
wire.

Crab canon. A CANON performed backwards; *crab movement* is thus backwards movement of a MELODY.

Cracovienne (Fr., krăh-koh-v'yen'). A Polish dance for a large company, the music in DUPLE TIME with frequent SYNCOPATIONS; RHYTHM:

Credo (L., crā'doh). "I believe"; part of the MASS.

Crescendo (It., krĕh-shen'dŏh). Swelling, increasing in loudness.

Crescendo pedal. A PEDAL mechanism drawing all STOPS successively up to "full organ." Also, the swell-pedal.

Crescent; also **Chinese crescent**, **Chinese Pavilion**. An instrument of Turkish origin, used in military music; it has crescent-shaped brass plates hung around a staff and surmounted by a cap or pavilion; around the plates little bells are hung, which are jingled in time with the music. Also sometimes called *Jingling Johnny*.

Croche (Fr., krohsh). An EIGHTH NOTE.

Cromorne (Fr., kroh-mahrn'). KRUMMHORN.

Crook. A short tube, bent or straight, which can be fitted to the main tube of a HORN or TRUMPET to lower the PITCH. In common use before VALVES were introduced on modern horns.

Crooner. A popular singer who intones his songs in a soft, seductive manner.

Crossbar. The upper support or yoke that serves as the anchor for the strings on a LYRE.

Cross flute. One held *across* the mouth, and blown from the side.

Cross relation. FALSE RELATION.

Crossrhythm. Regular shifting of some of the BEATS in a rhythmic pattern to points ahead of or behind their usual position, i.e., the division of a MEASURE of 9/8 into 2+3+2+2 instead of the expected 3+3+3.

Crotales. Small hollow-sphere CYMBALS of definite PITCH; also known as "ancient cymbals."

Crotchet. A QUARTER NOTE. *Crotchet-rest*, a QUARTER REST.

Crucifixus (L., kroo-chē-fĕx'oos). Part of the MASS, in the CREDO section.

Crwth (krŭth). An ancient Welsh or Irish bowed LYRE, probably the oldest European instrument of its class. Its square body was terminated by two parallel arms joined at the end by a CROSSBAR, the center of which supported the FINGERBOARD; it had originally three, in modern times six, strings. Also spelled *Crouth* or *Crouch*.

Csárdás (Hungarian, char'dahsh). A national Hungarian dance, distinguished by its passionate character and changing TEMPO. Commonly misspelled *czárdás*.

Cue. A PHRASE, from a vocal or instrumental PART, occurring near the end of a long pause in another part, and inserted in small notes *in the latter* to serve as a guide in timing its reentrance.

Cuivré (Fr., kyuh-eev-ray'). With a brassy tone, as played particularly on the FRENCH HORN.

Cupo,-a (It., koo'pŏh,-päh). Dark, deep, obscure; reserved. *Con voce cupa*, with a veiled, intense TONE.

Cupped mouthpiece. The shallower, cup-shaped form of MOUTHPIECE for BRASS INSTRUMENTS; the *conical* (cone-shaped) mouthpiece is the deeper form.

Cut time. ALLA BREVE.

Cyclical forms. Forms that embrace a cycle or set of MOVEMENTS, such as the CLASSICAL SUITE or PARTITA, or the SONATA, SYMPHONY, and CONCERTO.

Cymbals. The orchestral cymbals are two concave plates of brass or bronze, with broad, flat rims, and holes for the straps by which they are held; used to make strong accents, or to produce peculiar effects.

D

D. (Ger. *D*; Fr. *ré*; It. *re*). The second TONE and DEGREE in the typical DIATONIC SCALE of *C* MAJOR. In music THEORY, capital *D* designates the *D*-major TRIAD, small *d* the *d*-MINOR triad. *D.* also stands for *Da* (D.C. = *Da capo*) and *Dal* (D.S. = *Dal segno*).

Da. (It., dah). By, from, for, of. *Da capo*, from the beginning; *D. capo al fine*, repeat from beginning to end (that is, to the word *Fine*, or to a hold); *D. capo al segno*, from the beginning to the sign (𝄋); *D.C. al segno, poi (segue) la coda*, from the beginning to the sign, then play the coda; *D.C. dal segno*, repeat from the sign; *D.C. senza replica* (or *senza ripetizione*), play through from the beginning without noticing the repeats; *D. eseguirsi*, to be executed.

Dactyl(e) (L., *dactylus*, a finger). A metrical foot with syllables arranged like the finger-joints, one long and two short; the accent on the first: ´◡◡.

Dactylion. An apparatus for finger-gymnastics invented by Henri Herz in 1835.

Dagli (dăhl'yē), **dai** (dah'ē), **dal, dall', dalla, dalle, dallo** (It.). To the, by the, for the, from the, etc.

Dal segno (It., dăhl sān'yŏh). From the sign. *Dal segno al fine*, from the sign to the end.

Damenisation. Carl Heinrich Graun's system of SOLMISATION using the syllables *da, me, ni, po, tu, la, be*.

Damper. 1. A mechanical device for checking the vibration of the PIANO-string. *Damper-pedal*, the right, or loud,

PEDAL. 2. The MUTE of a BRASS INSTRUMENT. *Also* **Dämpfer** (Ger., däm'pfer). DAMPER or MUTE.

Dance band. An instrumental ENSEMBLE accompanying ballroom dancing and often composed of SAXOPHONES, TRUMPETS, TROMBONES, and PERCUSSION.

Danse champêtre (Fr., dahns shan-petr'). A peasant dance in an open field.

Danza. Italian and Spanish word for *dance*.

DAT (Digital Audio Tape). A late 20th-century technology allowing digital information to be recorded to a small, cassette-sized tape; DAT players offer sound close in quality to a CD player, but, unlike CD players, they also allow for original material to be recorded.

D dur (Ger., dä door). D MAJOR.

Deaconing. A practice in early American Protestant churches of reading aloud a line of a HYMN before singing it.

Debile or **Debole** (It., dä'bē-lĕh, dä'boh-lĕ). Feeble, weak.

Début (Fr., dä-bü'). A first appearance.

Débutant,-e (Fr., dä-bü-tän' [masc.], -tähn't [fem]). A performer who appears for the first time.

Decay. The gradual extinction of a sound.

Decibel. A scientific unit for the measurement of loudness or intensity of sound.

Decima (L., dehs'ĭ-mŭ). 1. The INTERVAL of a tenth. 2. An ORGAN STOP pitched a TENTH higher than the 8' stops.

Deciso (It., dä-chē'zŏh). Decided, energetic, with decision.

Declamando (It., dä-klăh-măhn'dŏh). "Declaiming"; in declamatory style.

Declamation. In vocal music, clear and correct enunciation of the words.

Declamato (It., dä-klăh-mah'tŏh). "Declaimed"; in declamatory style.

Decrescendo (It., dā-crĕh-shen'dŏh). Decreasing in loudness.

Decuplet. A group of ten equal NOTES executed in the TIME proper to eight of like value, or to four notes of the next highest value, in the established RHYTHM; marked by a SLUR and the figure 10.

Deficiendo (It., dā-fē-ts'yen'dŏh). Dying away.

Degree. 1. One of the eight consecutive TONES in a MAJOR or MINOR DIATONIC SCALE, counted upward from the KEYNOTE. 2. A line or space on the STAFF. 3. A STEP.

Dehnen (Ger., dā'nen). To prolong.

Dehors, en (Fr., än dĕ-or). "Outside"; with emphasis.

Del, dell', della, delle, dello (It.). Of the, than the.

Deliberato (It., dĕh'lē-bĕh-**r**ah'tŏh). Deliberately.

Delicato (It., dĕh-lē-kah'tŏh). Delicately; in a delicate, refined style.

Delirio, con (It., kŏhn dĕh'lē'rē-ŏh). Raving; deliriously, frenziedly.

Demiquaver. A SIXTEENTH NOTE.

Demisemiquaver. A THIRTY-SECOND NOTE.

Depress. 1. To lower (as by a ♭ or ♭♭). *Depression*, CHROMATIC lowering of a NOTE. 2. To press down on a KEY, as on the PIANO.

Derivative. 1. Same as *derivative chord*, that is, the INVERSION of a FUNDAMENTAL CHORD. 2. The ROOT of a chord.

Derived set. A twelve-note set created by subjecting a smaller subset to the serial transformations of INVERSION, RETROGRESSION, and TRANSPOSITION.

Des (Ger., dess). D flat.

Descant. 1. The first attempts at POLYPHONY characterized by CONTRARY MOTION in the PARTS (12th century); opposed to the ORGANUM, in which PARALLEL MOTION was the rule. 2. TREBLE or SOPRANO voice; the highest part in PART-MUSIC.

Des dur (Ger., dess door). *D* flat major.

Deses (Ger., dess'ess). *D* double flat.

Desiderio, con (It., kŏhn dĕh-sē-dâ′rē-ŏh). With desire; longingly, yearningly.

Desto (It., dĕh′stŏh). Sprightly.

Destra (It., dês′străh). Right. *Mano destra (destra mano, colla destra),* "play with the right hand" (abbreviated *m.d.*).

Détaché (Fr., dā-tăh-shā′). In VIOLIN playing, "detached," that is, playing successive NOTES with DOWN-BOW and UP-BOW in alteration, but not STACCATO. *Grand détaché,* a whole STROKE of the BOW to each note.

Determinato (It., dĕh-târ-mē-nah′tŏh). Determined, resolute.

Deux (Fr., dö). Two. *À deux mains,* for two hands; *d. temps,* or *Valse à d. temps,* a "two-step" WALTZ.

Development. The working out or evolution (elaboration) of a THEME by presenting it in varied melodic, harmonic, or rhythmic treatment.

Devozione, con (It., kŏhn dĕh-vŏh′tsē-oh′nĕh). In a devotional style; devoutly.

D flute. The orchestral or German FLUTE.

Di (It., dē). Of, from, to, by; than.

Diapason. 1. An OCTAVE. 2. Either of the two principal foundation-STOPS of the ORGAN, both of 8′ pitch. *Pedal diapasons* are usually 16′ stops. 3. COMPASS of a voice or instrument (in poetical usage). 4. A fixed PITCH; the "normal diapason" is an accepted standard of pitch.

Diapason tone. ORGAN TONE.

Diaphony. Literally, "sounding through"; a form of medieval COUNTERPOINT allowing certain liberties in crossing of PARTS and in using passing DISSONANCES.

Diatonic. By, through, with, within, or embracing the TONES of the standard MAJOR or MINOR SCALE. *Diatonic harmony* or *melody*, that employing the TONES of but one scale; *d. instrument*, one yielding only the tones of that scale of which its FUNDAMENTAL tone is the KEYNOTE; *d. interval*, one formed by two tones of the same scale; *d. modulation*, see MODULATION; *d. progression*, stepwise PROGRESSION within one scale; *d. scale*, see SCALE.

Di colta (It., dē kôl'tăh). Suddenly, at once.

Dies iræ (L. "day of wrath"). SEQUENCE of the REQUIEM MASS.

Diesis (It., dē-ā-sis); **Dièse** (Fr., dē-ez). SHARP; the sign ♯.

Differential tone. A TONE produced by the difference of the frequencies of VIBRATION between two NOTES when played loudly on a STRINGED INSTRUMENT; such a tone lies well beneath the original two sounds, and produces a jarring effect; sometimes called "wolf tone."

Difficile (It., dĕf-fē'chē-lĕh); **Difficile** (Fr., dē-fē-sēl'). Difficult.

Di gala (It., dē gäh'lăh). Gaily, merrily.

Digital (dĭ'jĭ-tăl). 1. A KEY on the KEYBOARD of the PIANO, ORGAN, etc. 2. A recording in which musical tones are translated into binary information, as in a CD.

Dignità, con (It., kŏhn dēn-ye-tah'). With dignity.

Dilettante (It., dē-let-tăhn'tĕh). AMATEUR.

Diligenza, con (It., kŏhn dē-lē-jen'dzăh). "With diligence"; carefully.

Diluendo (It., dē-loo-en'dŏh). Growing softer, dying away.

Diminished interval. A perfect or MINOR INTERVAL contracted by a CHROMATIC SEMITONE. *Diminished chord*, one whose highest and lowest TONES form a diminished interval; *d. subject* or *theme*, one repeated or imitated in DIMINUTION; *d. triad*, a ROOT with minor THIRD and diminished FIFTH.

Diminished seventh chord. A CHORD consisting of three conjunct MINOR THIRDS, forming the INTERVAL of the DIMINISHED SEVENTH between the highest and lowest NOTES.

Diminuendo (It., dē-mē-noo-en′dōh). Diminishing in loudness. *Diminuendo pedal*, a PEDAL-mechanism for gradually pushing in the STOPS (ORGAN).

Diminution. The repetition or IMITATION of a THEME in NOTES of smaller TIME value.

Di molto (It., dē mōhl′tōh). Very, extremely. *Allegro di molto*, extremely fast.

Di nuovo (It., dē nô′vōh). Anew; over again.

Direct. The sign ∾ or ᴠ set at the end of a STAFF to show the position of the first NOTE on the next staff.

Dirge. A funeral HYMN, or vocal or instrumental COMPOSITION written in commemoration of the dead.

Diritto,-a (It., dē-rit′tōh,-tăh). Direct, straight. *Alla diritta*, in direct motion.

Dis (Ger., dĭs). *D* sharp.

Discant. DESCANT.

Discord. DISSONANCE.

Discotheque. 1. A gathering place where people dance to the sounds of amplified recordings; commonly, "disco." 2. Popular musical style of the 1970s characterized by a mechanically repeated emphasis of the BEAT, and the elaborate dance style that accompanied it.

Discrezione, con (It., kŏhn dē-skrĕh-tsē-oh′nĕh). "With discretion"; discreetly, cautiously.

Disinvoltura, con (It., kŏhn dē-zin-vŏhl-too′rah). With ease, grace; flowingly.

Disis (Ger., dĭs′ĭs). *D* double sharp.

Disjunct motion. Progression by leaps.

Disk (or **Disc**). 1. A PHONOGRAPH record. 2. A COMPACT DISC.

Dis moll (Ge., dĭs mohl). *D* sharp minor.

Disperazione, con (It., kŏhn dē-spěh-**r**ăh-tsē-oh'něh). In a style expressive of desperation or despair.

Dissonance. A combination of two or more TONES requiring RESOLUTION. *Dissonant interval*, two tones forming a dissonance, i.e., the SECONDS, SEVENTHS, and all DIMINISHED and AUGMENTED INTERVALS; *dissonant chord*, one containing one or more dissonant intervals.

Distanza (It., dē-stăhn'tsăh). INTERVAL; distance. *In distanza*, at a distance, marking music to be performed as if far away.

Distintamente (It., dē-stin-tăh-men'těh). Distinctly.

Dital (dīt'al). A KEY that, on pressure by the finger or thumb, raises the PITCH of a GUITAR or LUTE string by a SEMITONE. *Dital harp*, a guitar-shaped lute with twelve to eighteen strings, each having a dital to raise its pitch a semitone; invented by Light in 1798.

Divertimento (It., dē-vâr-tē-men'tŏh); **Divertissement** (Fr., dē-vâr-tēs-măh**n**'). A light and easy piece of instrumental music. Also, an instrumental COMPOSITION in six or seven MOVEMENTS, like a SERENADE. Also, an ENTR'ACTE in an OPERA, in the form of a short BALLET, etc.

Divide. To play DIVISIONS.

Divisi (It., dē-vē'zē). "Divided." Signifies that two PARTS written on one STAFF are not to be played as DOUBLE STOPS, but by the division into two bodies of instruments playing from that staff. *Divise* (dē-vē'zěh) is the feminine form.

Division. A "dividing up" of a melodic series of TONES into a rapid COLORATURA PASSAGE; if for voice, the passage was to be sung in one breath (obsolete). *To run a division*, to execute such a passage; *d.-viol*, the VIOLA DA GAMBA.

Division mark. The SLUR or bracket written for DUPLETS, TRIPLETS, QUADRUPLETS, etc., with a figure 2, 3, 4, etc.

Dixieland. An American JAZZ style that began around 1915 and became prominent in the 1920s. Its instruments are typically TRUMPET (or CORNET), CLARINET, PIANO, BANJO, and DRUMS, and it is characterized by collective IMPROVISATION, dotted RHYTHMS, and SYNCOPATION. Dixieland enjoyed a revival after World II, and continues to be played from time to time.

D moll (Ger., deh mohl). *D* minor.

Do (It., doh). 1. The NOTE *C*. 2. In SOLMISATION, the usual syllable name for the first DEGREE of the SCALE. In the FIXED DO method of teaching, *Do* is the name for all notes bearing the letter name *C*, whether KEYNOTES or not; in the MOVABLE DO method, *Do* is always the keynote, regardless of letter name.

Dodecuplet. A group of twelve equal NOTES, to be performed in the time of eight notes of the same kind in the established RHYTHM.

Dodecaphony. Technique of COMPOSITION developed by Arnold Schoenberg and others about 1925 in which the basic THEME of a given composition contains twelve different NOTES; the name is derived from the Greek words *dodeca*, "twelve," and *phone*, "sound." In dodecaphonic writing, the KEY SIGNATURE is abolished and the concept of TONALITY undergoes a radical change; furthermore, DISSONANCES are emancipated and are used on a par with CONSONANT combinations. See also TWELVE-NOTE COMPOSITION.

Doigté (Fr., doo-ah-teh'). Fingering.

Dolce (It., dŏhl'chĕh). 1. Sweet, soft, suave. 2. A sweet-toned ORGAN STOP.

Dolcemente (It., dŏhl-chā-men'tĕh). Sweetly, softly.

Dolcian (Ger., dŏhl-tsiahn'); **Dolciano** (It., dŏhl-chah-nŏh). An early kind of FAGOTTO or BASSOON; in modern times, an 8' or 16' REED STOP in the ORGAN.

Dolciato (It., dŏhl-chah'tŏh). Softer, calmer.

Dolcissimo (It., dŏhl-chis'sē-mŏh). Very sweetly, softly; also, a very soft-toned 8' FLUTE STOP in the ORGAN.

Dolentemente (It., dŏh-len-tĕh-men'tĕh). Dolefully, plaintively.

Doloroso (It., dŏh-lŏh-roh'sŏh). In a style expressive of pain or grief; pathetically.

Dominant. The FIFTH TONE in the MAJOR or MINOR SCALE. *Dominant chord*, (*a*) the dominant TRIAD, or (*b*) the dominant SEVENTH CHORD; *d. section* of a MOVEMENT, one written in the KEY of the dominant, lying between and contrasting with two others in the key of the TONIC; *d. triad*, one having the dominant as the ROOT.

Domra. A Russian BALALAIKA.

Dopo (It., doh'pŏh). After.

Doppel (Ger., dohp'pĕl). Double.

Doppelfuge (Ger., dŏhp'pel'foo-gĕ). DOUBLE FUGUE.

Doppelgriff (Ger., dŏhp'pel'grēf). DOUBLE STOP (VIOLIN); also *Doppelgriffe*, THIRDS, SIXTHS, etc., played with one hand (PIANO).

Doppelkreuz (Ger., dŏhp'pel-kroytz). DOUBLE SHARP.

Doppio (It., dô'pĭ-ŏh). Double. *Doppio movimento*, twice as fast; *d. note* or *d. valore*, twice as slow (with the absolute TIME value of the notes doubled); *d. pedale*, PEDAL PART in OCTAVES.

Dorian mode. The church MODE that corresponds to the SCALE from *D* to *D* played on the white KEYS of the PIANO.

Dot. A dot set after a NOTE prolongs its time value by half: $\left(\right)$;

a second or third dot prolongs the time value of the dot immediately preceding it by half: $\left(\right)$

Double. 1. A VARIATION. 2. Repetition of words in a SONG. 3. In ORGAN playing, a 16' STOP (accompanying the 8' stops) in the lower OCTAVE. 4. A substitute singer. 5. In CHANGE-RINGING, changes on five BELLS. 6. (*adjective*) "Producing a TONE an octave lower"; as DOUBLE-BASSOON, DOUBLE-BOURDON, etc. 7. (*verb*) To add the higher or lower octave (to any tone or tones of a MELODY or HARMONY).

Double bar. The two vertical lines drawn through the STAFF to indicate the end of a SECTION, MOVEMENT, or PIECE.

Double bass. The largest and deepest-toned instrument of the VIOLIN family, with either three (G_1-D-A being the Italian, A_1-D-G the English tuning) or four (E_1-A_1-D-G) STRINGS.

Double bassoon. A popular instrument among 20th-century orchestral composers; in B-flat, an OCTAVE below the BASSOON.

Double chorus. One for two CHOIRS, or divided choir, usually in eight PARTS.

Double counterpoint. COUNTERPOINT in which the upper and the lower VOICES are inverted so that the low voice becomes the top voice and vice versa. See COUNTERPOINT.

Double croche (Fr., doo-ble crosh'). A SIXTEENTH NOTE.

Double flat. The sign ♭♭.

Double fugue. One with two THEMES.

Double note. A BREVE; ‖O‖, a note twice the length of a WHOLE NOTE.

Double octave. A FIFTEENTH, or the INTERVAL of two OCTAVES.

Double quartet. A QUARTET for two sets of four solo voices, or of four solo instruments.

Double reed. The REED used for instruments of the OBOE family; two separate pieces of cane bound together to produce a characteristic vibration.

Double repetition mark. The symbol , which divides a SECTION of a COMPOSITION into two PARTS and calls for the repetition of each part.

Double sharp. The sign ×.

Double stop. In VIOLIN playing, to stop two strings together, thus obtaining two-part HARMONY.

Douce or **Doux** (Fr., doos, doo). Soft, sweet, suave.

Doucement (Fr., doos-măhn'). Softly, sweetly, suavely.

Downbeat. 1. The downward stroke of the hand in beating TIME, marking the primary or first ACCENT in each MEASURE. 2. Hence, the accent itself (strong BEAT, THESIS).

Down-bow. In playing STRINGED INSTRUMENTS, the downward stroke of the BOW from NUT to POINT. Usual sign ⊓ .

Doxology. A SONG of praise to God in Roman Catholic liturgy, and also used in a modified form in Protestant church services. The word comes from the Greek *Doxa*, "glory," and *Logos*, "saying."

Drabant. A ceremonial 18th-century Polish dance.

Dramatic music. 1. PROGRAM MUSIC. 2. Music accompanying and illustrating a drama on the stage.

Drame lyrique (Fr., drăhm lē-rēk'). French designation for OPERA.

Dramma per musica (It., drahm-măh pĕr moo'zē-kăh). Literally, "drama by music"; a designation used at the birth of OPERA in Italy about 1600.

Drammatico (It., drăhm-măh'tē-kŏh). Dramatically; in a vivid, dramatic style.

Drängend (Ger., dreng'ent). Pressing, hastening; STRIN-GENDO.

Drei (Ger., drī). Three.

Dreifach (Ger., drī-făyh). Triple.

Drohend (Ger., drŏh'ent). Menacing.

Dröhnend (Ger., drö'nent). Thundering; TONANTE.

Droit, Droite (Fr., drwăh, drwăh't). Right. *Main droite,* right hand.

Drone. In the BAGPIPE, a continuously sounding pipe of constant PITCH; a DRONE-pipe. *Drone-bass,* a BASS on the TONIC, or tonic and DOMINANT, which is persistent throughout a MOVEMENT or PIECE.

Drum. A PERCUSSION instrument consisting of a cylindrical, hollow *body* of wood or metal, over one or both ends of which a membrane (the *head*), is stretched tightly by means of a *hoop,* to which is attached a *cord* tightened by leather *braces,* or by rods and screws. *Rhythmical* drums (side drum, snare drum, bass drum) do not vary in PITCH; *musical* drums (the KETTLEDRUM) produce musical TONES distinct in pitch.

Drum machine. An electronic SYNTHESIZER specifically designed to simulate different types of PERCUSSION sounds. Usually equipped with some type of built-in SEQUENCER to allow rhythmic patterns to be created and stored so that they may be replayed at a later time.

Due (It., doo'ĕh). Two. *A due,* (*a*) for two, as *a due voci,* for two parts or voices; (*b*) both together (after *Divisi*); *due corde,* see CORDA; *due volte,* twice; *I due pedali,* both (PIÁNO-) PEDALS at once.

Duet. 1. A COMPOSITION for two voices or instruments. 2. A composition for two performers on one instrument, as the PIANO. 3. A composition for the ORGAN, in two PARTS, each to be played on a separate MANUAL.

Duetto (It., doo-et'tŏh). DUET 1, 2.

Dulciana. 1. An ORGAN STOP, having metal pipes of a somewhat sharp, thin tone. 2. A small REED stop of delicate tone. 3. A small BASSOON.

Dulcimer. 1. An ancient STRINGED INSTRUMENT, having wire strings stretched over a SOUNDBOARD or SOUNDBOX, and struck with mallets or hammers; a precursor of the PIANO. 2. The *Appalachian dulcimer* is a small ZITHER, usually with three strings; one plays the MELODY, the other two DRONES. The player uses a small stick or *noter* to fret the strings, and strums across them using a feather or PICK.

Dumb piano. A small KEYBOARD instrument resembling a PIANO, but without hammers and strings; intended for silent finger practice.

Dumka (Polish, dŏŏm'kăh). A sort of vocal or instrumental ROMANCE, of a melancholy cast; a lament or ELEGY.

Dummy pipes. PIPES that do not speak, displayed in the front of the ORGAN for show.

Duo (It., doo'ŏh). A DUET. *Duo* is sometimes distinguished from *Duet* by applying the former term to a two-PART COMPOSITION for two voices or instruments of *different* kinds, and the latter to a two-part composition for two voices or instruments of the *same* kind. Also, a composition in two parts for *one* instrument, i.e., a VIOLIN-*duo*, in contradistinction to a violin-*duet* for *two* violins.

Duodecima (It., doo-ŏh-dā'chē-măh). 1. The INTERVAL of the TWELFTH. 2. An ORGAN STOP.

Duodrama. A kind of MELODRAMA, or spoken dialogue accompanied by music.

Duolo, con (It., kŏhn dŏŏ-ô'lŏh). Dolefully, grievingly.

Duple. Double. *Duple rhythm*, RHYTHM of two BEATS to a MEASURE; *d. time*, see TIME.

Duplet. See COUPLET, 2.

Dur (Ger., door). MAJOR, as in *C dur* (C major), *F dur* (F major), etc.

Duration. Length of a sound, MOVEMENT, or COMPOSITION.

Dur(e) (Fr., dür). Harsh, unpleasing in TONE.

Duramente (It., doo-**räh**-men'teh). Sternly, harshly.

Durchkomponiert (Ger., door**h**-kom-poh-neert'). THROUGH-COMPOSED.

Durchführung (Ger., door**h**'für-öŏng^k). "Through leading." 1. The DEVELOPMENT section in SONATA FORM. 2. The EXPOSITION in a FUGUE.

Duro,-a (It., doo'rŏh,-räh). Hard, harsh.

Düster (Ger., dü'ster). Gloomy, mournful.

Dutch concert. The singing of an entire company in which each person sings whatever he or she pleases; or the persons present sing in alternation any VERSE that comes into their heads, the REFRAIN by the whole company being a regular repetition of some popular verse.

Dux. The SUBJECT in a FUGUE; literally, "leader" in Italian.

Dyad. A group of two PITCH CLASSES, usually with reference to a 12-NOTE SET.

Dynamics. The varying and contrasting degrees of intensity or loudness in musical TONES.

E

E (Ger. *E*; Fr. and It. *mi*). The third TONE and DEGREE in the typical DIATONIC SCALE of *C* major.

E (It., ā). And. When preceding a word beginning with "e," it should be written *ed*; before other vowels, either *e* or *ed* may be used; before consonants, only *e*.

Early music. Generic term used in modern times to describe CLASSICAL MUSIC of the Medieval and early Renaissance periods.

Ebollimento (It., ā-bŏhl-lē-men'tŏh). Ebullition; a sudden and passionate expression of feeling.

Eccheggiare (It., ā-kĕd-jē-āh'rĕh). To echo.

Eccitato (It., et-chē-tah'tŏh). Excited.

Ecclesiastical modes. The OCTAVE SCALES employed in medieval church music; also called *church modes*.

Ecco, Eco (It., ek'kŏh, ĕ'kŏh). ECHO.

Echo. 1. A subdued repetition of a strain or PHRASE. 2. An echo STOP.

Echo organ. A separate set of PIPES, either enclosed in a box within the ORGAN, or placed at a distance from the latter, to produce the effect of an echo.

Echo stop. An ORGAN STOP producing an echo-like effect.

Écossaise (Fr., ā-kŏh-säz'). Originally, a Scottish round dance in 3/2 or 3/4 TIME; now, a lively CONTRADANSE in 2/4 time. Compare SCHOTTISCHE.

Edel (Ger., ā'del). Noble; refined, chaste.

E dur (Ger., eh door). *E* major.

Effetto (It., ef-fet'tŏh). Effect, impression.

Effusione, con (It., kŏhn ef-foo-zē-oh'nēh). With effusion; with warmth.

Eguale (It., ā-guah'lĕh). Equal; even, smooth.

Eighth. An OCTAVE.

Eighth note. A note equal to one-half of the duration of a QUARTER NOTE. Also called QUAVER.

Eilen (Ger., ī'len). To hasten, accelerate, go faster.

Eilend (Ger., ī'lent). Hastening; STRINGENDO.

Eilig (Ger., ī'lĭyh). Hasty, hurriedly; rapid, swift.

Ein, Eins (Ger., īn, īns). One.

Einfach (Ger., īn'fäh). Simple; simply; SEMPLICE.

Eingang (Ger., īn'gähng^k). INTRODUCTION.

Einklang (Ger., īn'klähng^k). UNISON, CONSONANCE.

Einlage (Ger., īn'lähge). An INTERPOLATION or inserted PIECE.

Einleitung (Ger., īn'lī-toong^k). Introduction.

Einsatz (Ger., īn'sähtz). 1. An ATTACK. 2. An entrance of a vocal or instrumental PART.

Einstimmung (Ger., īn'shtĭm-mĭyh). MONOPHONIC, one-voiced.

Eis (Ger., ā'iss). *E* sharp.

Élan, avec (Fr., äh-vek' ā-lähn'). With dash; CON ISLANCIO.

Élargissez (Fr., ā-lar-zhē-sē'). ALLARGATE.

Electric guitar. Electronically amplified GUITAR, often with a solid body, widely used in modern ROCK groups.

Electrochord. An instrument invented by Peter Eötvos consisting of a fifteen-string Hungarian ZITHER amplified by a SYNTHESIZER.

Electronic instruments. A class of musical instruments, generally assignable to one of four categories: (1) original inventions (THEREMIN, ONDES MUSICALES or Martenot, etc.); (2) altered ACOUSTIC instruments (electric GUITAR, electronic ORGAN, etc.); (3) acoustic instruments joined to electronic equipment (electronic VIOLA or VIOLIN, etc.); and (4) ordinary objects joined to electronic equipment (i.e., Trimpin's "Klompen" [wooden shoes], etc.).

Electronic music. A body of COMPOSITIONS created out of a new, resourceful method of tone production by electronic means. The earliest electronic instrument, the THEREMIN, was demonstrated by the Russian inventor of the same name in 1920; a few years later the French composer Martenot introduced a keyboard electronic instrument known as ONDES MUSICALES (musical waves) or martenot. The most advanced electronic instruments are the SYNTHESIZERS, capable of generating any desired PITCH, SCALE, RHYTHM, TONE COLOR, or degree of loudness.

Electronic organ. A powerful modern ORGAN activated not by pipes but by electrical devices and capable of unlimited TONE production.

Electrophones. A class of musical instruments that produce their sound by electronic means.

Elegante (It., ā-lā-gähn'těh). In an elegant, graceful, refined style.

Elegie (Ger., ā-lā-zhe'); **Élégie** (Fr., ā-lā-zhe'); **Elegy.** A vocal or instrumental COMPOSITION of a melancholy cast, having no fixed FORM.

Elevator music. MUZAK.

Elevazione, con (It., kŏhn ā-lā-väh-tsē-oh'něh). In a lofty, elevated style.

Embellishment. GRACE.

Embouchure (Fr., ähn-boo-shür'). The MOUTHPIECE of a WIND INSTRUMENT; also, the manipulation of the lips and tongue in playing a wind instrument.

E moll (Ger., eh mohl). *E* minor.

Emozione (It., ā-mŏh-tsē-oh'něh). Emotion.

Empfindung, mit (Ger., mit em-pfin'dŏŏngᵏ). With emotion, feelingly; full of feeling.

Emphase, avec (Fr., ă-vek'ähn'fahz'); **Emphase, mit** (Ger., mit em-fah'zě). With emphasis.

Enchaînez (Fr., ähn-shä-nā'). "Go on directly"; ATTACCA.

Encore (Fr., ähn-kor'). "Again!" So used by English-speaking audiences when recalling an actor or singer to the stage (the French cry "Bis!"). Also, the PIECE or performance repeated or added.

En dehors (Fr., ahn de-or'). "Outside"; to emphasize, or bring out the MELODY.

En élargissant (Fr., ăhn ā-lar-zhē-sähn'). ALLARGANDO.

Energia, con (It., kŏhn ā-nâr-jē'äh); **Énergie, avec** (Fr., āh-vek' ā-nâr-zhi'); **Energisch** (Ger., ā-nâr'gish). With energy and decision, energetically. A PASSAGE so marked is to be vigorously accented and distinctly phrased.

Enfatico (It., en-fäh'tē-kŏh). With emphasis, emphatic.

English horn. An instrument of the OBOE family which TRANSPOSES a FIFTH below the written NOTE.

Enharmonic tones. TONES derived from different SCALE DEGREES, but practically identical in PITCH, like $c\sharp$ and $d\flat$ on the PIANO or ORGAN. *Enharmonic chords*, CHORDS differing in NOTATION but alike in sound; such chords are called "enharmonically changed," and passing from one to the other is an "enharmonic MODULATION"; *e. interval*, one formed between two enharmonic tones.

En mesure (Fr., ăhn mu-zür'). MISURATO.

Ensemble (Fr., ăhn-sähn'bl'). 1. General effect (of a COMPOSITION). 2. Style of performance (of a body of musicians). 3. Any group of three or more musicians. *Morceau d'ensemble*, concerted PIECE.

Entr'acte (Fr., ăhn-trăhkt'). "Interval between acts"; hence, a light instrumental COMPOSITION or short BALLET, for performance between acts.

Entrata (It., en-trah'tăh); **Entrée** (Fr., ăhn-trā'). 1. The orchestral PRELUDE to a BALLET, following the OVERTURE. 2. A division in a ballet like a "scene" in a play. 3. An old dance like a POLONAISE, usually in 4/4 TIME.

Entschlossen (Ger., ent-shlŏshs'sen). Resolutely, in a determined manner.

Entusiasmo, con (It., kŏhn en-too-zē-ăhz'mŏh). With enthusiasm.

Envelope. The shape of a sound's AMPLITUDE, changing over time; an important determinant of sound quality. Most SYNTHESIZERS allow modification of a sound's envelope, from ATTACK through DECAY.

Epic theatre or **opera**. A noninterpretive, highly dramatic theatrical form of music, developed most prominently by Bertolt Brecht and his musical collaborator, Kurt Weill.

Episode (ep'ĭ-sōd). An intermediate or incidental SECTION; in the FUGUE, a digression from the principal THEME, interpolated between the developments of the latter.

Epistle. A recited section of the MASS that comes directly before the GRADUAL.

Epithalamium. A wedding HYMN.

Equabile (It., ā-kwah'bē-lĕh). Equable; even, uniform.

Equal counterpoint. COUNTERPOINT in equal TONES; see TEMPERAMENT.

Equal temperament. See TEMPERAMENT.

Equal voices. Voices of the same class; that is, either women's and boy's (SOPRANO and ALTO) or men's (TENOR and BASS).

Equivocal chord. A DISSONANT CHORD of uncertain RESOLUTION, like the DIMINISHED SEVENTH.

Ergriffen (Ger., âr-grif'fen). Affected, stirred.

Erhaben (Ger., âr-hab'ben). Lofty, exalted.

Erklingen (Ger., âr-kling'en). To resound.

Ermattet (Ger., âr-măht'tet). Exhausted, wearied.

Ernst (Ger., ârnst). Earnest, grave.

Eroico,-a (It., ā-rôh'ē-kŏh,-kăh). Heroic; strong and dignified.

Erschüttert (Ger., âr-shüt'tert). Shaken, agitated.

Erzählung (Ger., âr-tsä'lŏŏng^k). Story, tale, narration.

Es (Ger., ess). *E* flat.

Esaltazione, con (It., kŏhn ā-zăhl-tăh-tsē-oh'nĕh). With exaltation; in a lofty, fervent style.

Escapement. Device in the PIANO mechanism that allows the hammer to strike the strings two or more times before returning to its resting position, thus allowing rapid repetition of the same NOTE.

Esclamato (It., ĕh-sklăh-mah'tŏh). "Exclaimed"; forcibly declaimed.

Es dur (Ger., ess door). *E* flat major.

Eses (Ger., ess'ess). *E* double flat.

Es moll (Ger., ess mohl). *E* flat minor.

Espandendosi (It., ĕh-spăhn-den'dŏh-sē). Growing broader and fuller; with growing intensity.

Espansione, con (It., kŏhn ĕh-spăhn-sē-oh'nĕh). With intense feeling.

Espirando (It., ĕh-spē-răhn'dŏh). Dying away, expiring.

Espressivo (It., ĕh-spres-sē-vŏh). With expression, expressively. *Con molto* (or *molt'*) *espressione*, very expressively.

Esquisse (Fr., es-keese'). A sketch.

Essential. Any ♯ or ♭ belonging to a KEY SIGNATURE, as in *essential note, chord-* or *melody-note*; *essential seventh*, the leading-tone; also, the DOMINANT SEVENTH CHORD.

Estinguendo (It., ĕh-stin-gwen'dŏh). Extinguishing; dying away.

Estinto (It., ĕh-stin'tŏh). Barely audible; the extreme of PIANISSIMO.

Estremamente (It., ĕh-strā-măh-men'tĕh). Extremely.

Estro poetico (It., â'strŏh pŏh-â'te-kŏh). Poetic fervor.

Ethnomusicology. The study of non-Western musical forms, practices, and behaviors. Originally, the term was developed to distinguish this study from standard, i.e., "Western" MUSICOLOGY, although many now object to referring to non-Western groups as "ethnic," and feel the term "World Musicology" would be preferable.

Étude (Fr., ā-tüd'). A study; especially, one affording practice in some particular technical difficulty. *Étude de concert*, one designed for public performance.

Etwas (Ger., et'vähss). Rather, somewhat.

Euphonium. 1. A valved BRASS INSTRUMENT, resembling a shrunken TUBA, taking the BARITONE PART in a brass BAND. 2. An instrument invented by Chladni in 1790, consisting of graduated glass tubes made to sound by the moistened fingers, and connected with steel rods.

Eurhythmics. A system of musical training introduced by Jaques-Dalcroze in 1910 in which pupils are taught to represent complex rhythmic movement with their entire bodies, to the ACCOMPANIMENT of specially composed music.

Evening song, Evensong. In the Anglican Church, a form of worship to be spoken or sung at evening; known as VESPERS in the Roman Catholic Church.

Execution. 1. Style, manner of performance. 2. Technical ability.

Exercise. A short technical study for training the fingers (or vocal organs) to overcome some special difficulty. Also, a short study in COMPOSITION.

Experimental music. Music that departs from the usual expectations of style, FORM, and genre as these have developed through history; as distinct from the work of the primarily European AVANT-GARDE, its proponents begin with Satie and Ives, and move through and beyond the work of Cage, Cowell, and Cardew.

Exposition. 1. The opening SECTION of a SONATA MOVEMENT, in which the principal THEMES are presented for the first time. 2. Sections of a FUGUE that present the SUBJECT.

Expressionism. A modern movement in music, beginning around 1910, giving expression to the inner state of a composer's mind and emotion; the term itself originated in painting. Expressionism reflects anxious moods characteristic of modern life in a musical idiom that frequently uses atonally constructed MELODIES and spasmodic, restless RHYTHMS.

Expression mark. A written direction (a sign, word, or phrase) for the performance of a PIECE.

Expression stop. In the HARMONIUM, a STOP that closes the escape-valve of the bellows, so that wind pressure and intensity of tone are partly controlled by the PEDALS.

Expressive organ. HARMONIUM.

Extemporize. To perform spontaneously in the manner of IMPROVISATION.

Extended compass. TONES beyond the usual range of a voice or instrument.

Extension pedal. The loud (right) PIANO PEDAL.

Extravaganza. An elaborate stage show with music, often marked by exaggerated comic effects.

F

F (Ger. *F*; Fr. and It. *fa*). The fourth TONE and DEGREE in the typical DIATONIC SCALE of *C* MAJOR. Also, *f* = FORTE; *ff* or *fff* = FORTISSIMO.

Fa or Fah. 1. In SOLMISATION, the usual name for the fourth

DEGREE of the SCALE. 2. Name of the TONE *F* in Italy, France, Spain, and Russia.

Faburden. Old English term describing a PROGRESSION in consecutive 6/3 CHORDS, similar but not identical to FAUX-BOURDON.

Facile (It., fah′chē-lĕh); **Facile** (Fr., făh-sēl′). Facile, easy, fluent.

Fackeltanz (Ger., făhkl′tants). Torch dance.

Fado. A popular Portuguese SONG.

Fagott (Ger., făh-gŏht′). A predecessor of the BASSOON. Also, a reed STOP in the ORGAN.

Fagotto (It., făh-gŏht′tŏh). BASSOON.

False relation. The CHROMATIC contradiction of a TONE in one PART by another; it consists in sounding, either together or in succession, a TONE and its chromatically altered OCTAVE.

Falsetto. The highest of the vocal REGISTERS.

Fancy. Type of 17th-century English instrumental music. See FANTASIE.

Fandango (Sp.). A lively dance in triple TIME, for two dancers of opposite sex, who accompany themselves with CASTA-NETS or TAMBOURINE.

Fanfare (fan′fâr). A flourish of TRUMPETS or a trumpet-call.

Fantasie (Fr., făhn-tä-zē′); **Fantasia** (It., făhn-tăh-zē′äh);**Fantasie** (Ger., făhn-tăh-zē). 1. An IMPROVISATION. 2. An instrumental PIECE in free IMITATION (17th and 18th centuries). 3. A COMPOSITION free in form and more or less fantastic in character; a fantasy. 4. A potpourri or PARAPHRASE.

Fantastico (It., făhn-tăh′stē-kŏh). Fantastic, fanciful.

Farandola (It., făh-răhn-doh'lăh); **Farandole** (Fr., făh-răhn-dŏhl'). A circle-dance in 6/8 TIME and very rapid TEMPO.

Farce. A one-act OPERA or OPERETTA of ultracomical or burlesque character.

Fastosamente (It., făh-stŏh-săh-men'těh). Pompously; in a stately style.

Fauxbourdon (Fr., foh-boor-dŭn). A CONTRAPUNTAL technique of the 15th century, marked by parallel PROGRESSIONS in THIRDS and SIXTHS. This practice eventually led to the use of consecutive 6/3 CHORDS, common in classical usage. The reason for the name, "false DRONE," is probably owed to the introduction of the "false BASS," which was not the (usual) TONIC of the chord but its MEDIANT.

F clef. The bass CLEF: 𝄢 or 𝄢

F dur (Ger., ĕff door). F MAJOR.

Feedback. The whining or howling sound created by the interference of two electrical sources, such as a microphone and speaker. Feedback as an expressive device is commonly used in ROCK music; guitarist Jimi Hendrix is generally credited with this innovation.

Feierlich (Ger., fī'er-lĭyh). Ceremonial, solemn, grave.

Fermamente (It., fâr-măh-men'těh). Firmly, with decision.

Fermata (It., fâr-mah'tăh); **Fermate** (Ger., fâr-mah'tĕ). The sign ⌒ over, or ⌣ under, a NOTE or REST, indicating the prolongation of its TIME VALUE at the performer's (or conductor's) discretion. Placed over a BAR, indicates a slight pause or breathing-spell before attacking what follows. Also called *hold*.

Fermezza, con (It., kŏhn fâr-met'săh). In a firm, decided, energetic style.

Fermo (It., fâr'mŏh). Firm, decided; fixed, unchanged. *Canto fermo*, same as CANTUS FIRMUS.

Ferne (Ger., fâr-nĕ). Distance. *Wie aus der Ferne,* as from a distance.

Feroce (It., fā-roh'chĕh). Wild, fierce, vehement.

Fervente (It., fâr-ven'tĕh). Fervently, ardently, passionately.

Fes (Ger., fess). *F* flat.

Festlich (Ger., fest'lĭyh); **Festivo** (It., fĕh-stē'vŏh). Festive, festal.

Festivamente (It., fĕh-stē-vǎh-men'tĕh). In a gay, festive style.

Festschrift (Ger., fĕst'shrĭft'). An offering in honor of a musical scholar or composer on the occasion of an advanced birthday or retirement, in the form of a published volume of collected articles by his or her students and colleagues.

Festspiel (Ger., fĕst'shpēl). German term for a stage play in which music is included.

Feuerig (Ger., fahü'ĕ-rĭyh). With fire; fiery, impetuous.

F holes. The two *f*-shaped SOUNDHOLES in the BELLY of the VIOLIN, etc.

Fiacco (It., fē-ăhk'kŏh). Languishing, feeble.

Fiato (Itl., fē'ăh'tŏh). "Breath." *Stromenti a fiato,* WIND IN-STRUMENTS.

Fibonacci Series. A sequence of numbers in which each is the sum of the preceding pair, i.e., ...2,3,5,8,13,21...

Fiddle. A VIOLIN. Also, *Fiddle-bow, Fiddlestick*; see BOW.

Fieramente (It., fē-ĕh-răh-men'tĕh). Wildly, boldly.

Fife. An OCTAVE CROSS-FLUTE with six holes and without KEYS; compass d^2 to d^4. Also, a piccolo-STOP on the ORGAN.

Fifteenth. A double OCTAVE. Also, an organ STOP of 2′ PITCH.

Fifth. An INTERVAL of five DIATONIC DEGREES (see INTERVAL). Also, the fifth degree of any diatonic SCALE (the DOMINANT). *False fifth,* a DIMINISHED fifth.

Figuration. Rapid FIGURES or PHRASES, containing passing and changing NOTES.

Figure. A group of NOTES in a MELODY.

Figured bass. One of the most important methods of indicating the HARMONY to be used in the KEYBOARD PART in BAROQUE MUSIC, in which the BASS line alone is given, annotated with numbers that indicate the INTERVALS to be used from the bass up, and thus determining the harmony. Numerous elaborations were also in use, such as FLATS or SHARPS after the figures, etc. The practice of figured bass disappeared in the 19th century. Also called *thoroughbass, throughbass,* or *basso continuo*.

Filar la voce (It., fē-lar' lăh voh-chĕh); **Filer la voix** (Fr., fē-lā' lăh vwăh). To prolong a TONE, slowly swelling and diminishing.

Filato (It., fē-lah'tōh). Long, drawn out.

Film music. Music improvised, adapted, or composed for use with film.

Filo di voce (It., fē'lŏh dē voh'chĕh). The very softest and lightest vocal TONE.

Finale (It., fē-nah'lĕh). The last MOVEMENT in a SONATA or SYMPHONY; the closing number(s) of an act (OPERA) or PART (ORATORIO).

Fine (It., fē'nĕh). End; close; indicates either the end of a "repeat" (after the *Da capo* or *Dal segno*), or the end of a PIECE.

Fingerboard. The neck or extension of a LUTE on which the player frets or STOPS the STRINGS.

Fingering. 1. The method of applying the fingers to the KEYS, holes, STRINGS, etc., of musical instruments. 2. The marks guiding the performer in placing his fingers. *English fingering* (for the PIANO), that in which NOTES taken by the thumb are marked **×** with 1,2,3,4 for the fingers; *German* (or *Continental*) *f.*, the thumb marked 1, and the fingers 2,3,4,5.

Fingerpicking. A style of GUITAR playing in which the player PICKS the STRINGS with the fleshy tips of the fingers (or with steel metal picks placed on the fingers), rather than strumming across the strings. Commonly heard in ACOUS-TIC BLUES, FOLK, and soft-ROCK styles.

Fingersatz (Ger., fin′ger-sähts). FINGERING.

Fino (It., fē′nŏh). Till, up to, as far as.

Fioritura (It., fē-ŏh-rē-too′räh; pl. *fioriture*). An EMBELLISH-MENT; an ornamental TURN, flourish, or PHRASE, introduced into a MELODY.

Fipple flute. A vertical FLUTE, now obsolete, blown from the end; the word is derived from fipple, a plug in the MOUTH-PIECE. See RECORDER.

First. Of voices and instruments of the same class, the highest, as *first* SOPRANO, *first* VIOLIN. In the STAFF, the lowest, as *first* line, *first* space. The *first* STRING of an instrument is the highest.

Fis (Ger., fiss). *F* sharp.

Fis dur (Ger., fiss door). *F* sharp major.

Fisis (Ger., fiss′iss). *F* double sharp.

Fis moll (Ger., fiss mohl). *F* sharp minor.

Fistel, Fistelstimme (Ger., fis′tel-shtim′mě). FALSETTO.

Fixed Do. In the Fixed Do system of SOLMISATION, the TONE *C*, and all its CHROMATIC derivatives (*C♯*, *C♭*, *C*×, *C♭♭*), are called *Do*, *D* and its derivatives are called *Re*, etc., in whatever KEY or HARMONY they may appear. As opposed to MOVABLE DO.

Fixed-tone instrument. One (like the PIANO or ORGAN) the PITCH of whose TONES cannot be modified at the player's pleasure, like (for example) those of the VIOLIN. Such an instrument is said to have "fixed INTONATION."

Flag. A HOOK on the STEM of a NOTE.

Flageolet. A small end-blown FLUTE, a WIND INSTRUMENT of the WHISTLE family. The French flageolet has a COMPASS of two OCTAVES and three SEMITONES, from g^1 to $b^{3}\flat$. Also, a small flute STOP in the ORGAN, of 1' or 2' PITCH. *Flageolet-tones*, HARMONICS.

Flamenco. A typical dance of the Andalusian gypsies and Spanish dancers elsewhere characterized by vigorous heel stamping and passionate gesticulation.

Flat. The character ♭, that lowers the PITCH of the NOTE before which it is set by a SEMITONE; the double flat lowers its note by two semitones. *Flat chord*, one whose TONES are performed simultaneously (a *solid* CHORD, as opposed to *broken*); *f. fifth*, DIMINISHED FIFTH.

Flatterzunge (Ger., fläht-ter-tsoon'gheh). FLUTTER-TONGUE.

Flautando (It., fläh-ŏŏ-tähn'dŏh). A direction in VIOLIN music to play near the FINGERBOARD so as to produce a some-what "fluty" TONE.

Flauto (It., flah'ŏŏ-tŏh). FLUTE; also the name of ORGAN STOPS, as *Flauto amabile*, etc. *Flauto traverso*, CROSS-FLUTE.

Flebile (It., flâ'bē-lĕh). Tearful; plaintive, mournful.

Flehend (Ger., flā'hent). Pleading.

Flexible notation. A modern type of NOTATION that allows some aspect of a COMPOSITION to be determined during performance.

Fliessend (Ger., flē'sent). Flowing, smooth; SCORRENDO.

Fling. A Scottish dance resembling the REEL, in QUADRUPLE TIME.

Flourid. Embellished with RUNS, PASSAGES, FIGURES, GRACES, etc.

Flourish. A trumpet FANFARE.

Flüchtig (Ger., fl*ü*yh'tīyh). Flightily, hastily; lightly, airily.

Flügel (Ger., flü'gel). "Wing." The GRAND PIANO or HARPSICHORD is so-called because of its winged shape.

Flügelhorn. A BRASS INSTRUMENT similar to but larger than the CORNET.

Flute. The orchestral flute (*Boehm flute*) has a wooden or metal tube of cylindrical bore, with fourteen holes closed by KEYS and a COMPASS from c^1 to c^4; it is blown through an oval orifice near the upper end. This is the so-called *Cross-flute*, being held across the mouth; the *Direct f.* is blown from the end, like a WHISTLE.

Flute à bec. RECORDER.

Flute stop. An ORGAN STOP with flute TONE.

Flutter-tongue. A special effect on the FLUTE and occasionally other WIND INSTRUMENTS consisting of the rapid insertion of the tongue into the blowhole resulting in a rapid STACCATO. Single (performed t-t-t...), double (performed t-k/t-k/t-k/...), and triple (performed t-k-t/t-k-t/t-k-t/...) are varieties.

Fluxus. New York art movement of the early 1960s giving birth to highly original, mostly theatrical, and often humorous mixed-media stage works frequently involving novel uses of sound.

F moll (Ger., ef mohl). *F* minor.

Foco (It., fô'kŏh). Fire. See FUOCO.

Folgend (Ger., fŏhl'ghent). Following.

Folia (Sp., fŏh-lē'äh); **Follia** (It., fohl-lē'äh). A Spanish dance for one person, in slow TEMPO and 3/4 TIME.

Folk music. Music that is indigenous to a people, region, state, or country, often MODAL and having strong ties to language; in subsequent compositional use, seen 1) in simple ARRANGEMENT; 2) as material for imitation; and

3) as subject for analysis and reinterpretation. See also
FOLK SONG.

Folk song. A SONG of the people, tinged by the musical peculi-
arities of the nation, and usually in simple, unaffected
BALLAD FORM. See also FOLK MUSIC.

Follower. A CONSEQUENT.

Foot. 1. A group of syllables having one ACCENT like a simple
MEASURE in music. 2. That part of an ORGAN PIPE below
the mouth. 3. The unit of measure in designating the
PITCH of organ STOPS, and of the several OCTAVES in the
musical SCALE.

An 8' stop is one whose longest pipe
produces the TONE *C* and is about 8' in
length, that is, a stop whose pipes pro-

duce tones corresponding in pitch to the KEYS touched;
4' stop is an octave stop; a 16' stop yields tones an octave
lower than indicated by the keys touched. The 8' octave
embraces the tones from *C* upwards. See ABSOLUTE PITCH.

Footing. The method of applying the heels and toes to the
ORGAN PEDALS.

Foreign chords or **tones**. Those that do not belong to a
given KEY.

Forlana (It., fohr-lah'năh); **Forlane** (Fr., fohr-lăhn'). A lively
Italian dance in 6/8 or 6/4 TIME.

Form. In music, a concept or organization governing the
order, character, METER, and KEY of a COMPOSITION. The
most elementary is BINARY, in which only two elements
are presented; TERNARY form evolves from binary by the
interpolation of a middle SECTION. In a large work, such
as a SONATA or SYMPHONY, formal elements often intermin-
gle and are distinguished by their similarities or contrasts.

Formalism. A pejorative term used in former times by USSR authorities to denigrate offending music, i.e., that of Shostakovich, Prokofiev, et al., as "artificial."

Formant. A characteristic of TIMBRE; the variation produced in AMPLITUDE over a range of FREQUENCIES.

Forte (It., fôhr'tĕh). Loud, strong; usually written *f. Piu forte*, louder; *piano f. (pf)*, begin softly and swell rapidly; *poco f.*, rather loud; *f. piano (fp)*, ACCENT strongly, instantly diminishing to PIANO; *f.mente* (for-tĕh-mēn'tĕh), loudly, forcibly; *f. possibile* (pŏhs-sĕ-be-lĕh), as loud as possible. Also, *f.-stop* (HARMONIUM), a slide opened by a draw STOP or knee-lever, to produce a *forte* effect; *f. generale*, the full ORGAN combination stop.

Fortepiano. Literally, "loudsoft." A term used to denote the 18th-century PIANO, to distinguish it from the modern instrument.

Fortissimo (It., fohr-tis'sē-mŏh). Extremely loud (usually written *ff* or *fff*).

Forza, con (It., kŏhn fôr'tsäh). With force, forcibly.

Forzando (It., fohr'tsähn'dŏh). With force, energy; means that the NOTE or CHORD is to be strongly accented; usually written *fz*.

Four-hand piano. Pieces written for two PIANO players at one piano; one player plays the TREBLE PARTS and the other the BASS.

Fourth. An INTERVAL embracing four SCALE DEGREES. Also, the fourth degree in the DIATONIC scale; the SUBDOMINANT.

Fox trot. A popular ballroom dance, in DUPLE (or QUADRUPLE) METER, that originated in the 1920s.

Française (Fr., frähn-säz'). A dance in TRIPLE TIME, resembling the COUNTRY DANCE.

Francamente (It., frähn-käh-men-tĕ). Free in delivery; boldly; frankly, ingenuously.

Frase large (It., frah′zĕh lar′gäh). "Broad phrase"; LAR-GAMENTE.

Freddamente (It., fred-däh-men′tĕh). Coldly; coolly, indifferently.

Freddo (It., fred′dŏh). Cold; indifferent.

Free fugue. One written with more or less disregard of strict rules.

Free reed. A metal reed that vibrates freely in its frame, such as those used in the HARMONICA or ACCORDION.

Free jazz. A JAZZ style of the 1960s and 1970s characterized by collective IMPROVISATION without reference to preset harmonic or formal structures.

Free part. One added to a CANON or FUGUE to complete the HARMONY.

Free style (of composition). That in which the rules of strict COUNTERPOINT are relaxed.

Frei (Ger., frī). Free. *Frei im Vortrag*, free in style (delivery).

Fremente (It., frä-men′tĕh). Furiously.

French horn. BRASS INSTRUMENT in the shape of a spiral with a tunnel-shaped opening. The modern French horn possesses a mellow TONE capable of great expressive power.

French sixth. The common name for a CHORD containing the INTERVAL of the AUGMENTED SIXTH between the highest and lowest NOTES, other intervals from the bottom being a MAJOR THIRD and an AUGMENTED FOURTH, as in *A* flat, *C*, *D*, and *F* SHARP. See AUGMENTED SIXTH.

French overture. A type of OVERTURE developed in France in the 18th century, consisting of three SECTIONS: the first in slow TEMPO, the second rather quick, and the third again slow.

Frequency. The rate of vibration of a given TONE; the scientific correlate to the sensation of PITCH.

Frequency modulation (FM). Change made to the FREQUENCY of a wave enabling information transfer to electromagnetic wave.

Fret. One of the narrow wedges of wood, metal, or ivory crossing the FINGERBOARD of the MANDOLIN, GUITAR, ZITHER, etc., on the which the strings are "stopped."

Fretta, con (It., kŏhn fret'tâh). With haste; hurriedly.

Freude (Ger., froy'-deh). Joy.

Freudig (Ger., froy'dĭyh). Joyous.

Frisch (Ger., frish). Brisk, vigorous; *brioso*.

Friss. The rapid section of the Hungarian dance CSÁRDÁS.

Fröhlich (Ger., frö'lĭyh). Gay, glad, joyous.

Frosch (Ger., frŏsh). NUT (of a BOW).

Frottola (It., froht'toh-lah). A type of CHORAL MADRIGAL popular in Italy in the 16th century.

Frülingslied (Ger., frü'lings-lēt). Spring SONG.

F-Schlüssel (Ger., shlüsel). The BASS or *F* CLEF.

Fuga (L. and It., foo'găh). FUGUE.

Fugato (It., fŏŏ-gah'tŏh). "In FUGUE style"; a PASSAGE or MOVEMENT consisting of fugal IMITATIONS, but not worked out as a regular fugue.

Fuge (Ger., foo'gĕ). FUGUE.

Fughetta (It., fŏŏ-get'tăh). A short FUGUE; a fugue EXPOSITION.

Fuging (or **Fuguing**) **tune**. A CHORAL HYMN with an imitative, though not truly fugal, SECTION. Very popular in late 18th-century New England.

Fugue (fewg). The most highly developed form of contrapuntal IMITATION, based on the principle of the equality of the PARTS, a THEME proposed by one part being taken up successively by all participating parts, thus bringing each in turn into special prominence. The elements essential

to every fugue are (1) SUBJECT, (2) ANSWER, (3) COUN-
TERSUBJECT, (4) STRETTO; to these are commonly added
(5) EPISODES, (6) an ORGAN POINT, and (7) a CODA. In a *real
fugue*, the answer is an exact TRANSPOSITION of the subject;
in a *tonal fugue*, the subject is modified in the answer
in order to lead back to the original KEY.

Full anthem. One for CHORUS without soli. *Full band*, a military BAND, or an ORCHESTRA, having all the customary
instruments; *f. cadence*, a perfect CADENCE; *f. choir* (Great,
Swell), draw all STOPS of Choir (Great, Swell) ORGAN; *f.
chord*, a CHORD having one or more of its original three
or four TONES doubled in the OCTAVE; *f. orchestra*, compare
FULL BAND; *f. organ*, with all stops and COUPLERS drawn; *f.
score*, see SCORE; *f. to fifteenth*, draw all stops but MIXTURES
and REEDS.

Fundamental. 1. The ROOT of a CHORD. 2. A TONE which produces a series of HARMONICS; a GENERATOR (or fundamental BASS [NOTE, tone]). *Fundamental chord*, triad (see
"Chords," pp. xvi–xvii); *f. position*, any arrangement of
chord notes in which the root remains the lowest.

Funèbre (Fr., fu-nä′br); **Funebre** (It., fŏŏ′nâ-brĕh). Funereal,
mournful, DIRGE-like.

Funeral march. A MARCH in slow 4/4 TIME in a MINOR KEY,
sometimes used as a part of a larger work. The most
famous funeral march is the slow MOVEMENT from Chopin's piano sonata in *B* flat minor, often played at the
funerals of important persons.

Funky. A JAZZ style of the 1950s and 1960s which returns to
the relative simplicities of the BLUES; a reaction against
the complexities and sophistication of BEBOP and COOL.

Fuoco, con (It., kŏhn fŏŏ-ô′kŏh). With fire; fiery, spirited.

Furioso (It., foo-rē-oh′sŏh). Furiously, wildly.

Furiant, Furie. A rapid Bohemian dance with alternating RHYTHMS and changing accentuation.

Furlana (It., foor-lah′nǎh). FORLANA.

Furniture music. A descriptor introduced by the whimsical French composer Erik Satie (as *musique d'amueblement*) to denote purposely unindelible (i.e., background) music.

Furore (It., foo-roh′rĕh). Fury, passion; also a rage, mania (for anything). *Con furore*, passionately.

Fusion. JAZZ-ROCK.

Futurism. A literary and musical movement originating in Italy early in the 20th century. It declared a rebellion against traditional art of all kinds, and preached the use of noises in musical composition.

Fuzztone. An effect commonly available on ELECTRIC GUITAR to add distortion or "fuzz" to the sound produced. Some say fuzztone was created to simulate the cheesy sound of inexpensive AMPLIFIERS often used by local ROCK musicians.

G

G. The fifth TONE and DEGREE in the typical DIATONIC SCALE of *C* MAJOR. *G.* stands for *gauche in m.g. (main gauche*, left hand); *G.O.* (or simply *G*), for *Grand-orgue* (Great ORGAN).

Gagaku. Orchestral music of the Japanese court dating back to the 12th century whose instruments include the Shinobue (transverse FLUTE), hichiriki (SHAWN), shō (MOUTH ORGAN), and taiko (barrel DRUMS).

Gagliarda (It., gǎhl-yar′dǎh); **Gagliarde** (Ger., gǎhl-yar′dĕ). GALLIARD.

Gal (Fr., gä). Gay, lively, brisk.

Gaiamente (It., gǎh-yah-men′tĕh); **Gaiement** (Fr., gä-mǎhn′). Gaily, briskly.

Gaillarde (Fr., găh-yard'). GALLIARD.

Gala, di (It., dē găh'lăh). Gaily, merrily.

Galant (Fr., gah-lan'). Gallant. See STYLE GALANT.

Galanter stil (Ger., găh-lant'er shtēl). STYLE GALANT.

Galanterien (Ger., găh-lan-ter-ē'ehn). The movements in the CLASSICAL SUITE typically placed before the last MOVEMENT, principally the MINUET, GAVOTTE, BOURRÉE, POLONAISE, and AIR.

Galliard. An old French dance for two dancers, gay and spirited, but not rapid, in 3/4 TIME.

Galop (Fr., găl-lŏh'); **Galopp** (Ger., găh'lŏhp'). A lively round dance in 2/4 TIME.

Gamba (It., gahm'băh). 1 A VIOLA DA GAMBA. 2. An ORGAN STOP similar in TONE.

Gamelan. An Indonesian ORCHESTRA, variously comprised of tuned GONGS, CHIMES, DRUMS, FLUTES, CHORDOPHONES, XYLOPHONES, and small CYMBALS.

Gamme (Fr., găhm). A SCALE.

Gamut. 1. A SCALE or PITCH range. 2. A collection of sounds available to a composer.

Ganz (Ger., găhnts). 1. Whole; *ganze Note*, WHOLE NOTE. 2. Very; *ganz langsam*, very slowly.

Garbamente (It., gar-băh-men'tĕh). Gracefully, elegantly; in a refined style.

Gathering note. In CHANTING, a hold on the last syllable of the RECITATION.

Gato. One of the most popular COUNTRY DANCES of Argentina, in 6/8 and 3/4 TIME.

Gauche (Fr., gohsh). Left.

Gaudioso (It., găh-ŏŏ-dē-oh'sŏh). Joyous, jubilant.

Gavotta (It., găh-vôht′tăh); **Gavotte** (Fr., găh-vŏht). A Gavot; an old French dance in strongly marked DUPLE TIME (ALLA BREVE), beginning on the UPBEAT.

G clef. The TREBLE CLEF; see "The Clefs," p. x.

G dur (Ger., gä door). G MAJOR.

Gebrauchsmusik (Ger., gĕ-browhs′moo-zīk). "Utility music"; that is, music for AMATEUR or home use, a chief proponent of which being Paul Hindemith.

Gebunden (Ger., gĕ-bŏŏn′den). Tied; LEGATO.

Gedackt (Ger., gĕ-dăhkt′). Stopped (of ORGAN PIPES).

Gedämpft (Ger., gĕ-dempft′). Damped; muffled; muted.

Gedehnt (Ger., gĕ-dānt′). Sustained, prolonged; slow, stately; LARGAMENTE, STESO.

Gefallen, nach (Ger., năh gĕ-fähl′len). AD LIBITUM.

Gefällig (Ger., gĕ′fel-līyh). Pleasing, graceful.

Gefühl, mit (Ger., mit gĕ-fül′). With feeling, expressively.

Gehalten (Ger., gĕ-hähl′ten). Held, sustained.

Gehaucht (Ger., gĕ-howht′). "Sighed"; very softly and lightly sung or played.

Geheimnisvoll (Ger., gĕ-hīm′nĭs′fŏhl). Mysterious.

Gehend (Ger., gä′ent). ANDANTE.

Geige (Ger., gī′gĕ). VIOLIN. *Geigenprinzipal*, violin-diapason (ORGAN STOP).

Geist (Ger., gīst). Spirit, soul; essence.

Gelassen (Ger., gĕ-lähs′sĕn). Calm, placid, easy.

Geläufig (Ger., gĕ-lähü′fīyh). Fluent, easy. *Geläufigkeit* (gĕ-lähü′fīyh-kīt), fluency, velocity.

Gemächlich (Ger., gĕ-mĕyh′līyh). Easy, comfortable; COMODO.

Gemässigt (Ger., gĕ-mä′sīyht). Moderate (in TEMPO).

Gemendo (It., jā-men'dŏh). Moaning.

Gemessen (Ger., gĕ-mes'sen). Measured(ly), moderate(ly); MODERATO.

Gemischte Stimmen (Ger., gĕ-mĭsh'te shtĭ'mmen). Mixed voices.

Gemüt(h), mit (Ger., mit gĕ-müt'). With feeling; soulfully.

Gemüt(h)lich (Ger., gĕ-müt'lĭyh). Easily and cheerily; DISINVOLTURA, CON; COMODO (of TEMPO).

Generalpause (Ger., gĕh-nĕh-rahl-pow'-zŭ). A REST for an entire ORCHESTRA.

Generator. 1. A ROOT, or FUNDAMENTAL TONE. 2. A tone that produces a series of HARMONICS.

Generoso (It., jĕh-nĕh-roh'sŏh). Free, ample.

Gentilmente (It., jen-tēl-men'tĕh). In a graceful, refined style.

German flute. The CROSS-FLUTE.

German sixth. A CHORD with the INTERVAL of an AUGMENTED SIXTH between the highest and lowest NOTES. Other INTERVALS from the bottom are a MAJOR THIRD and a PERFECT FOURTH, as in *A* flat, *C*, *E* flat, *F* sharp. See AUGMENTED SIXTH.

Ges (Ger., gess). *G* flat.

Gesang (Ger., gĕ-zăhngᵏ'). Singing, SONG; a song; MELODY; VOICE (vocal PART).

Gesamtkunstwerk (Ger., gĕ-zampt-kunst-werk). "Total artwork"; a late Romantic call, and most particularly by Wagner, for operatic reform through restoration of the unity of the arts of music, literature, and painting as were believed to have existed in Greek practices.

Gesangreich (Ger., gĕ-zăhngᵏ'rĭyh). Very singingly; CANTABILE.

Geschleift (Ger., gĕ-shlĭft'). Slurred; LEGATO.

Geschmackvoll (Ger., gĕ-shmăhk'fŏhl). Tastefully.

Geschwindt (Ger., gĕ-shvint'). Swift(ly), rapid(ly).

Ges dur (Ger., gĕs door). *G* flat minor.

Geses (Ger., gess'ess). *G* double flat.

Gesteigert (Ger., gĕ-shtī'gert). Intensified; RINFORZATO.

Gestopft (Ger., gĕ-shtŏ'pft). Stopped. The modification of the TONE of a HORN caused by inserting the hand into the BELL of the instrument, which raises the tone a HALF STEP.

Gestossen (Ger., gĕ-shtŏh'sen). 1. STACCATO. 2. DÉTACHÉ.

Geteilt (Ger., gĕ-tīl't). Divided.

Getragen (Ger., gĕ-trah'gen). Sustained; SOSTENUTO.

Gezogen (Ger., gĕ-tsoh'gen). Drawn out; LARGAMENTE, SOSTE-NUTO, STESO.

Ghiribizzoso (It., gē-rē-bid-zoh'sŏh). Whimsical.

Giga (It., jē'găh); **Gigue** (Fr., zhig). A JIG.

Gioco (or **Giuoco**, etc.), **con** (It., kŏhn jô'kŏh). Playfully, sportively, merrily.

Giocondamente (It., jŏh-kŏhn-dăh-men'tĕh). In a jocund, joyous style.

Giocosamente (It., jŏh-kŏh-săh-men'tĕh). Playfully, sportively, merrily.

Gioia (or **Gioja**, etc.), **con** (It., kŏhn jô'yăh). Joyfully, joyously, gaily, merrily.

Gioviale (It., jŏh-vē-ah'lĕh). Jovial, cheerful.

Giovialità, con (It., kŏhn jŏh-vē-ăh-lē-tah'). Jovially, cheerfully.

Gis (Ger., giss). *G* sharp.

Gisis (Ger., gĭss'ĭs). *G* double sharp.

Gis moll (Ger., mohl). *G* sharp minor.

Giubilante (It., jŏŏ-bē-lăhn'tĕh). Jubilant.

Giubilo (It., jŏŏ′bē-lŏh). Joy, rejoicing, jubilation.

Giustamente (It., jŏŏ-stäh-men′tĕh). Exactly, with precision.

Giusto (It., jŏŏ′stŏh). Strict, appropriate, proper (*tempo giusto*), exact, correct. *Allegro giusto*, moderately fast.

Glass harmonica. A set of glasses of different sizes that are rubbed on the rim with wet fingers producing a gentle ethereal sound. It was so popular in the 18th century that Mozart wrote a piece for it. Developed by Benjamin Franklin.

Glee. A secular COMPOSITION for three or more unaccompanied solo voices, peculiar to England. Serious glees are written as well as merry ones.

Glissando (It., glis-sähn′dŏh). 1. On bowed instruments, (*a*) demands a flowing, unaccented execution of a PASSAGE; (*b*) same as PORTAMENTO. 2. On the PIANO, a rapid SCALE effect obtained by sliding the thumb, or thumb and one finger, over the KEYS. Also *Glissato, Glissicando, Glissicato*.

Gloche (Ger., glŏh′kĕ). A BELL.

Glockenspiel (Ger., glŏh′ken-shpēl′). 1. CARILLON. 2. A set of BELLS or steel bars, tuned diatonically and struck with a small hammer. 3. An ORGAN STOP having bells instead of pipes.

Glottis. The aperture between the vocal cords when they are drawn together in singing.

G moll (Ger., gä mohl). *G minor*.

Golden Section. Division of a whole into two unequal parts such that the ratio of the smaller to the larger is the same as that of the larger to the whole; evidence suggests compositional applications by Debussy and Bartók.

Gondellied (Ger., gŏhn′del-lēt′); **Gondoliera** (It., gŏhn-dŏh-lē-â′räh). A BARCAROLE.

Gong. A suspended circular metal plate, struck with a mallet, producing a sustained reverberation.

Goose. A harsh break in the TONE of a CLARINET, OBOE, or BASSOON.

Gopak. A Ukrainian folk dance in rapid 2/4 TIME. Same as *Hopak*.

Gospel song. A Protestant church HYMN. See also SPIRITUAL.

G.P. Abbreviation for GENERALPAUSE.

Grace. A vocal or instrumental ORNAMENT or EMBELLISHMENT not essential to the MELODY or HARMONY of a COMPOSITION. *Grace note*, a note of embellishment, usually written small.

Gracile (It., grah′tsē-lĕh). Graceful, delicate.

Gradatamente (It., grăh-dăh-tăh-men′tĕh). By degrees, gradually.

Gradevole (It., grăh-dā′vŏh-lĕh). Pleasingly, agreeably.

Gradual. 1. An ANTIPHON (responsorial chant) following the EPISTLE. 2. A book of CHANTS containing the GRADUALS, INTROITS, and other antiphons of the Roman Catholic MASS.

Gramophone. A trademark commonly used in England for the PHONOGRAPH.

Gran, Grand′, or **Grande** (It., grăhn, grăhnd, grăhn′dĕh). Large, great, full, complete. (*Grande* is the regular form, used after nouns; it is abbreviated to *grand′* before vowels, and to *gran* before consonants.)

Gran cassa (It., grăhn cah′săh). Bass DRUM; literally, "big box."

Grand. Technical term for GRAND PIANO.

Grand(e) (Fr., grăhn). Large; great; full. *Grand barré*, a STOP of over three NOTES; *grand bourdon*, double-BOURDON; *grand choer*, full ORGAN; *grand jeu*, (*a*) full organ, (*b*) an HARMO-

NIUM stop for full power; *à grand orchestre*, for full ORCHES-TRA; *grande-orgue*, (*a*) full organ, (*b*) Great organ, (*c*) pipe organ.

Grandioso (It., grähn-dē-oh'sŏh). With grandeur; majestically, pompously, loftily.

Grandisonante (It., grähn-dē-sŏh-nähn'tĕh). Loud or long sounding, sonorous; pompous, affected.

Grand opera. A type of OPERA, usually in five acts, treating a heroic, mythological, or historical subject, sumptuously costumed, and produced in a large opera house.

Granulato (It., gräh-nŏŏ-lah'tŏh). Non-LEGATO.

Graphic notation. Symbols of NOTATION other than those traditionally seen in musical SCORES, often to indicate extremely precise (or intentionally imprecise) PITCH or to stimulate musical behavior or actions in performance.

Grave (It., grah'vĕh). 1. Grave or low in PITCH. 2. Heavy, slow, ponderous in movement. 3. Serious.

Gravemente (It., gräh-vĕh-men'tĕh). Slowly, ponderously; seriously, gravely.

Gravicembalo (It., gräh-vē-chĕm-bahl'oh). HARPSICHORD.

Grazia, con (It., kŏhn grah'tsē-äh). With grace; elegantly.

Great octave. Common name for the OCTAVE beginning on *C*, two LEGER LINES below the STAFF of the BASS CLEF. See "Table of Clefs," p. xii.

Great organ. The chief MANUAL of an ORGAN, and the PIPES controlled by it.

Gregorian chant. See CHANT (2).

Grido (It., grē'dŏh). Cry, shout.

Grosso (It., grô'sŏh). Great, grand; full, heavy.

Grottesco (It., grŏht-tĕh'skŏh). Grotesque, comic.

Ground bass. A continually repeated bass PHRASE of four or eight MEASURES; a BASSO OSTINATO.

Group. 1. A short series of rapid NOTES, especially when sung to one syllable. 2. A section of the ORCHESTRA (or SCORE) embracing instruments of one class, i.e., the strings. 3. A pop-music ENSEMBLE.

Grunge. 1990s-era ROCK, originating in Seattle and spreading East, with bands playing music in the style of HEAVY METAL, but with more thoughtful, although still nihilistic, lyrical content.

Gruppetto, Gruppo (It., grŏŏp-pet'tŏh, grŏŏ-pŏh). Formerly, a TRILL; now, a TURN; also, any "group" of GRACE NOTES.

G string. The lowest STRING on the VIOLIN. On the VIOLA and CELLO, it is the second string above the lowest; on the DOUBLE BASS, it is the highest.

Guaracha (Sp., gwăh-**rah**'chăh). Lively Spanish dance, partly in 3/4 or 3/8, partly in 2/4 TIME.

Guerriero (It., gwĕr-rē-â'**r**ŏh). Martial, war-like.

Guide. A DIRECT; also, a SUBJECT or ANTECEDENT.

Guitar. An instrument of the LUTE family. The modern Spanish guitar has six STRINGS, and a COMPASS of three OCTAVES and a FOURTH, from E to a^2. The music is written an octave higher than it sounds, in the G CLEF. The *Spanish* or *Classical g.* is strung with GUT or nylon strings, has a wide FINGERBOARD, and a slotted PEGHEAD. The *folk* or *acoustic g.*, with a narrower fingerboard and larger body, is strung with steel strings and has a solid peghead.

Gusli. An ancient Russian ZITHER-type instrument.

Gusto (It., gŏŏ'stŏh). Taste.

Gut (Ger., goot). Good.

Gymel. A type of "twin" singing (gymel comes from the Latin word *gemellus*, "a twin") common during the Middle Ages, harmonized in THIRDS.

H

H. In SCORES, *H* stands for HORN; in ORGAN music, for *Heel*; in music for KEYBOARD instruments, for *Hand* (*r.h.*, *l.h.*).

H (Ger., hah). The NOTE *B*.

Habanera (Sp., hăh-băh-nâ'răh). A Cuban dance, in DUPLE METER, characterized by dotted or syncopated RHYTHMS.

Halb (Ger., hăhlp). Half.

Half note. A NOTE one-half the TIME VALUE of a WHOLE NOTE and represented by a white circle with a STEM ♩.

Half step. A SEMITONE.

Hallelujah (Hebr.). "Praise ye the Lord!"

Halling. A national Norwegian dance in 2/4 TIME.

Hammerclavier (Ger., hăhm'mer'klăh-vēr'). Old name for the PIANOFORTE.

Hanacca. A Moravian dance in 3/4 TIME, like the POLONAISE, but quicker.

Handle piano. A mechanical PIANO that operates on the principle of the BARREL ORGAN.

Hand organ. A portable BARREL ORGAN.

Happening. A multimedia event often taking place in unusual settings; Cage's 1954 theater piece at Black Mountain College in North Carolina is usually cited as the first; later enriched by FLUXUS practitioners.

Harfe (Ger., har'fĕ). HARP.

Harmonic. 1. (*adjective*) Pertaining to CHORDS (either CONSONANT or DISSONANT), and to the THEORY and practice of HARMONY. *Harmonic curve*, the curved figure described by a vibrating string; *h. figuration*, broken chords; *h. flute*, see H. STOP; *h. mark*, in music for VIOLIN, etc., a sign (○) over a NOTE, calling for an harmonic TONE; *h. note*, see H. TONE; *h. reed*, *h. stop*, an ORGAN STOP having PIPES double the ordinary length, and pierced mid-way, so that a 16' pipe yields an 8' tone; *h. scale*, (*a*) the succession of harmonic tones, (*b*) MINOR SCALE with MINOR SIXTH and MAJOR SEVENTH; *h. tone*, or *Flageolet-tone*, see HARMONIC 2 (*b*).

Harmonic. 2. (*noun*) (*a*) One of the series of TONES (the so-called PARTIAL TONES) that usually accompany, more or less faintly, the prime tone (GENERATOR) produced by a string, an ORGAN PIPE, the human voice, etc. The *prime tone* (*fundamental*, or *generator*) is the strong tone produced by the vibration of the whole string, or the entire column of air in the pipe; the *partial* tones are produced by the vibration of fractional parts of that string or air column; (*b*) These same harmonics (harmonic tones) are obtained, on any stringed instrument that is stopped (VIOLIN, ZITHER), by lightly touching a nodal point of a string.

Harmonica. A set of graduated metal reeds mounted in a narrow frame, blown by the mouth, and producing different tones on exhalation and inhalation. Also called *mouth harmonica* or *mouth organ*.

Harmonic minor scale. A MINOR SCALE with the raised SEVENTH DEGREE providing a LEADING TONE.

Harmonicon. 1. A HARMONICA. 2. An ORCHESTRION. 3. A keyed harmonica combined with a flue STOP or stops.

Harmonie. French term for WIND INSTRUMENTS.

Harmonic series. A natural series of OVERTONES, sounding an OCTAVE above the FUNDAMENTAL TONE, then a FIFTH higher than that, a FOURTH higher, a MAJOR THIRD higher, a MINOR THIRD higher, etc. The first six members of the natural harmonic series form the harmony of the MAJOR CHORD, fundamental to all acoustic phenomena.

Harmonisch (Ger., har-moh'nish). Harmonic (*adj.*); harmonious.

Harmonium. A popular REED ORGAN, activated by two pedals with both feet operating one after another to pump the air. Once very popular at home and in small churches as a substitute for the organ.

Harmony. 1. A musical combination of TONES or CHORDS. 2. A chord, either CONSONANT or DISSONANT. 3. The HARMONIC texture of a PIECE, as two-PART, three-part harmony. *Chromatic harmony* has CHROMATIC tones and MODULATIONS; *close h.* (in four-part writing) has the three highest parts within the COMPASS of an OCTAVE; *compound h.* has two or more essential chord tones doubled; *dispersed, extended h.*, see OPEN HARMONY; *essential h.*, (*a*) the fundamental TRIADS of a KEY, (*b*) the harmonic frame of a COMPOSITION minus all FIGURATION and ORNAMENTS; *false h.*, (*a*) the inharmonic or FALSE RELATION, (*b*) DISCORD produced by imperfect PREPARATION or RESOLUTION, (*c*) discord produced by wrong NOTES or chords; *figured h.* varies the simple chords by figuration of all kinds; *open h.* (in four-part writing) spreads the three highest parts beyond the compass of an octave; *pure h.*, music performed with pure (not tempered) INTONATION, as by a STRING QUARTET, or unaccompanied voices; *spread h.*, open harmony; *strict h.*, composition according to strict rules for the preparation and resolution of dissonances; *tempered h.*, music performed with tempered intonation, as on the ORGAN or PIANO.

Harp. 1. A STRINGED INSTRUMENT of ancient origin. By definition, a harp has strings that run perpendicular to the SOUNDBOX; compare LYRE. 2. The modern orchestral harp

(Erard's double-action harp) has a nearly three-cornered wooden *frame*, the *foot* of which is formed by an upright *pillar* meeting the hollow *back* (the upperside of which bears the SOUNDBOARD) in the *pedestal*; the upper ends of pillar and back are united by the curving NECK. The GUT strings are 46 (or 47) in number; its COMPASS is 6 1/2 octaves, from $C_1\flat$ to $f^4\flat$ (or $g^4\flat$).

Harpsichord. A KEYBOARD STRINGED INSTRUMENT in which the STRINGS are plucked by quills or bits of hard leather. A predecessor of the PIANO, it was popular as a solo and ensemble instrument in the 18th century.

Haupt (Ger., howpt). Head; chief, principal. *Hauptsatz,* PRINCIPAL MOVEMENT or THEME.

Hauptstimme (Ger. howpt'shtim-meh; "chief voice"). A term first used by Schoenberg to indicate the main POLYPHONIC VOICE in a COMPOSITION, abbreviated in his scores as "H." See NEBENSTIMME.

Hautbois (Fr., ŏh-bwăh'). OBOE.

Havanaise (Fr., ăh-văh-năz'). A HABANERA.

H dur (Ger., hah door). *B* major.

Head. 1. POINT (of a BOW). 2. In the VIOLIN, etc., the part comprising PEGHEAD and scroll. 3. In the DRUM, the membrane stretched over one or both ends. 4. In a NOTE, the oval (or square) part which determines its place on the STAFF.

Head tones (or **voice**). The vocal TONES of the head REGISTER.

Heavy metal. A type of ROCK music characterized by simple, loud MELODIES, blaring GUITAR solos, frequently misogynous lyrics, and a thunderous BEAT. The least subtle of all rock forms.

Heckelphone. A BARITONE OBOE with a range an OCTAVE below the oboe; invented by Heckel.

Heftig (Ger., hef'tĭyh). Vehement, impetuous, passionate.

Heimlich (Ger., hĭm'lĭyh). Secret, mysterious; MISTERIOSO; furtive, stealthy.

Heiter (Ger., hī'ter). Serene; cheerful; glad; GIOIOSO.

Heldentenor. In German, "heroic tenor," requiring a robust voice for highly demanding operatic parts, particularly in Wagner's MUSIC DRAMAS.

Helicon. A BRASS WIND INSTRUMENT, used chiefly in military music as a BASS; its tube is bent in a circle, and it is carried over the shoulder.

Hell (Ger., hel). Clear, bright.

Hemidemisemiquaver. A SIXTY-FOURTH NOTE. *Hemidemisemiquaver-rest*, a sixty-fourth REST.

Hemiola. In mensural NOTATION of the Middle Ages, the use of three NOTES of equal duration in a BAR alternating with two notes of equal value, in the same bar length, so that the longer notes equal 1 1/2 shorter ones (the word comes from the Greek, meaning "one-and-a-half"). In modern notation, the hemiola is represented by a succession of bars alternating between 6/8 and 3/4 TIME.

Hervorgehoben (Ger., hâr-fŏhr'gĕ-hō'ben). Emphasized.

Hervortretend (Ger., hâr-fŏhr'trā-tent). A term indicating that the VOICE or PART to which it is applied is to be brought to the fore, in contrast to the other parts that are accompanying.

Herzig (Ger., hâr'tsĭyh). Hearty, heartily; tenderly.

Hesitation waltz. See BOSTON.

Heterophony (from the Greek *heteros*: "other" or "different"; and *phonē*: "voice"). Generally descriptive of simultaneous variations of a single MELODY; prominent in accompanied vocal music of the Near East and the Orient.

Hexachord. 1. The six tones *ut, re, mi, fa, sol, la* in SOLMISA-TION. 2. A set of six different PITCH CLASSES, usually the first (or last) six of a TWELVE-NOTE SET.

Hidden fifths, octaves. PROGRESSIONS of INTERVALS leading towards an open FIFTH, or an OCTAVE, from the same direction, forbidden in strict, common-practice HARMONY.

Hip hop. An outgrowth of RAP, hip hop has more complicated RHYTHMS and MELODIES, usually featuring a combination of sung and recited sections, with a rich background of SAMPLED RIFFS and sounds. It is also more dance-oriented than is rap.

His (Ger., hĭss). *B* sharp.

H moll (Ger., hĭss mohl). *B* minor.

Hochzeitlied (Ger., hōh′-tsĭt-lēt). Wedding SONG.

Hocket. A curious CONTRAPUNTAL device much in vogue in the Middle Ages, in which one voice stops and another comes in, sometimes in the middle of a word, creating the effect of hiccuping (*hocket* is an old word for *hiccup*).

Hold. FERMATA.

Holding note. A NOTE sustained in one PART while the other parts are in motion.

Homophonic. Alike in sound or PITCH. In modern music, a style in which one MELODY or PART, supported to a greater or lesser extent by CHORDS or chordal combinations (that is, an *accompanied melody*), predominates, is called homophonic; opposed to POLYPHONIC.

Homophony. HOMOPHONIC music; the homophonic style; opposed to ANTIPHONY and POLYPHONY.

Hook. A stroke attached to the STEMS of EIGHTH NOTES, SIXTEENTH NOTES, etc.

Hopak. The Ukrainian spelling of GOPAK.

Hoquet (Fr., oh-keh′). HOCKET.

Horn. The orchestral horn is a BRASS WIND INSTRUMENT, having a conical tube variously bent upon itself (the smallest horn generally used, in high B♭, has a tube nearly nine feet long; that an OCTAVE lower, nearly eighteen feet); wide and flaring BELL; the tone rich, mellow, and sonorous. The old *natural* horn yields only the natural TONES supplemented by stopped TONES and CROOKS, giving a total possible COMPASS of three and one-half octaves, from B♭ to f♭. The modern *Valve-horn*, played like a CORNET, is much easier to handle. The horn is a TRANSPOSING INSTRUMENT. Also called *French horn*.

Horn band. A band of TRUMPETERS. *Russian horn band*, a band of performers on hunting HORNS, each of which produces but one TONE.

Hörner (Ger., hör′ner). HORNS (*corni*).

Hornpipe. An old English dance in lively TEMPO, the earlier ones in 3/2 TIME, the later in 4/4.

Huqin. A Chinese bowed LUTE; also called *Erhu*.

Humoresque. A light, whimsical instrumental PIECE, often for PIANO.

Hurdy-gurdy. A STRINGED INSTRUMENT having two MELODY and from two to four DRONE STRINGS. The melody-strings are "stopped" by KEYS touched by the left hand; the right hand turns a crank that turns a rosined wheel, which scrapes the strings and produces the musical TONES.

Hurtig (Ger., hŏŏr′tĭyh). Swift, headlong.

Hymn. A religious or sacred SONG; usually, a metrical poem to be sung by a congregation. In foreign usage, a national song of lofty character, like the *Marseillaise*.

Hypo-. In the system of church MODES, the prefix *hypo-* indicates the starting point of a mode a FOURTH below its

TONIC; therefore, if the DORIAN mode begins on *D*, then the HYPODORIAN mode will begin on *A*, a fourth below.

I

I (It., ē; *masc. pl.*). The.

Iambus. A metrical foot of two syllables, one short and one long, with the accent on the long: ⌣ —́ .

Ictus. A separation mark in GREGORIAN CHANT before and after an important note in the MELODY; in poetic usage, a "stress."

Idée fixe. In French, "fixed idea"; a term used by Berlioz with reference to his *Symphonie fantastique* to denote its recurrent THEME.

Idiophones. A class of musical instruments that produce their sound by the vibration of the instrument itself, i.e. CASTENETS, RATTLES, GLASS HARMONICAS, etc.

Idyl. A COMPOSITION of a pastoral or tenderly romantic nature, without set FORM. *Also* **Idillio** (It., ē-dil'lē-ōh); **Idylle** (Fr., ē-dil'); **Idylle** (Ger., ē-dil'lĕ).

Il (It., ēl; *masc. sing.*). The. *Il più*, the most.

Im (Ger., im). In the. *Im tempo*, in the regular TEMPO (*a tempo*).

Imbroglio (It., em-broh'lyo). Literally, "confusion"; a term used to describe scenes in OPERA where several groups of singers or instrumental ensembles perform together, each serving a different dramatic purpose.

Imitando (It., ē-mē-tähn'dōh). Imitating.

Imitation. The repetition of a MOTIVE, PHRASE, or THEME proposed by one PART (the ANTECEDENT) in another part (the CONSEQUENT), with or without modification. *Free i.*, that in which changes of the antecedent are permitted in the consequent; *canonic* or *strict i.*, that in which the consequent answers the antecent NOTE for note and INTERVAL for interval.

Immer (Ger., im'mer). Always; continually. *Immer stärker werdend*, continually growing louder; *i. langsamer*, slower and slower; *i. langsam*, slowly throughout.

Impazientemente (It., im-păh-tsē-en'tĕh-men-tĕh). Impatient, impatiently.

Imperioso (It., im-pĕh-rē-oh'sŏh). Imperious, haughty, lofty.

Impetuoso (It., im-pĕh-tŏŏ-oh'sŏh). Impetuously, vehemently.

Imponente (It., im-pŏh-nen'tĕh). Imposing, impressive.

Impresario (It., im-prĕh-sah'rē-ŏh). The agent or manager of an OPERA or CONCERT company.

Impressionism. A term used to describe modern French compositions of the early 20th century, in which subtle impressions rather than programmatic descriptions are conveyed through the use of ethereal HARMONIES in free MODULATION and colorful INSTRUMENTATION.

Impromptu. 1. An IMPROVISATION. 2. A COMPOSITION of loose and extemporaneous FORM and slight development; a FANTASIA.

Improvisation. Extemporized musical performance.

Incalzando (It., in-kăhl-tsăhn'dŏh). "Pursuing hotly"; growing more vehement. *Incalzando e stringendo*, growing more vehement and rapid.

Incarnatus, Et. Part of the CREDO. See MASS.

Incidental music. Music supplementary to a spoken drama, such as an OVERTURE, INTERLUDES, SONGS, etc.

Inciso (It., in-chē'sŏh). Incisive; sharply marked. *Incise*, "mark the notes sharply."

Incomplete stop. A half STOP.

Indeciso (It., in-dĕh-chē'sŏh). Irresolute, undecided.

Independent chord, harmony, triad. One which is CONSONANT (contains no DISSONANCE) and is, therefore, not obliged to change to another CHORD by PROGRESSION or RESOLUTION.

Indeterminacy. With reference to a COMPOSITION, denoting a conventional SCORE produced by CHANCE methods; with reference to performance, denoting a score that leaves much to be determined by performers.

Indifferente (It., in-dif-fĕh-**r**en'tĕh). Indifferently, carelessly.

Infernale (It., in-fâr-nah'lĕh). Infernal.

Infinite canon. One without a closing CADENCE, that may be repeated indefinitely (at pleasure).

Infinite melody. One that avoids CADENCE; often associated with the melodic meanderings of Wagner in his mature MUSIC DRAMAS.

Infino (It., in-fē'nŏh). Up to, as far as, until you reach.

Ingenuamente (It., in-jĕh-nŏŏ-ăh-men'tĕh). Naturally, ingenuously.

Inharmonic relation. FALSE RELATION.

Iniziale (It., ē-nē-tsē-ah'lĕh). Initial; the first.

Inner parts. PARTS in HARMONY lying between the highest and lowest.

Inner pedal. A PEDAL POINT on an inner PART.

Innig (Ger., in'nĭyh). Heartfelt, sincere, fervent, intense; INTIMO, CON AFFETTO.

Inniglich (Ger., in'nĭyh'lĭyh). With deep emotion; fervently.

Innocente (It., in-nŏh-chen'tĕh). Innocently, artlessly.

Inquieto (It., in-kwē-ĕh'tŏh). Unrestful, uneasy.

Insensible (It., in-sen-sē'bē-lĕh). Imperceptible.

Insensibilmente (It., in-sen-sē-bĕl-men'tĕh). Insensibly.

Inständig (Ger., in'shten'dih); **Instante** (It., in'stähn'těh). Urgent, pressing.

Instrumentation. The THEORY and practice of composing, arranging, or adapting music for a body of instruments of different kinds, especially for ORCHESTRA.

Intabulation. Arranging vocal music for STRINGED INSTRUMENTS or KEYBOARD; more recently, the arrangement of a vocal composition for keyboard or stringed instruments. *Also* **Intabulierung** (Ger., in'tä-boo-lee'er-oongᵏ); **Intavolatura** (It., in-tă-voh-lă-too'räh).

Intenzione, con (It., kŏhn in-ten-tsē-oh'něh). With stress, emphasis.

Interlude. 1. An INTERMEZZO. 2. An instrumental strain or PASSAGE connecting the lines or STANZAS of a HYMN, etc. 3. An instrumental piece played between certain portions of the church service (*Interludium*).

Intermezzo (-med'zŏh). 1. A light musical entertainment alternating with the acts of the early Italian tragedies. 2. INCIDENTAL MUSIC in modern dramas. 3. A short MOVEMENT connecting the main DIVISIONS of a SYMPHONY. 4. Many instrumental compositions take the name "Intermezzo" for want of a better title, not being "characteristic" pieces.

Intermodulation. Electronic technique of sound manipulation inspired by the interference of two signals; used extensively, in principle, by such modern composers as Stockhausen.

Interruzione, senza (It., sen'tsäh in-tĕr-rŏŏ-tsē-oh'něh). Without interruption.

Interval. The difference in PITCH between two NOTES. INTERVALS are regularly measured from the lower TONE to the higher. *Augmented interval*, wider by a CHROMATIC SEMITONE than MAJOR or PERFECT; *chromatic i.*, AUGMENTED or

DIMINISHED (except augmented FOURTH, and diminished FIFTH and SEVENTH); *compound i.*, wider than an OCTAVE; *consonant i.*, not requiring RESOLUTION; *diatonic i.*, occurring between two notes belonging to the same KEY (except the augmented SECOND and fifth of the HARMONIC MINOR SCALE); *diminished i.*, chromatic semitone narrower than major or perfect; *dissonant i.*, requiring resolution; *enharmonic i.*, see ENHARMONIC TONES; *extended*, or *extreme, i.*, augmented; *flat i.*, diminished; *harmonic i.*, both tones sounded together; *imperfect i.*, diminished; *inverted i.*, the higher tone is lowered, or the lower tone raised, by an octave; *major i*, equal to the standard second, THIRD, SIXTH, and seventh of the major scale; *melodic i.*, both tones sounded in succession; *minor i.*, a chromatic semitone narrower than major or perfect; *parallel i.* (with an interval preceding), two tones progress in the same direction and at the same interval; *perfect* (or *perfect major*) *i.*, equal to the standard prime, fourth, fifth, and octave of the major scale; *redundant i.*, augmented; *simple i.*, not wider than an octave; *standard i.*, measured upward from the KEYNOTE; *superfluous i.*, augmented.

Intimissimo (It., in-tē-mis'sē-mŏh). Very tenderly, warmly.

Intimo (It., in'tē-mŏh). Heartfelt, fervent.

Intonarumori. Musical instruments (literally "noisemakers") invented c. 1913 by FUTURIST musician Luigi Russolo, all of which were destroyed in Paris during World War II.

Intonation. 1. The production of TONE, either vocal or instrumental. 2. The method of CHANTING employed in PLAINCHANT. 3. The opening NOTES leading up to the RECITING TONE of a CHANT. *Fixed intonation*, see FIXED-TONE INSTRUMENT.

Intoning. The chanting by the minister, in MONOTONE, of parts of the Anglican church service.

Intrada (It., in-trăh′dăh). A short INTRODUCTION or PRELUDE.

Intrepidezza, con (It., kŏhn in-trâ-pē-det′săh). Boldly, daringly, dashingly.

Introduction. A PHRASE or DIVISION preliminary to and preparatory of a COMPOSITION or MOVEMENT.

Introit (L., ĭn-trō′ĭt, "entrance"). An ANTIPHON sung while the priest is approaching the altar to celebrate the MASS. In the modern Anglican Church, an ANTHEM or PSALM, sung as the minister approaches the Communion table.

Invention. A short PIECE in FREE CONTRAPUNTAL style, developing one MOTIVE in an IMPROMPTU fashion.

Inversion. The TRANSPOSITION of the NOTES of an INTERVAL or CHORD. (*a*) In a simple interval, the higher note is set an OCTAVE lower, or the lower note an octave higher. (*b*) A chord is *inverted* when its lowest note is not the ROOT (see "Chords," p. xvi–xvii). (*c*) IN DOUBLE COUNTERPOINT, the transposition of two PARTS, the higher being set below the lower, or vice versa; this inversion may be by an octave or some other interval, and is called "inversion in the octave," "in the tenth," "in the fifth," etc. (*d*) An ORGAN POINT is *inverted* when in some other part than the lowest. (*e*) A MELODY is *inverted* when ascending intervals are made to descend by the same DEGREE, and vice versa. The melody is therefore turned upside down. (*f*) One of the three standard techniques in 12-NOTE COMPOSITION (RETROGRADE, inversion, TRANSPOSITION) wherein all intervals of a set are reversed in their direction.

Invertible counterpoint. A type of POLYPHONIC writing in which CONTRAPUNTAL parts could be INVERTED and placed in different VOICES without forming forbidden DISCORDS. Also called DOUBLE COUNTERPOINT.

Ionian mode. The ecclesiastical MODE corresponding to a MAJOR SCALE.

Ira, con (It., kŏhn ē′răh). With wrath; passionately.

Irlandais,-e (Fr., ēr-lăhn-dä,-däz′). Hibernian, Irish.

Ironicamente (It., ē-rŏh-nē-kăh-men′tĕh). Ironically.

Irregular cadence. See CADENCE.

Irresoluto (It., ir-rĕh-sŏh-loo′tŏh). Irresolute, undecided; vacillating.

Islancio, con (It., kŏhn ē-zlăhn′chŏh). Vehemently, impetuously; with dash.

Isorhythm. In the 14th and 15th centuries, a technique using a repeated PITCH (COLOR) and RHYTHM (TALEA) patterns. The color and talea do not necessarily coincide, so that the repeated pitches are presented in different rhythms and PHRASES.

Istesso (It., ē-stes′sŏh). Same. *L'istesso tempo*, "the same tempo" (or "time"); signifies that (*a*) the TEMPO of either the MEASURE or measure NOTE remains the same after a change of TIME SIGNATURE, or (*b*) a MOVEMENT previously interrupted is to be resumed.

Italian overture. An OVERTURE current in the 17th and 18th centuries consisting of three sections — quick, slow, quick — in contradistinction to the FRENCH OVERTURE in which the sections are slow, quick, slow.

Italian sixth. A CHORD of three NOTES, containing the INTERVAL of the AUGMENTED SIXTH between its highest and lowest NOTES and a MAJOR THIRD from the bottom to its middle notes, as in *A* flat, *C*, and *F* sharp. See AUGMENTED SIXTH.

Ite, missa est. "Go, ye are dismissed." The final words of the MASS.

J

Jack. In the HARPSICHORD and CLAVICHORD, an upright slip of wood on the rear end of the KEY lever, carrying (in the former) a bit of crow-quill or hard leather set at a right angle so as to pluck or twang the string, or (in the latter) a metallic TANGENT. 2. In the PIANO, the ESCAPEMENT lever, or hopper.

Jagdhorn (Ger., yăht′horn). Hunting HORN.

Jagdstück (Ger., yăh′shtük). Hunting PIECE.

Jägerchor (Ger., yă′ger-kohr′). Hunters' CHORUS.

Jaleo (Sp., hăh-lā′ŏh). A Spanish dance for one performer, in 3/8 TIME and moderate TEMPO.

Jam session. A free IMPROVISATION by a JAZZ group.

Jankò keyboard. A PIANO KEYBOARD invented by Paul von Jankò of Totis, Hungary, in 1882. It has six rows of KEYS so arranged that any given TONE can be struck in three different places, that is, on every other row.

Jarábe (Sp., hăh-răh′bě). Type of Mexican dance of Spanish origin.

Jazz. A term covering a wide variety of African-American styles: RAGTIME, BLUES, DIXIELAND, SWING, BEBOP, COOL, THIRD STREAM, FREE JAZZ, FUNKY, JAZZ-ROCK, and other styles less amenable to specific categorization. Most are characterized by IMPROVISATION and a "swinging" BEAT composed of a steady, prominent METER and dotted or SYNCOPATED RHYTHMS.

Jazz-rock. A style of the late 1960s and 1970s that merges the electric amplification and heavy beat of ROCK with some of the more sophisticated improvisatory features of JAZZ. Also called *fusion*.

Jeu (Fr., zhö). 1. Style of playing. 2. A STOP of an ORGAN, i.e., *grand* or *plein jeu*, full organ or power; *demi-jeu*, half power.

Jew's harp. A small instrument with rigid iron frame, having a thin vibratile metal tongue; the frame is pressed against the slightly opened teeth, and the metallic tongue plucked with the finger.

Jig. A kind of COUNTRY DANCE, with many modifications of step and gesture, in TRIPLE or COMPOUND TIME, and rapid TEMPO. In the CLASSICAL SUITE, the *Gigue* is usually the last MOVEMENT.

Jingling Johnny. A noise-making exotic instrument, consisting of a stick overhung with jingles and bells. It is also known as a Turkish CRESCENT or Chinese Pavilion, indicating its supposed outlandish provenance.

Jodel. YODEL.

Jongleur (Fr., zhon'glör'). A wandering medieval minstrel employed by royalty and aristocracy to provide light entertainment; the word itself corresponds to the English "juggler," implying that such a minstrel also performed acrobatic acts.

Jota (Sp., hoh'täh). A national dance of northern Spain, danced by couples, in triple TIME and rapid movement, something like a WALTZ.

Just intonation. Singing or playing music precisely to true PITCH; opposed to tempered INTONATION.

K

K. An abbreviation for Köchel, as in Ludwig Köchel, the Austrian botanist, mineralogist, and music bibliographer known today for his monumental catalog of Mozart's works, *Chronologisch-thematisches Verzeichnis sämtlicher Tonwerke Wolfgang Amade Mozarts* (1862), in which each composition is identified with a *K.* number instead of the more usual *Op.*

Kalimba. See LAMELLAPHONES.

Kammer (Ger., kähm'mer). "Chamber"; "court." *Kammermusik*, CHAMBER MUSIC; *K.musiker*, court musician; *K.kantate*, chamber CANTATA.

Kantate (Ger., kähn-tah'tĕ). CANTATA.

Kantele. National Finnish instrument, plucked with fingers like a ZITHER.

Kapelle (Ger., käh-pel'lĕ). 1. A private BAND or CHOIR. 2. An ORCHESTRA.

Kapellmeister (Ger., käh-pel'mīs'ter). CONDUCTOR of an ORCHESTRA or a CHOIR.

Kavatine (Ger., käh-väh-tē'nĕ). CAVATINA.

Kazoo. A toy-like instrument consisting of a short tube with membranes at one end, into which the player hums, producing a curiously nasal tone; also known as MIRLITON. In the 17th century, it was called a *flûte-eunuque* ("eunuch flute").

Keckheit, mit (Ger., mit kek'hīt). Boldly, confidently.

Kettledrum. An orchestral DRUM consisting of a hollow brass or copper hemisphere (the kettle) resting on a tripod, with a head of vellum or plastic stretched by means of an iron ring and tightened by a set of screws, or by cords and braces. It is generally played in pairs, the larger *drum* yielding any TONE from *F* to *c*, and the smaller from *B♭* to *f*.

Key. (1) The series *of* TONES forming any given MAJOR or MINOR SCALE, considered *with* reference to their HARMONIC relations, particularly the *relation* of the other tones to the TONIC or KEYNOTE. *Attendant key*, see ATTENDANT; *chromatic k.*, one having SHARPS or FLATS *in the* KEY SIGNATURE; *extreme k.*, a remote key; *major k.*, one *having* a major THIRD and SIXTH; *minor k.*, one having a minor *third* and sixth; *natural k.*, one with neither sharps nor flats in the key signature, as in *C* major; *parallel k.*, (*a*) a minor key with the same keynote as the given major key, or vice versa, (*b*) a *relative k.* (see RELATIVE); *remote k.*, an indirectly related key. (2) (*a*) A digital or finger lever in the KEYBOARD of a PIANO or ORGAN; (*b*) A PEDAL or foot key in the organ or pedal piano. (3) A flat padded disk attached to a lever worked by the finger or thumb, closing the soundholes of various WIND INSTRUMENTS. A wrest, or tuning key.

Key action. In the KEYBOARD of a PIANO or ORGAN, the KEYS and the entire mechanism connected with and set in action by them.

Keyboard. The range of KEYS on any "keyboard" instrument, i.e., ORGAN, PIANO, HARPSICHORD.

Key bugle. See BUGLE.

Key chord. The TONIC TRIAD.

Key harp. An instrument formed like a PIANO, but having TUNING FORKS in lieu of STRINGS. Invented in 1819 by Dietz and Second.

Keynote. The first NOTE of a KEY or SCALE.

Key signature. The SHARPS or FLATS at the head of the STAFF.

Key stop. A KEY attached to the FINGERBOARD of a VIOLIN so as to replace the fingers in stopping the strings; the instrument is called a *key-stop* or *keyed-stop violin.*

Key trumpet. A TRUMPET provided with KEYS.

Kindlich (Ger., kint′lĭyh). Childlike, artless.

Kirchenmusik (Ger., kĭryh′en-moo-zĭk). Church music.

Kit. The small VIOLIN used by dancing masters, about sixteen inches long, and tuned c^1-g^1-d^2.

Kithara. An ancient Greek instrument of the LYRE family, with several STRINGS stretched over the SOUNDBOX.

Klagend (Ger., klah'ghent). Mournfully, plaintively.

Klang (Ger., klăng^k). 1. A sound. 2. A composite musical TONE (a FUNDAMENTAL tone with its HARMONICS). 3. A CHORD, as in *Dreiklang* (TRIAD).

Klangfarbe (Ger., klăng^k'far-bĕ). TONE COLOR.

Klangfarbenmelodie (Ger., klăng^k-fahr-bĕn-mel'oh-dē). A technique of the 20th-century Viennese school in which MELODIES have wide and DISSONANT SKIPS and changing TONE COLORS.

Klappe (Ger., klăhp'pĕ). See KEY (3). *Klappenhorn*, key BUGLE.

Klarinette (Ger., klăh-rē-net'te). CLARINET.

Klavier (Ger., klăh-vēr'). 1. A KEYBOARD. 2. A keyboard stringed instrument; in the 18th century, a CLAVICHORD; now, a PIANOFORTE of any kind.

Klavierauszug (Ger., klăh-vēr'ows'tsŏŏh). PIANO ARRANGEMENT.

Klaviermässig (Ger., klăh-vēr'mä'sīyh). Suitable for the PIANO; in piano style.

Knabenstimme (Ger., knăh'bĕn-shtĭ'mĕ). A boy's voice.

Knee stop. A knee lever under the MANUAL of the REED ORGAN. There are usually two, used to (*a*) open and shut the swell-box (make the sound louder or softer), and (*b*) draw all the STOPS.

Kniegeige (Ger., knē'gī-gŭh). VIOLA DA GAMBA; literally, "knee violin."

Konzert (Ger., kŏhn'tsârt'). 1. CONCERTO. 2. CONCERT.

Konzertmeister (Ger., kŏhn-sârt'mī-ster). CONCERTMASTER.

Konzertstück (Ger., kŏhn-tsârt'shtük). 1. A CONCERT PIECE. 2. A short CONCERTO in one MOVEMENT and free FORM.

Koppel (Ger., kŏhp'pel). COUPLER. *Koppel ab*, off coupler; *K. an*, draw coupler, couple.

Koto. A Japanese thirteen-stringed instrument similar to a ZITHER.

Kräftig (Ger., kref'tĭyh). Forceful, vigorous, energetic; CON FORZA.

Krakowiak. CRACOVIENNE.

Krebsgang (Ger., krĕps'gähng). Literally, "crab walk"; a RETROGRADE motion of a given THEME or PASSAGE.

Kreuz (Ger., kroytz). The sharp sign (♯).

Krummhorn (Ger., krŏŏm'horn). An obsolete WOODWIND INSTRUMENT with double REED. Hence, an ORGAN STOP of similar (mournful) TONE.

Kujawiak. A Polish dance in the RHYTHM of a MAZURKA, but executed at a faster TEMPO.

Kulturbolschewismus. "Cultural bolshevism"; a term used by Nazi officials to denigrate music, particularly that of Schoenberg and Stravinsky, but also others, as artistically radical and thus revolutionarily political.

Kurz (Ger., kŏŏrts). Short. *Kurz und bestimmt*, short and decided.

Kyrie (Gk., kü'rē-ĕh). "Lord"; the first word in the opening division (the "Kyrie") of the MASS.

L

L. Stands for *left* (or *links*, Ger.) in the direction *l.h.* (left hand).

La. 1. The sixth Aretinian syllable. 2. The note *A* in French and Italian. 3. (It., läh). The.

Lacrimosa (L., läh-crē-mŏh'zäh). A part of the REQUIEM MASS.

Lage (Ger., lah'gĕ). Position (of a CHORD); position, shift (in VIOLIN playing). *Enge (weite) Lage*, close (open) POSITION or HARMONY.

Lagrimoso (It., lăh-grē-moh'sŏh). "Tearful," plaintive, like a lament.

Lah. Stands for *La* in TONIC SOL-FA.

Lamellaphones. A class of handheld musical instruments indigenous to Africa whose sound is produced by the vibration of thin tongues of metal or wood plucked by the thumbs; well known are the *mbira* and *kalimba*; also called *thumb pianos*.

Lamentoso (It., lăh-men-toh'sŏh). Lamentingly, plaintively, mournfully.

Lamento (It., lăh-men'tŏh). A lament, complaint.

Ländler (Ger., lent'ler). A slow WALTZ of South Germany and the Tyrol (whence the French name *Tyrolienne*), in 3/4 or 3/8 TIME, and the RHYTHM

Langsam (Ger., lăhng^k'zăhm). Slow. *Langsamer*, slower.

Languendo (It., lăhn-gwen'dŏh). Languishing, plaintive.

Languore, con (It., kŏhn lăhn-gô'rĕh). Languidly, languishingly.

Largamente (It., lar-găh-men'tĕh). Largely, broadly; in a manner characterized by a vigorous and sustained TONE and general breadth of style, without change of TEMPO.

Largando (It., lar-găhn'dŏh). "Growing broader"; that is, slower and more marked; generally a CRESCENDO is implied.

Large. A PLAINCHANT NOTE equal to two (or three) LONGS.

Larghetto (It., lar-get'tŏh). The diminutive of LARGO, demanding a somewhat more rapid TEMPO, nearly ANDANTINO.

Largo (It., lar'gŏh). Large, broad; the slowest TEMPO-MARK, calling for a slow and stately movement with ample breadth of style. *Largo assai*, very slowly and broadly (also *Largo di molto*, *Molto largo*, or *Larghissimo*); *Poco largo*, "with some breath"; can occur even during an ALLEGRO.

Lassú. The slow SECTION of the CSÁRDÁS.

Lauda (Latin). A laud (HYMN or SONG of praise). *Laudes*, lauds; together with MATINS, the first of the seven Canonical Hours.

Laudamus te. "We praise Thee"; part of the GLORIA of the MASS.

Laudi spirituali. Medieval SONGS of devotion.

Launig (Ger., low'nĭyh). 1. With light, gay humor. 2. With facile, characteristic expression.

Laute (Ger., low'te). LUTE.

Lavolta. A dance of Italian origin (properly *la volta*, "a turn"), popular in Shakespeare's time in England.

Lay. A MELODY or TUNE.

Le (It., lā; Fr., lŭ). The.

Lead. 1. The giving-out or proposition of a THEME by one PART. 2. A CUE.

Leader. 1. CONDUCTOR, director. 2. In the ORCHESTRA, the first VIOLIN; in a BAND, the first CORNET; in a MIXED CHORUS, the first SOPRANO. 3. An ANTECEDENT.

Leading. 1. (*noun*) The MELODIC PROGRESSION or CONDUCT of any PART. 2. (*adjective*) Principal, chief; guiding, directing. *Leading chord*, the DOMINANT SEVENTH CHORD; *l. melody*, principal MELODY or THEME; *l. motive*, see LEITMOTIV; *l. note*, *l. tone*, the SEVENTH DEGREE of the MAJOR and HARMONIC MINOR SCALE.

Leaning note. APPOGGIATURA.

Leap. 1. In PIANO playing, a spring from one NOTE or CHORD to another. 2. In HARMONY, a SKIP.

Lebhaft (Ger., lāb'hăft). Lively, animated. *Lebhaft, aber nicht zu sehr*, lively, but not too much so.

Lebhaftigkeit (Ger., lāg'hăhf-tīyh-kīt). Animation. *Mit Lebhaftigkeit und durchaus mit Empfindung und Ausdruck*, with animation, and with feeling and expression throughout.

Ledger line. A LEGER LINE.

Legando (It., lĕh-găhn'dŏh, "binding"). 1. LEGATO. 2. An EXPRESSION MARK calling for the smooth execution of two or more consecutive TONES by a single "stroke of the GLOTTIS" (vocal), in one BOW (VIOLIN, etc.), a single stroke of the tongue (WIND INSTRUMENTS), or LEGATISSIMO (on ORGAN or PIANO).

Legate (It., lĕh-gah'tĕh). Slurred; played or sung smoothly and evenly.

Legatissimo (It., lĕh-găh-tis'sē-mŏh). Very smoothly and evenly. On the PIANO, an indication that each finger is to hold its NOTE as long as possible.

Legato (It., lĕh-gah'tŏh). Bound, slurred; a direction to perform the PASSAGE in a smooth and connected manner, with no break between the TONES; also indicated by the "legato mark," a curving line under or over notes to be so executed.

Legend (lē- or lĕj'end); **Lengende** (Ger., lĕh-gen'dĕ); **Légende** (Fr., lā-zhahnd'). A vocal or instrumental COMPOSITION depicting the course of a short tale of legendary character.

Legendenton, im (Ger., im lĕh-gen'den'tohn). In the tone (style) of a LEGEND.

Leger line. A short line used for writing notes that lie above or below the STAFF. *Leger space*, a space bounded on either side or both sides by a leger line. (Pronounced, and often written, *Led'ger line*.)

Leggeramente (It., led-jĕh-**răh**-men'tĕh). Lightly, briskly.

Leggero (It., led'jâ'**r**oh). Light, airy.

Leggiadramente (It., led'jâh-drăh-men'tĕh). Neatly, elegantly, gracefully.

Legno, col (It., kŏhl lān'yŏh). "With the stick"; let the stick of the BOW (of the VIOLIN, etc.) fall on the STRINGS.

Lehrstück. Literally, "teaching piece." Musico-dramatic stageworks conceived and developed by Bertolt Brecht, in collaboration with Hindemith, Weill, Eisler, and others, as exercises for amateur performers meant to raise political and/or artistic consciousness.

Leicht (Ger., līyht). Light, brisk; easy, facile. *Leicht bewegt,* lightly and swiftly; with slight agitation.

Leichtlich (Ger., līyht'līyh). Lightly, easily.

Leidenschaftlich (Ger., lī'den-shăhft'līyh). With passion; passionately.

Leidvoll (Ger., līt'fŏhl). Sorrowful, mournful.

Leise (Ger., lī'zĕ). Low, soft; PIANO.

Leiser (Ger., lī'zer). Softer. *Immer leiser,* softer and softer.

Leitmotiv (Ger., līt'mŏh-tēf'). Leading motive; any striking musical MOTIVE (THEME, PHRASE) characterizing or accompanying one of the actors in a drama, or some particular idea, emotion, or situation in the latter.

Lenezza, con (It., kŏhn lĕh-net'săh). Faintly, gently, quietly.

Leno (It., lā'nŏh). Faint, gentle, quiet.

Lentamente (It., len-tăh-men'tĕh). Slowly.

Lentando (It., len-tăhn'dŏh). Growing slower.

Lento (It., len'tŏh). Slow; calls for a TEMPO between ANDANTE and LARGO. *Adagio non lento,* slowly, but not dragging.

Lesson. English instrumental PIECE of the 17th and 18th centuries composed for the HARPSICHORD or ORGAN.

Lesto (It., lâ'stǒh). Gay, lively, brisk.

Liberamente (It., lē-běh-**r**äh-men'těh). Freely, boldly.

Libretto (It., lē-bret'tǒh). A "booklet"; the words of an OPERA, ORATORIO, etc. The author is called a *librettist* (It., *li-bretti'sta*).

Licenza (It., lē-chen'tsäh). Freedom, license. *Con alcuna licenza*, with a certain (degree of) freedom.

Lieblich (Ger., lēp'līyh). Lovely, sweet, charming.

Lied (Ger., leed). 1. An art SONG; the plural is *lieder*. 2. Originally, any song in the German vernacular, as opposed to religious (Latin) texts. 3. In the 19th century, a song expressing deep emotion, lyrically and musically, written for CONCERT (RECITAL) performance.

Liedertafel. A general name for a German male CHORAL society.

Ligature. 1. A TIE, joining two or more NOTES together, thus lengthening the original TIME VALUE and occasionally resulting in a SYNCOPATION. 2. An indication that a group or series of notes is to be executed in one breath, to one syllable, or as a LEGATO PHRASE.

Light opera. An OPERETTA.

Limpido (It., lim'pē-dǒh). "Limpid"; clearly, distinctly.

Linear counterpoint. A modern term describing a type of contrapuntal writing in which individual lines are the main considerations in the ENSEMBLE.

Lip. 1. The upper and lower lips of an ORGAN'S flue PIPE are the flat surfaces above and below the mouth. 2. Lipping; that is, the art of so adjusting the lips to the MOUTHPIECE of a WIND INSTRUMENT as to get a good tone.

Lirico. Italian word for LYRIC.

Liscio (It., lē'shǒh). Smooth, flowing.

L'istesso (It., lē-stes'sŏh). The same. *L'istesso tempo*, the same TEMPO.

Litany. A song of supplication, with priests and choir alternating.

Liturgy. The total service of the Christian church.

Liuto (It., lē-oo'tŏh). A LUTE.

Live electronic music. Music that requires ELECTRONIC MUSIC in its performance beyond simple tape playback or amplification of sound.

Lo (It., loh). The.

Lobgesang (Ger., lŏhb'gĕ-săng^k). SONG of praise.

Loco (It., lô'kŏh). "Place"; following *8va*, it means "perform the NOTES as written."

Locrian mode. The ecclesiastical MODE that corresponds to the SCALE from *B* to *B* on the white KEYS of the PIANO.

Lointain (Fr., loo-an-tehn'). Distant; faint sounding.

Long. A PLAINCHANT NOTE equal to two (or three) BREVES.

Lontano (It., lŏhn-tah'nŏh). Far away. *Da lontana*, from a distance.

Loud pedal. The right PIANOFORTE PEDAL that lifts the DAMPERS.

Lourdement (Fr., lŏŏr-deu-män'). Heavily.

Loure (Fr., loor). A dance in 6/4 or 3/2 TIME and slow TEMPO, the DOWNBEAT strongly marked.

Louré (Fr., loorā). Slurred, LEGATO, *non staccato*.

Luftig (Ger., lŏŏf'tīyh). Airy, light.

Lugubre (It., lŏŏ-goo'brĕh). Mournful.

Lunga (It., lŏŏn'gah). Long; sustained, prolonged. Written over or under a FERMATA (⌒), it means that the pause is to be decidedly prolonged; often written *Pausa lunga*, long pause.

Lur. A primitive wooden TRUMPET in use by shepherds in Scandinavia.

Lusinghiero (It., loo-zin-gē-â′rŏh). Coaxingly, caressingly, flatteringly, seductively.

Lustig (Ger., lŏŏs′tīyh). Merry, merrily.

Lute. 1. A general term for a variety of plucked, STRINGED INSTRUMENTS, popular from the 16th through 18th centuries, often featuring bowl-shaped backs and PEGHEAD set at right angles to the FINGERBOARD. Also *laute* (Ger., low′te); *liuto* (It., lē-oo′tŏh). 2. Generally, any musical instrument with STRINGS that run parallel to the SOUNDBOX, and an extended NECK coming out of the BODY, featuring a FINGERBOARD for stopping or fretting the strings.

Luthier (Fr., leu-tieh′). A maker of LUTES, and generally speaking, of any STRINGED INSTRUMENTS.

Luttuosamente (It., lŏŏt-tŏŏ-ŏh-săh-men′tĕh). Mournfully, plaintively.

Luttuoso (It., lŏŏt-tŏŏ-oh′sŏh). Mournful, doleful, plaintive.

Lydian mode. The church MODE that corresponds to the SCALE from *F* to *F* on the white KEYS of the PIANO.

Lyre. 1. An ancient Greek STRINGED INSTRUMENT, the BODY being a SOUNDBOARD, from which rose two curving arms joined above by a CROSSBAR; the STRINGS, from three to ten in number, were stretched from this crossbar to or over a BRIDGE set on the soundboard, and were plucked with a PLECTRUM. 2. The lyre of military bands consists of loosely suspended steel bars tuned to the SCALE and struck with a hammer.

Lyric, lyrical. Pertaining to or proper for the LYRE, or for ACCOMPANIMENT on (by) the lyre; hence, adapted for singing, or for expression in song; opposed to *epic* (narrative) and *dramatic* (scenic, accompanied by action). *Lyric* *drama*, the OPERA; *l. opera*, one in which the lyric form predominates; *l. stage*, the operatic stage.

Lyrics. A colloquial term for the text of a POPULAR SONG or stage MUSICAL.

M

M. Stands for It. *mano* or Fr. *main* (hand); for MANUAL (ORGAN); and for METRONOME (usually *M.M.*).

Ma (It., măh). But. *Allegro ma non troppo*, rapidly, but not too fast.

Mächtig (Ger., mäyh'tĭyh). Powerful, mighty.

Madrigal. A short LYRIC poem; also, a vocal setting of such a poem, in from three to eight PARTS, CONTRAPUNTAL, and usually for unaccompanied CHORUS; there are also madrigals in simple HARMONY, in dance RHYTHMS, etc., or accompanied by instruments.

Maestoso (It., măh-ĕ-stoh'sŏh). Majestic, dignified; in a style characterized by lofty breadth.

Maestro (It., măh-ĕh'strŏh). Master. *Maestro di cappella*, CHOIRMASTER; CONDUCTOR.

Maggiore. In Italian, MAJOR.

Maggot. A MADRIGAL, in old English; the word meant "a whimsical notion," and was used in the sense of a SONG dedicated to a lady.

Magic Square. An arrangement of numbers placed in such a way that each of its horizontal or vertical rows equals the same sum, i.e.,

$$
\begin{array}{ccc}
1 & 2 & 3 \\
2 & 3 & 1 \\
3 & 1 & 2
\end{array}
$$

Magnificat (L., măhg-nē'fē-kăht). "Magnificat anima mea dominum" (my soul doth magnify the Lord), the CANTICLE of the Virgin Mary (Luke I, 46–55) sung as part of the Office of VESPERS in the Roman Catholic Church.

Main (Fr., măn). Hand. *Main droite* (*gauche*), right (left) hand; often written *m.d.* (*m.g.*).

Maître (Fr., mä'tr). Master. *Maître de chapelle*, CHOIR MASTER; CONDUCTOR.

Majestätisch (Ger., măh-yes-tä'tish). MAESTOSO.

Majeur. French for MAJOR.

Major. "Greater"; opposed to minor, or "lesser." See INTERVAL. *Major cadence*, one closing on a major TRIAD; *m. chord* or *triad,* one having a MAJOR THIRD and PERFECT FIFTH.

Major scale. A SCALE consisting of two MAJOR SECONDS, one MINOR second, three major seconds, and one minor second, in this order.

Malagueña (Sp., măh-lă-gay'nyăh). A type of Spanish FOLK MUSIC originating in the provinces of Malaga and Murcia.

Malinconicamente (It., măh-lin-kŏh-nē-kăh-men'tĕh). With melancholy expression; dejectedly.

Malinconico (It., măh-lin-kô'nē-kŏh). Melancholy, dejected. Also *con malinconia, malinconioso, malinconoso.*

Mambo. A ballroom dance of West Indian origin similar to the CHA-CHA and RUMBA.

Mancando (It., măhn-kăhn'dŏh). Decreasing in loudness, dying away.

Mandocello. The CELLO-ranged member of the MANDOLIN family.

Mandola (It., măhn-dô'lăh). A large MANDOLIN, tuned like a VIOLA. Also *mandora, mandore.*

Mandolin(e). 1. A small kind of LUTE, the BODY shaped like half a pear; with wire STRINGS tuned pairwise, like a

VIOLIN, played with a PLECTRUM and stopped on a FINGER-BOARD. 2. Modern mandolins as used in BLUEGRASS music have a slightly raised (curved) back, like a violin's.

Mandolinata (It., măhn-dŏh-lē-nah′täh). 1. A MANDOLIN PIECE of quiet character, like a SERENADE. 2. A direction in PIANO playing to play with a mandolin effect.

Mandolino (It., măhn-dŏh-lē′nŏh). A MANDOLIN.

Maniera (It., măh-nē-â′räh). Manner, style, method. *Con dolce maniera*, in a suave, delicate style.

Mano (It., mah′nŏh). Hand. *Mano destra (sinistra)*, right (left) hand.

Manual. An ORGAN KEYBOARD; opposed to PEDAL.

Manualiter (L., mă-nü-ăl′i-tŭr). On the MANUAL(S) alone.

Maracas. Latin American RATTLES, usually in pairs, shaken vigorously.

Marcato,-a (It., mar-kăh′tŏh,-täh). With distinctness and emphasis.

Marcatissimo (It., mar-kăh-tis′sē-mŏh). With very marked emphasis.

March. A COMPOSITION of strongly marked RHYTHM, suitable for timing the steps of a body of persons proceeding at a walking pace. *March form* is in DUPLE (2/4), COMPOUND DUPLE (6/8), or QUADRUPLE (4/4) TIME, with REPRISES of four, eight, or sixteen MEASURES, followed by a TRIO section, and ending with a repetition of the march. *Also* **Marche** (Fr., marsh); **Marcia** (It., mar′chäh). *Alla marcia*, in march style.

Marche funèbre. Funeral MARCH.

Marimba. South American and African XYLOPHONE with tuned resonators placed underneath the wooden bars.

Markiert (Ger., mar-keert′). Accented, marked.

Marsch (Ger., ma**r**sh). MARCH.

Martellato (It., ma**r**-tel-lah'tŏh). "Hammered"; on the VIOLIN, a direction to play the NOTES with a sharp, decided stroke (♪) ; on the PIANO, to strike the KEYS with a heavy, inelastic plunge of the finger, or (in OCTAVE playing) with the arm STACCATO.

Mattinata (It., măh-tē-năh'tă). Morning song.

Marziale (It., ma**r**-tsē-ah'lĕh). Martial, war-like.

Masque. A kind of musical drama, popular in the 16th and 17th centuries; a spectacular play with vocal and instrumental music.

Mass. In the Roman Catholic Church, the musical service taking place during the consecration of the elements, with five divisions: (1) Kyrie, (2) Gloria (including the Gratias agimus, Qui tollis, Quoniam, Cum Sancto Spiritu), (3) Credo (with the Et incarnatus, Crucifixus, Et resurrexit), (4) Sanctus and Benedictus (with the Hosanna), and (5) Agnus Dei (with the Dona nobis). *High Mass*, one celebrated at church festivals, with music and incense; *Low Mass*, one without music.

Mässig (Ger., mä'sīy**h**). Measured; moderate. *Mässig langsam*, moderately slow; *m. geschwind*, moderately fast.

Matins. The music sung at morning prayer; the first of the Canonical Hours.

Mazurka (Polish, măh-zoor'kăh). A Polish national dance in TRIPLE TIME and moderate TEMPO with a variable ACCENT on the third BEAT.

Mbira. See LAMELLAPHONES.

M.d. Abbreviation of "main droite," *right hand* in French, or "mano destra" in Italian.

Me. Stands for Mi in TONIC SOL-FA.

Measurable music. MENSURABLE MUSIC.

Measure. The NOTES and RESTS comprised between two BARS; the metrical unit in a COMPOSITION, with regular accentuation, familiarly called a "bar." *Measure note*, a note shown by the TIME SIGNATURE to be an even divisor of a MEASURE; thus 3/4 shows that each measure has three QUARTER NOTES, and the measure note is then a quarter note; *m. rest*, see REST.

Mechanical instrument. An instrument that is played mechanically, rather than by a human performer, such as a MUSIC BOX or PLAYER PIANO.

Mechanism. A literal (and bad) translation of the French *mécanisme*, which means technical ability or skill, mechanical dexterity, or training.

Medesimo (It., mĕh-dä′zē-mŏh). The same.

Mediant. The third DEGREE of the SCALE.

Medley. POTPOURRI.

Meistersinger (Ger., mī′ster-zing′er; *sing. and pl.*). Mastersinger(s); in Germany, the 15th-16th century artisan successors to the 12th-14th century aristocratic MINNE-SINGERS(S).

Melancolia (It., mä-lăhn-kŏl-lē′äh). Melancholy.

Mélange (Fr., mä-lahn′zh). A medley; see POTPOURRI.

Melisma. A MELODIC ORNAMENT or GRACE; COLORATURA. *Melismatic*, ornamented, embellished; *melismatic song*, that in which more than one TONE is sung to a syllable; opposed to syllabic SONG.

Melodeon. 1. The original American ORGAN. See REED ORGAN. 2. A family of usually single-row button ACCORDIONS that play a different NOTE on the press or draw.

Melodia (It., mĕh-lŏh-dē′äh). MELODY. *Marcata la melodia*, the melody (should be) marked.

Melodic. 1. In the style of a MELODY; progressing by single TONES. 2. Vocal, singable; as a melodic INTERVAL.

Melodic minor scale. A MINOR SCALE that eliminates the INTERVAL of an AUGMENTED SECOND between the sixth and seventh DEGREES of the HARMONIC MINOR SCALE, thereby providing a smoother melodic progression. When ascending, the sixth and seventh degrees are raised; when descending, these notes are unaltered.

Melodioso (It., mĕh-lŏh'dē-oh'sŏh). Melodious, singing.

Melodion. A PIANO in which steel bars pressing against a revolving cylinder take the place of STRINGS; invented by J.C. Dietz of Emmerich, Germany.

Melodrama. Originally, a musical drama; now (1) stage-declamation with a musical accompaniment; (2) a romantic and sensational drama in which music plays a subordinate part.

Melody. 1. The ordered and rational PROGRESSION of single TONES; contrasted with HARMONY, the ordered and rational combination of several tones. 2. The LEADING PART (usually the SOPRANO). 3. An AIR or TUNE.

Melos (Gk., mä'lŏhs, "song"). The name bestowed by Wagner on the style of RECITATIVE employed in his mature MUSIC DRAMAS.

Membranophones. A class of musical instruments that produce their sound by the vibration of a membrane or HEAD, i.e., DRUMS.

Même (Fr., mäm). Same. *À la même*, TEMPO primo (i.e., the original tempo).

Meno (It., mā'nŏh). Less; not so. *Meno allegro*, not so fast; *m. mosso*, not so fast (usually shortened to simply *meno*).

Mensurable notation (or **Mensuration**). The late Medieval system of NOTATION governing the relationships between the single LONG, BREVE, and SEMIBREVE.

Menuet (Fr., mŭ-nü-ā'); **Menuett** (Ger., mā-noo-et'). A MINUET.

Messa (It., mes'säh); **Messe** (Fr., mess); **Messe** (Ger., mes'se). A MASS.

Messa di voce (It., mes'säh dē voh'chēh). The attack of a sustained vocal tone PIANISSIMO, with a swell to FORTISSIMO, and slow decrease to *pianissimo* again.

Mestamente (It., mĕh-stäh-men'tĕh). Plaintively, grievingly.

Mesto (It., mĕh'stŏh). Pensive, sad, melancholy.

Mesuré (Fr., mŭ-zü-rā'). 1. Measured, moderate. 2. In exact TIME.

Meter, Metre. 1. In music, the symmetrical grouping of musical RHYTHMS. 2. In verse, the division into symmetrical lines. The metre of English HYMNS is classified according to the kind of feet used, as IAMBIC, TROCHAIC, or DACTYLIC.; the figures show the number of syllables in each line:

IAMBIC METRES: *Common metre* (C.M.), 8 6 8 6; *Long metre* (L.M.), 8 8 8 8; *Short metre* (S.M.), 6 6 8 6. These have regularly four lines to each stanza; when doubled to 8 lines they are called *Common metre double* (C.M.D.), *Long metre double* (L.M.D.), and *Short metre double* (S.M.D.). They may also have six lines in each stanza and are then named *Common particular metre* (C.P.M.), 8 8 6 8 8 6; *Long particular metre* (L.P.M.), or *Long metre 6 lines*, 8 8 8 8 8 8; and *Short particular metre* (S.P.M.), 6 6 8 6 6 8. Besides the above, there are *Sevens and Sixes*, 7 6 7 6; *Tens*, 10 10 10 10; *Hallelujah metre*, 6 6 6 6 8 8 (or 6 6 6 6 4 4 4 4), etc.

TROCHAIC METRES: *Sixes*, 6 6 6 6; *Sixes and Fives*, 6 5 6 5; *Sevens*, 7 7 7 7; *Eights and Sevens*, 8 7 8 7, etc.

DACTYLIC METRES: *Elevens*, 11 11 11 11; *Elevens and Tens*, 11 10 11 10, etc.

Metric modulation. A modern compositional technique, initiated by Elliott Carter, of progressing from one metric pulse to another by introducing the new rhythmic character within the established RHYTHM as a CROSS-RHYTHM.

Metronome. The familiar "timekeeper" of music students; a double pendulum moved by clockwork, and provided with a slider on a graduated scale marking the number of beats the metronome makes per minute. M.M. stands for "Maelzel's Metronome" after the reputed inventor, Maelzel of Vienna (1816). The number following such an indication in a score, as in "M.M. = 60," instructs the player to perform at a moderate TEMPO of sixty beats per minute. Modern metronomes are electric and have no pendulum. Another modern innovation is the *trinome*, capable of marking two BEATS at once.

Mezzo,-a (It., med'zŏh,-zäh). 1. Half. Written alone, as an EXPRESSION MARK, it refers to either an *f* or a *p* just preceding, thus meaning "mezzo *forte*" or "mezzo *piano*." *Mezzo forte*, half-loud; *m. legato*, in PIANO playing, calls for a light touch with less pressure than in legato; *m. piano*, half-soft (less loud than *mezzo forte*); *m. voce*, "with half the power of the voice."

Mezzosoprano (It., med'zŏh-sŏh-prah'nŏh). The female voice between SOPRANO and ALTO, partaking of the quality of both, and usually of small COMPASS (a-f^2, or a-g^2), but very full toned in the medium REGISTER.

M.g. Abbreviation for "main gauche," *left hand* in French.

Mi. The third Aretinian syllable; name of the note *E* in France, Italy, etc.

Microtones. Division of the OCTAVE into INTERVALS smaller than the HALF-TONE, the smallest interval used within the tempered scale. Examples include Fokker's thirty-one-NOTE ORGAN, Partch's forty-three-note PERCUSSION INSTRUMENTS, etc. *Microtonal music*, compositions based on microtones. See also QUARTER-TONES.

Middle C. The *C* in the middle of the PIANO KEYBOARD:

MIDI (Musical Instrument Digital Interface). The digital language used for connecting COMPUTERS, SYNTHESIZERS, SEQUENCERS, and other modern electronic musical instruments so that they may "communicate with" (send data to) each other. *M. compatible*, able to understand/read MIDI data; *M. jack*, *M. port*, the connecting device on a computer, synthesizer, sequencer, etc., where the *M. plug* is inserted.

Militarmente (It., mē-lē-tar-men'tĕh). In military (MARCH) style. *Alla militare*, in the style of a march.

Military band. An ORCHESTRA attached to a branch of the military service consisting of WOODWINDS, BRASS, and PERCUSSION.

Military music. Music for instruments of PERCUSSION and WIND only, admitting the CORNET, BUGLE, SAXOPHONES, etc.

Mimodrama. A dramatic or musical spectacle in which the performers convey the dramatic action by gestures and choreography, without speaking; same as PANTOMIME.

Minaccioso (It., mē-năht-choh'sŏh). In a menacing or threatening manner.

Miniature score. An orchestral SCORE reproduced in a small size so that it can be easily used for study purposes; also called "study score."

Minim. A HALF NOTE. *Minim rest*, a HALF REST.

Minimal music. A term used to denote works based on the repetition and gradual alteration of short rhythmic and/or melodic figures; main proponents include Young, Riley, Reich, and Glass; also referred to as *process music*.

Minnesänger, **Minnesinger** (Ger., min'ne-zeng'er, -zing'er; *sing. and pl.*). The German aristocratic poet-musicians of the 12th–14th centuries.

Minor. Latin word for "smaller," used in music in two different senses: 1. To indicate a *smaller* INTERVAL of a kind, as in MINOR SECOND, minor THIRD, minor SIXTH, minor SEVENTH, minor NINTH, and minor TENTH. 2. To define a KEY, as in *a* minor, or a SCALE, as in *a* minor scale, or a TRIAD, as a minor triad; in minor keys, the third of the scale forms an interval of a minor third from the ROOT.

Minore (It., mē-noh'rĕh). MINOR.

Minstrels. In the Middle Ages, professional musicians who sang or declaimed poems, often of their own composition, to a simple instrumental accompaniment.

Minuet. An early French dance form, in TRIPLE TIME; usually a "double" minuet, the first section repeated after the second (the TRIO). *Also* **Minuetto** (It., mē-noo-et'tŏh).

Miracle play. Sacred dramas, often with music, popular in England in the Middle Ages; the stories were usually on Biblical subjects or parables, which were also called *Moralities*.

Mirliton (Fr., meer-lĕ'tŏhn). KAZOO.

Mirror canon. A CANON that sounds the same when sung or played backwards; a musical palindrome.

Missa (L.). MASS. *Missa brevis*, short Mass; *M. solemnis*, high Mass.

Misterioso (It., mē-stĕh-**r**ē-oh'sŏh). In a style suggestive of mystery, or of hidden meaning.

Misurato (It., mĕ-zoo-**rah**'tŏh). With the MEASURE; in exact TIME.

Mit (Ger., mit). With. *Mit Ausdruck*, with expression; *m. Begleitung*, accompanied; *m. Bewegung*, with animation, CON MOTO; *m. halber Stimme*, mezza voce; *m. innigster Empfindung*, with deepest emotion; *m. Kraft*, powerfully, CON FORZA.

Mixed chorus. A CHORUS comprised of both male and female voices, traditionally with all four basic voice types represented (SOPRANO, ALTO, TENOR, BASS), with or without divisions.

Mixed media. A term used to describe works in which musical, dramatic, verbal, visual, literary, etc. elements are conjoined in a single COMPOSITION, usually in novel ways.

Mixolydian mode. A MODE corresponding to the progression from *G* to *G* on the white KEYS of the PIANO.

Mixture. A compound auxiliary ORGAN flue STOP with from three to six RANKS of PIPES sounding as many HARMONICS of any NOTE played.

M.M. METRONOME.

Mobile (It., mô'bē-lĕh). Readily responsive to emotion or impulse.

Mobile form. A term used, with obvious debt to sculptor Alexander Calder, to describe works composed in such a way that sections may be arranged variously in time without disturbing structural integrity; also referred to as "open form."

Modal harmony. The type of HARMONY that is derived from church, exotic, or invented MODES, apart from the common MAJOR and MINOR KEYS.

Mode. 1. A generic term applied to ancient Greek MELODIC PROGRESSIONS and to church SCALES established in the

Middle Ages and codified in the system of GREGORIAN CHANT. The INTERVALS of the Greek modes were counted downwards, and those of the medieval modes were counted upwards, so the intervallic contents were different between the Greek and the church systems. However, the church modes retained the Greek names of the modes. If played on the white KEYS of the PIANO, the church modes are: from *C* to *C*, Ionian; from *D* to *D*, Dorian; from *E* to *E*, Phrygian; from *F* to *F*, Lydian; from *G* to *G*, Mixolydian; from *A* to *A*, Aeolian; and from *B* to *B*, Locrian. The modes continued to underlie all western music through the 17th century, then gradually gave way to the common MAJOR and MINOR keys. 2. The distinction between a major key (mode) and minor key (mode). 3. Any scalar pattern of intervals, either traditional to a culture (Indian, Japanese, etc.) or invented. 4. A system of rhythmic notation used in the 13th century.

Moderato (It., mŏh-dĕh-**r**ah'tŏh). Moderate; that is, at a moderate TEMPO or rate of speed. *Allegro moderato*, moderately fast.

Moderazione, con (It., kŏhn mŏh-dĕh-**r**ăh-tsē-oh'nĕh). With moderation (of either TEMPO or emotion).

Modernism. Denoting the new sensibility of progress and "the new" that emerged c. 1910; often said to have been expressed in the paintings of Picasso and Kandinsky, the novels of Joyce and Proust, and the music of Schoenberg and Stravinsky.

Modern music. 1. Musical COMPOSITION as it developed at the turn of the 20th century, in which MODULATION from one KEY to another reached complete freedom of DIATONIC and CHROMATIC PROGRESSIONS, and DISSONANCES acquired equal rights with traditional CHORDS; several keys could be combined in a technique called POLYTONALITY, and the MELODY was allowed to veer away from its TONAL foundations becoming sometimes completely ATONAL. 2. Loosely speaking, all POPULAR MUSIC, particularly in America and England, including JAZZ and ROCK, as contrasted to traditional classical music.

Moderno,-a (It., mŏh-dâr′nŏh,-năh). Modern. *Alla moderna*, in modern style.

Modes of limited transpositions. For Messiaen, MODES that contain repeating intervallic units and thus can only be transposed a limited number of times before the identical SET is repeated.

Modulate. To pass from one KEY or MODE into another.

Modulation. Passage from one KEY or MODE into another. *Chromatic modulation*, one effected by use of CHROMATIC INTERVALS; *diatonic m.*, one effected by use of DIATONIC INTERVALS; *enharmonic m.*, one effected by using ENHARMONIC changes to alter the significance of TONES or intervals; *final m.*, one in which the new key is retained, or still another follows; *passing, transient, transitory m.*, one in which the original key is speedily regained.

Möglich (Ger., mö′glĭyh). Possible. *So rasch wie möglich*, as fast as possible.

Moll (Ger., mŏhl). MINOR.

Molto,-a (It., mŏhl′tŏh,-tăh). Very, much. *Molto adagio*, very slowly; *molto allegro*, very fast; *con molta passione*, with great passion; *di molto* or *molto molto*, exceedingly, extremely, as *crescendo molto molto*, growing very much louder.

Moment form. A short-lived structural concept developed by Stockhausen describing works that, in theory, rely less for their auditory coherence on relationships between movements than on the experience of "the moment."

Monochord. A very ancient musical instrument. As the name indicates, it had a single STRING, which was stretched over a SOUNDBOX, and a shifting BRIDGE that allowed the string to be adjusted to different PITCHES.

Monodrama. A dramatic or musical presentation, with a single performer.

Monody. The RECITATIVE-like accompanied SONG style of early 17th-century Italy.

Monophonic. "One sound" or "voice." 1. Music for a single voice or PART, as in GREGORIAN CHANT or unaccompanied SONG. 2. Early form of one-channel recording and playback of sound; compare STEREOPHONIC.

Monophonous. Capable of producing but one TONE at a time.

Monophony. Unaccompanied MELODY; as contrasted with POLYPHONY.

Monothematic. A COMPOSITION with a single SUBJECT.

Monotone. 1. A single unaccompanied and unvaried TONE. 2. Recitation (intoning, CHANTING) on such a tone.

Moralities. A later form of the MIRACLE PLAYS.

Morbido (It., môr'bē-dŏh). Soft, tender.

Morceau (Fr., mor-sōh'). A PIECE, COMPOSITION. *Morceau de genre* (zhahn**'r**), characteristic piece.

Mordant (Fr., mor-dähn'); **Mordent** (Ger., mor'dent). A GRACE consisting of the single rapid alternation of a principal NOTE with an AUXILIARY a MINOR SECOND below:

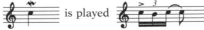

is played

Inverted mordent, the alternation of the principal note with the higher auxiliary:

played

Morendo (It., mŏh-**r**en'dŏh). Dying away.

Moresca (It., mŏh-rĕs'căh). A Moorish dance.

Morgenlied (Ger., mor'gĕn-lēt). Morning SONG.

Mormoroso (It., mor-mŏh-**r**oh'sŏh). Murmuring, murmurous; in a very gentle, subdued tone.

Mormorio (It., mor-mŏh-**r**ē'ŏh). Murmur. *Come un mormorio*, like a murmur.

Morris dance. An old English dance, often performed as part of a symbolic character play.

Mosso (It., môhs'sŏh). "Moved." Standing alone, as a TEMPO mark, it is the same as *con moto*. In the phrases *meno mosso* (less rapid), *più mosso* (more rapid), and *poco mosso* (somewhat rapid), it means "rapid." Also, *allegretto poco m.*, a rather lively ALLEGRETTO, almost ALLEGRO; *m. agitato*, a fast and agitated movement; *assai m. e agitato*, very rapid and agitated.

Motet. A sacred vocal composition in CONTRAPUNTAL style, without accompaniment. (Pieces in ANTHEM style are, however, sometimes called MOTETS.) *Also* **Motet** (Fr., mŏh-tā'); **Motette** (Ger., mŏh-tet'tĕ).

Motif (Fr., mŏh-tēf'). MOTIVE.

Motion. 1. The PROGRESSION or conduct of a single PART or MELODY; it is CONJUNCT when progressing by STEPS, DISJUNCT when progressing by SKIPS. 2. The movement of one part in relation to that of another; in *contrary* or *opposite* motion, one part ascends while the other descends; in *oblique* motion, one part retains its TONE while the other moves; in *parallel* motion, both parts move up or down by the same INTERVAL; in *similar* motion, both move up or down together by dissimilar intervals; in *mixed* motion, two or more of the above varieties occur at once between several parts.

Motive. 1. A short PHRASE or FIGURE used in DEVELOPMENT or IMITATION. 2. A LEADING motive. *Measure motive*, one whose ACCENT coincides with that of the MEASURE.

Moto (It., mô'tŏh). Motion; speed; movement, TEMPO. *Con moto*, with an animated and energetic movement; *m. precedente*, at the former tempo; *più (meno) m.*, same as *più (meno) mosso*.

Moto perpetuo. "Perpetual motion" in Italian, applied to short pieces in very fast TEMPO in RONDO FORM.

Motown. A popular music style of the 1960s and 1970s created by the black-owned, Detroit-based record label of the same name. The Motown name is synonymous with groups of this period, i.e., The Supremes, The Temptations, etc., noted for their fleet footwork and popish harmonies.

Motteggiando (It., mŏht-ted-jähn'dŏh). In a bantering, facetious style.

Mottetto (It., mŏht-tet'tŏh). MOTET.

Mouth organ. HARMONICA.

Mouthpiece. That part of a WIND INSTRUMENT that a player places upon or between the lips.

Mouvement (Fr., moov-mähn'). MOVEMENT; TEMPO.

Movable Do. A system of SOLFEGGIO in which the TONIC of every MAJOR SCALE is called Do, the second degree called Re, the third Mi, etc., following the scale of Guido d'Arezzo.

Movement. 1. TEMPO. 2. A principal division or section of a COMPOSITION.

Movendo il tempo (It., mŏh-ven'dŏh ēl tem'pŏh). Growing faster.

Movimento (It., mŏh-vē-men'tŏh). MOVEMENT.

Multiphonics. Any modern method of sound production resulting in two or more sounds being produced simultaneously by a single performer.

M.s. Abbreviation for "mano sinistra," *left hand* in Italian.

Munter (Ger., mŏŏn'ter). Lively, gay, animated.

Musette (Fr., mü-zet'). 1. A small OBOE. 2. A kind of BAGPIPE; also, a short PIECE imitating this bagpipe, with a DRONE BASS. 3. A REED STOP on the ORGAN.

Musica (It., moo'zē'kăh). Music. *Dramma per musica*, an OPERA.

Musica ficta (L., moo'zē-că fík'tah). In music from the 10th through the 16th centuries, theoretically questionable CHROMATIC alterations supposedly made in performance.

Musica figurata (It., moo'zē-căh fí-gyoor-a'tah). Music arranged in contrasting CONTRAPUNTAL FIGURATIONS.

Musica reservata (L., moo'zē-căh rĕ-zer-văh'tah). A 16th-century term applied to a particularly sophisticated type of CONTRAPUNTAL music, related to MUSICA FICTA and "reserved" for masters of the craft.

Music drama. The original description of OPERA as it evolved in Florence early in the 17th century (*dramma per musica*); in the 19th century, Wagner adopted this term in order to emphasize the dramatic element in his stage spectacles.

Musical. A colloquial description for an American or English musical theater piece or revue.

Music(al) box. The Swiss music box has a metal cylinder or barrel, studded with pins, and turned by clockwork; in revolving, the pins catch and twang a comb-like row of steel teeth, each tooth producing a TONE.

Musical saw. A special, quasimusical instrument, played by holding the handle of the saw against the inside of one leg and lightly flexing it with the other hand, while rubbing a VIOLIN BOW against its edge, creating an eerie, singing sound.

Musicology. The science of music. The concept includes all branches of music, i.e., theory, history, aesthetics, lexicography, bibliography, etc.

Music theatre. Any small-to-moderate musical stage work involving a dramatic element in its performance; frequently distinguished from OPERA by its relatively smaller scale and scope.

Music therapy. The study and use of musical stimuli and activity in the evaluation, remediation, or maintenance of health; it developed into a bona fide profession at about the time of World War II in the U.S., with university curriculae following within the decade.

Musique (Fr., mü-zēk'). Music.

Musique concrète (Fr., -con-crět'). "Concrete music"; a practice developed by French electrical engineers and radio men in 1948, in which all kinds of incidental musical, nonmusical, and unmusical sounds and noises are made use of in the composition of musical works. Specifically refers to assembling a musical composition on tape either through multiple-tracking or by literally pasting together smaller pieces of recording tape to form a COLLAGE of sound.

Muta (It., moo'tăh). "Change!" (CROOK or instrument).

Mutation. 1. Change of VOICE. 2. Change of POSITION, shifting (VIOLIN).

Mute. 1. A heavy piece of metal fitted to the BRIDGE of a VIOLIN, etc., to deaden the sound. The direction for putting on the mutes is "con sordini"; for taking them off, "senza sordini." 2. A leather covered pad, paste-board cone, or wooden cylinder inserted in the BELL of the HORN or TRUMPET to modify the TONE.

Mut(h)ig (Ger., moo'tǐyh). Spiritedly, boldly.

Muzak. Trade name for the first U.S. company to have license to produce, distribute, and transmit background music for public consumption. Also colloquially referred to as "elevator music," alluding to one of the many public spaces in which it may be heard.

Mysteries. Medieval bible plays, often with vocal and instrumental music. In the form called *Moralities*, abstract ideas were personified on the stage.

N

Nach (Ger., nǎh). After; according to.

Nachahmung (Ger., nǎh-ǎh'mǔng^k). IMITATION.

Nach Belieben (Ger., nǎh bě-lē'ben). An indication to the performer to play a PASSAGE so marked A PIACERE, or "at will."

Nachdrücklich (Ger., nǎh-drük'lǐyh). With emphasis, strongly marked.

Nachgebend (Ger., nǎh'gā'bent). Yieldingly, slower and slower; RALLENTANDO.

Nachgiebiger (Ger., nǎh'gē'bǐyh-er). Still slower.

Nachlässig (Ger., nǎh'les'sǐyh). Carelessly.

Nachschlag (Ger., nǎh'shlǎyh). The end NOTES of a TRILL.

Nachthorn (Ger., nǎh't-horn). A covered STOP in the ORGAN, having covered PIPES of 2', 4', or 8' PITCH.

Nachtmusik (Ger., nǎht'moo-zǐk). Night music, a SERENADE.

Nachtschall (Ger., nǎht'shähl). NACHTHORN.

Nachtstück (Ger., nǎht'shtük). "Night piece," a NOCTURNE.

Nach und nach (Ger., năh oont năh'). Little by little, gradually.

Nail fiddle. A primitive instrument in use for a time in the 18th century. It consisted of a wooden board with nails of different sizes affixed in a semicircle; it was played with an ordinary VIOLIN BOW on the nails.

Naked fifth. An HARMONIC FIFTH without an added THIRD.

Napolitana. An early type of Italian MADRIGAL, revived in modern times in the form of a popular SONG.

Narrante (It., năr-răhn'těh). Narrating; as if telling a story; calls for distinct declamation.

Nasard (Fr., năh-zar'); **Nasat** (Ger., năh-zaht'). The twelfth (ORGAN STOP) of 2 2/3-foot pitch (large sizes 10 2/3 and 5 1/3, smaller size 1 1/3).

Nationalism. A late 19th-century movement, prominent in Russia, Bohemia, etc., wherein composers consciously strived to embody and reveal aspects of national identity in their music.

Natural. 1. The sign ♮. 2. A white KEY on the KEYBOARD. *Natural harmonics*, those produced on an open STRING; *n. horn*, a HORN without valves; *n. interval*, an INTERVAL found between any two TONES of a DIATONIC MAJOR SCALE; *n. key*, one without SHARPS or FLATS in its KEY SIGNATURE, i.e., C major; *n. pitch*, the PITCH of any WIND INSTRUMENT when not overblown; *n. scale*, a SCALE having neither sharps nor flats, i.e., C major; *n. tone*, any tone obtained on a wind instrument with cupped MOUTHPIECE, without using keys, VALVES or the SLIDE.

Naturalmente (It., năh-too-răhl-men'těh). In a natural, unaffected style.

Natural minor scale. Any MINOR SCALE without CHROMATIC alterations and therefore lacking the LEADING TONE.

Neapolitan sixth. The first INVERSION of a flat two CHORD (♭II); in C major, the notes F, A♭, D♭.

Nebenstimme (Ger. nā-ben-shtim-meh; "next voice"). A term first used by Schoenberg to denote the second POLYPHONIC VOICE in a COMPOSITION, abbreviated in his scores as "N." See HAUPTSTIMME.

Neck. An extension of the BODY of a STRINGED INSTRUMENT on which the FINGERBOARD is mounted.

Negli (It., nāl'yē). In the.

Negligente (It., nĕh-glē-jen'tĕh). In a style expressive of negligence, carelessness.

Nei (nă'ē), **nel, nell', nella, nelle, nello** (It.). In the.

Neoclassicism. A revival, in 20th-century compositions, of 18th-century (or earlier) musical precepts, exemplified by many of the post-World War I works of both Stravinsky and Schoenberg.

Neoromanticism. A revival, in the 1930s and 1940s, of interest among composers in the gestures, forms, genres, and harmonies of the 19th century. A similar movement, *New Romanticism*, occurred in the United States in the 1970s.

Nervoso (It., nâr-voh'sŏh). In a forcible, agitated style.

Nettamente (It., net-tăh-men'tĕh). In a neat, clear, and distinct style.

Neumes. Signs used, in the early Middle Ages, to represent TONES.

New Age. A generic name given to spacey, ACOUSTIC, instrumental music, played primarily on either GUITAR or PIANO; also called *new acoustic music*.

New Music. A somewhat redundant term for music of the 20th century that is intended to be both distinct from music of the past and in advance of its own time.

New Romanticism. See NEOROMANTICISM.

New Simplicity. A 1970s movement, especially among German, Scandinavian, and Dutch composers, toward a simplified style of composition highly influenced by American MINIMALISM.

New Wave. American answer to PUNK ROCK. Artistically inclined bands like Talking Heads were leaders in this style, their music featuring poetic, oblique lyrics, and intentionally simple MELODIES and accompaniments.

Nicht (Ger., nīyht). Not. *Nicht zu langsam*, not too slow.

Niente (It., nē-en'těh). Nothing. *Quasi niente*, barely audible.

Ninth. The INTERVAL of an OCTAVE plus a MAJOR or MINOR SECOND.

Nobilmente (It., nŏh-bēl-men'těh). In a refined, chaste, and lofty style.

Noch (Ger., nŏh). Still; yet. *Noch rascher*, still faster.

Nocturne (Fr., nŏhk-tŭrn'). A piece of a dreamily romantic or sentimental character, without fixed FORM.

Nocturns. Services of the Church held during the night.

Nodal figures. The figures corresponding to the "nodal lines" of a vibrating object, rendered visible by strewing fine dry sand on the plate, this sand being tossed by vibrations into the "nodal lines," which are points of perfect or comparative rest. *Nodal point*, see NODE.

Node. A point or line in a vibrating body (such as a STRING, SOUNDBOARD, TRUMPET, BELL), which remains at rest during the vibration of the other parts of the body.

Noël (Fr., nŏĕl). A Christmas CAROL or HYMN.

Noire (Fr., nwăhr). QUARTER NOTE.

Noise. Scientifically speaking, sound with indefinite PITCH, but used as a compositional element in many 20th-century compositions. (*White noise* is sound with all possible frequencies in balance.)

Non (It., nŏhn). Not.

Nonet. A COMPOSITION for nine voices or instruments.

Nonnengeige (Ger., noh′nen-gī′gĕ). Literally, "nun violin"; a curious nickname for the TROMBA MARINA, which itself is a curious name for a MONOCHORD, a box with one string. German nuns supposedly favored this instrument.

Non-retrograde rhythm. For Messiaen, denotative of symmetrical rhythmic patterns that, by nature, exhibit no change upon INVERSION, i.e.,

Nota cambiata. A "changed NOTE" in Italian; an extra note inserted one diagonal DEGREE above the PRINCIPAL note before descending to the next (as the note *D* inserted between *C* and *B*).

Notation. The art of representing musical TONES, and their modifications, by means of written characters.

Note. One of the signs used to express the relative TIME VALUE and/or PITCH of TONES. *Note against note,* COUNTERPOINT in equal notes.

Note row. SET.

Notturno (It., nŏht-toor′nŏh). A NOCTURNE.

Novellette (Ger., nŏh-vel-let′tĕ). An instrumental piece free in FORM, bold in HARMONY, romantic in character, of considerable length, and with a variety of contrasting THEMES.

Nuane (Fr., nü-ahnss′). Shading; change in musical expression, either in the TONE COLOR, TEMPO, or degree of force.

Number. 1. A subdivision of an OPERA or ORATORIO. 2. A smaller, and more or less complete, portion of a large work, such as a SONG, ARIA, INTERLUDE, etc. 3. Any single PIECE on a program. 4. An OPUS number.

Number pieces. A designation for the late works of the American composer John Cage that bear numbers as titles (as *Seventy-four*, *Thirteen*, *One*[5], etc.). The numbers refer to the number of players (occasionally parts) called for in the score; superscript numbers are used to differentiate multiple compositions with the same number of players, and thus have the same number title (i.e., *Two*[4], Cage's *fourth* work composed for *two* players).

Nun's fiddle. NONNENGEIGE; TROMBA MARINA.

Nuovamente (It., nŏŏ-ŏh-văh-men'tĕh). Again, anew.

Nut. 1. The notched ridge over which the STRINGS of a VIOLIN, etc., pass at the end of the FINGERBOARD next to the PEG-HEAD. 2. The sliding projection at the lower end of the violin BOW, by means of which the hair is tightened or slackened. 3. The "lower nut" on the violin is the ridge between the TAILPIECE and tailpin (or button). Also referred to as the "frog."

O

O. A small circle signifies (*a*) an open string; (*b*) the HARMONIC mark; (*c*) the DIMINISHED FIFTH.

O (It., ŏh). Or. (Written before either vowels or consonants; *od* is an unusual form.)

Obbligato (It., ŏhb-blē-gah'tŏh). Required, indispensable. An *obbligato* PART is a concerted (and therefore essential) instrumental part; especially when accompanying and vying with a vocal solo.

Obligato (Ger., ŏh-blē-gah'tŏh). OBBLIGATO.

Oblique motion. A type of PROGRESSION in two-part COUNTERPOINT in which one VOICE moves and the other remains stationary.

Oboe (Ger. *Oboe* [oh-boh'ĕ]; It. *òboe* [oh'bŏh-ĕh]). 1. An orchestral instrument with conical wooden tube, nine to fourteen KEYS, and a double REED; its COMPASS is two OCTAVES and a SEVENTH, from bb to a^3, its TONE very reedy and penetrating, although mild. Only two kinds are in ordinary use, the TREBLE oboe (just described), and the ENGLISH HORN (ALTO oboe) of lower PITCH. 2. In the ORGAN, an 8' reed STOP, with conical PIPES surmounted by a bell and cap that produces an oboe-like sound.

Oboe da caccia (It., oh'boh-eh dǎh cǎh'tchǎh). Literally, "oboe of the hunt." An instrument tuned a FIFTH below the OBOE, in use during the Renaissance period but eventually replaced by the ENGLISH HORN.

Oboe d'amore (It., -dǎh-moh'reh). Literally, "oboe of love." An OBOE that sounds a MINOR THIRD below the written NOTATION; used in many early scores, and also in some modern revivals.

Ocarina (It., ô-kǎh-rē'nǎh). "Goose-pipe"; a bird-shaped WIND INSTRUMENT made of terra cotta, with FINGERHOLES and a whistle MOUTHPIECE.

Octave. 1. A series of eight consecutive DIATONIC TONES. 2. The INTERVAL between the first and eighth tones of such a series. 3. In the ORGAN, a STOP whose PIPES sound tones an octave higher than the keys touched; like the Principal. *Concealed, covered,* or *hidden octaves* (or *fifths*), parallel OCTAVES (or FIFTHS) suggested by the PROGRESSION of two PARTS in SIMILAR MOTION to the interval of an octave (or fifth); *rule of the o.,* a series of HARMONIES written over the diatonic scale as a BASS; *short o.,* the lowest octave of some old ORGAN MANUALS, in which some keys (and pipes) are omitted.

Octave coupler. A mechanism on the ORGAN that unites the 8' TONES of one KEYBOARD with those an OCTAVE higher on another.

Octave flute. 1. The PICCOLO. 2. An ORGAN STOP of 4′ PITCH.

Octave sign. OTTAVA.

Octave stop. See OCTAVE 3.

Octet. A COMPOSITION for eight voices or instruments.

Octuor (Fr., ŏhk-tü-ohr′). OCTET.

Ode. A CHORUS in ancient Greek plays; a musical work of praise.

Oder (Ger., oh′der). Or; or else.

Off. In ORGAN music, a direction to push in a STOP or COUPLET. *Off the pitch*, false in PITCH or INTONATION.

Offertoire (Fr., ŏh-fâr-twah′r); **Offertorio** (It., ŏhf-fâr-tô′rē-īh); **Offertorium** (L., ô-fūhr-tō′rē-ŭm); **Offertory**. In the Roman Catholic MASS, the verses or ANTHEM following the CREDO, and sung by the choir while the priest is placing the consecrated elements on the altar, during which the offerings of the congregation are collected.

Ohne (Ger., oh′nĕ). Without.

Oliphant. An ancient hunting HORN, sometimes made of elephant's tusk (*oliphant* is an old English word for "elephant").

Omnitonic. Having or producing all TONES; CHROMATIC (as in an instrument).

Ondeggiamento (It., ŏhn-ded-jäh-men′tŏh). Undulation; rocking (as by waves).

Ondeggiante (It., ŏhn-ded-jähn′tĕh). Undulating, billowy, rocking.

Ondes musicales. The name for the electronic musical instrument invented by Martenot; sometimes called *Ondes Martenot*.

Ondulé (Fr.). Undulated, wavy.

One step. An American ballroom dance of the 1910s and 1920s in 2/4 TIME.

Ongarese (It.). Hungarian.

Open form. MOBILE FORM.

Open harmony. In four-part HARMONY, an arrangement of VOICES such that the upper three have a total RANGE of more than an OCTAVE (as in *C, G, E, C*).

Open pedal. The loud PIANO PEDAL.

Open string. A string on the VIOLIN, VIOLA, or CELLO sounding its natural TONE without being stopped by the finger.

Opera. A form of drama, of Italian origin, in which vocal and instrumental music are essential and predominant. The several acts, usually preceded by instrumental introductions, consist of vocal scenes, RECITATIVES, SONGS, ARIAS, DUETS, TRIOS, CHORUSES, etc., accompanied by the ORCHESTRA. This is the *grand* or *heroic* opera; a *comedy* opera is a versified comedy set to music; a *comic* opera has spoken INTERLUDES.

Opéra bouffe (Fr., ŏh-pä-**răh** boof′); **Opera buffa** (It., ôh′pä-**răh** bŏŏf′fäh). Light comic OPERA.

Opéra comique (Fr., ŏh-pä-**răh** kŏh-mēk′). French OPERA with spoken dialogue instead of RECITATIVE. It is not necessarily comic in nature.

Opera seria (It., ôh′pä-**răh** sä′rē-äh). Serious (grand, heroic, tragic) OPERA.

Operetta (It., ŏh-pĕh-**ret**′tăh); **Opérette** (Fr., ŏh-pä-ret′). A "little OPERA"; the poem is in a comic, mock-pathetic, parodistic, or anything but serious vein; music is light and lively, often interrupted by dialogue.

Ophicleide (ŏf′ĭ′klīd). The BASS instrument of the key BUGLE family; now little used.

Oppure (It., ĭhp-poo′rĕh). Or; else; often written *opp*.

Opus (L.). Work; often written *Op.* or *op. Opus number*, one number in the series with which a composer marks ("numbers") his or her works.

Oratorio (It., ŏh-rāh-tô′rē-ŏh). An extended, more or less dramatic, COMPOSITION for vocal SOLOS and CHORUS, with ACCOMPANIMENT by ORCHESTRA and/or ORGAN, performed without stage play or scenery.

Orchester (Ger., or-kĕs′ter). ORCHESTRA.

Orchestra (or′kes-träh). A company of musicians performing on the instruments usually employed in OPERA, ORATORIO, or SYMPHONY; hence, also the instruments, taken together.

Orchestral (or-kĕs′tral, or or′kĕs-tral). Pertaining to, or resembling, the ORCHESTRA. *Orchestral piano playing*, the style of Liszt and his disciples, who try to imitate orchestral effects on the PIANO.

Orchestration. The art of writing music for performance by an ORCHESTRA; the science of combining, in an effective manner, the instruments constituting the orchestra.

Orchestrion. A large stationary BARREL ORGAN, generally played by clockwork, also featuring percussion and other special effects.

Order. The arrangement of the CHORD TONES above a given BASS, *open* and *close order* being the same as open and close HARMONY.

Organ. The church organ, or pipe organ, is a KEYBOARD WIND INSTRUMENT consisting of few or many sets of PIPES played from one or more KEYBOARDS; there may be five keyboards for the fingers (MANUALS), and there is generally one for the feet (PEDAL, or pedal keyboard). The pipes, of which there are two main divisions, flue and reed, are arranged in sets (registers, or STOPS), and made to "speak" by wind admitted from the bellows upon pressing the KEYS.

Organized sound. An inclusive term coined by Varèse to avoid the limitations and implications usually imposed by the term "music."

Organo (It., or'gäh-nŏh). ORGAN. *Organo pleno*, full organ.

Organ point. A TONE sustained in one PART to HARMONIES executed in the other parts, usually a BASS tone, TONIC and/or DOMINANT.

Organ tone. The tone of the 8' Open Diapason PIPE on the Great ORGAN MANUAL. Also called "Diapason tone."

Organum (L., ôr'gän-ŭm). 1. An ORGAN. 2. The earliest attempts at HARMONIC or POLYPHONIC MUSIC, in which two PARTS progressed in PARALLEL FIFTHS and FOURTHS.

Orgel (Ger., ohr'gel); **Orgue** (Fr., ohrg). ORGAN.

Orgue de barbarie. A street ORGAN, operated by a crank, and producing a "barbarous" crackling sound while playing a TUNE.

Ornament. A GRACE, embellishment.

Oscillator. An electronic device used to produce a WAVE FORM.

Osservato (It., ŏhs-sâr-vah'tŏh). Carefully observed. *Stile osservato*, strict style.

Ossia (It., ŏhs-sē'äh). Or; or else; indicates an alternative (or facilitated) reading or fingering of a PASSAGE. Also *Oppure, Ovvero*.

Ostinato (It., ŏh-stē-nah'tŏh). Obstinate. *Basso ostinato*, a GROUND BASS; hence, an "ostinato" is the incessant repetition of a THEME with a varying CONTRAPUNTAL ACCOMPANIMENT.

Ottava (It., ŏht-tah'väh). OCTAVE. *All' ottava* (written *8^(va)*-------- or *8*--------------), "at the octave," an octave higher; *coll' o.*, "with the octave," that is, in octaves; *o. alta*, the higher octave; *o. bassa* (*8^(va) bassa*), the lower octave, an octave below.

Ottavino. A PICCOLO.

Ottoni. In Italian, BRASS INSTRUMENTS.

Ottetto (It., ŏht-tet'tŏh). An OCTET.

Ou (Fr., oo). Or; or else.

Ouverture (Fr., oo-vâr-tür'); **Ouvertüre** (Ger., oo-var-tü'rĕ). OVERTURE.

Overblow. With respect to WIND INSTRUMENTS, to force the wind through the tube in such a way as to cause any HARMONIC to sound.

Overstring. To arrange the strings of a PIANO in two sets, one lying over and diagonally crossing the other; a piano so strung is called an *overstrung* piano, in contradistinction to *vertical*.

Overtone. HARMONIC TONE.

Overture. A musical introduction to an OPERA, ORATORIO, etc. A concert overture is an independent COMPOSITION, frequently in SONATA FORM.

Ovvero (It., ŏhv-vâh'rŏh). Or; or else.

P

P. Stands for *Pedal* (*P.* or *Ped.*); *piano (p)*, *pianissimo (pp* or *ppp)*; *P.F.*, pianoforte; *pf*, pianoforte (soft, increasing to loud); *fp*, forte piano (loud, diminishing to soft instantly); *mp*, mezzo piano (half soft); *Pointe* (Fr., "toe").

Padovana (It., păh-dŏh-vah'năh). A PAVANE. (Also *Padovane*, *Paduana*, *Paduane*, etc.)

Paired notes. Two parallel series of NOTES played on the PIANO with one hand.

Pandiatonicism. A modern term for a system of DIATONIC HARMONY making use of all seven DEGREES of the SCALE in DISSONANT combinations, as for instance in the concluding CHORD C, G, E, A, D, G.

Pandora. A STRINGED INSTRUMENT of great antiquity, plucked like a LUTE.

Panpipes. A set of REEDS of different sizes, the player blowing across the top to produce TONES. The name is explained by the legend that the god Pan invented it.

Pantomime. A BALLET-like performance without speech or singing, in which the action is suggested by gestures and CHOREOGRAPHY. The word *pantomime* means "all imitating" in Greek.

Pantonality. A term preferred to ATONALITY by Schoenberg, denoting the possibility of all tonalities, or the conscious absence of a single, preeminent TONALITY in a given COMPOSITION.

Parallel motion. Voice leading in HARMONY or COUNTERPOINT in which INTERVALS move in the same direction. In traditional, common-practice harmony, parallel THIRDS and SIXTHS are recommended, while parallel FIFTHS and OCTAVES are forbidden.

Parameter. A term denoting any one of the four aspects of musical sound, i.e., PITCH, DURATION, VOLUME, TIMBRE.

Paraphrase. A TRANSCRIPTION or rearrangement of a vocal or instrumental PIECE for an instrument (or instruments) other than that for which it was written, often with VARIATIONS.

Parlando (or **Parlante**) (It., par-lähn'dŏh [or -tĕh]). "Speaking"; singing with clear and marked enunciation. In PIANO playing, *parlante* calls for a clear, crisp *non* LEGATO.

Parody. As used in early music THEORY, this term meant "like something else," and was quite devoid of the contemporary sense of travesty. A *parody* MASS is a work with thematic materials taken from a work by another composer.

Part. 1. The series of TONES written for and executed by a voice or instrument, either as a solo or together with other voices or instruments. 2. A division of a HOMOPHONIC MOVEMENT devoted to the exposition of one MELODY, or musical idea; like the two-part and three-part SONG FORMS.

Parte (It., par'tĕh). PART. *Colla parte*, a direction to accompanists to follow yieldingly and discreetly the solo part or voice.

Partial stop. A half STOP.

Partial tone. An HARMONIC TONE.

Partita (It., par-tē'tăh). A SUITE.

Partition (Fr., păr-tē-si-ohn'); **Partitur** (Ger., păr-tē-toor). A SCORE.

Part music. CONCERTED or HARMONIZED vocal music.

Part singing. The singing of PART MUSIC, usually without instrumental ACCOMPANIMENT.

Part song. A COMPOSITION for at least three voices in HARMONY, without ACCOMPANIMENT, for equal or mixed VOICES. It is properly a MELODY with CHORAL harmony, with any reasonable number of voices to each PART.

Passacaglia (It., păhs-săh-cahl'yăh). An early Italian dance in TRIPLE TIME and stately movement, written on a GROUND BASS of four MEASURES. *Also* **Passacaille** (Fr., păh-săh-cah'ē).

Passage. 1. A portion or section of a PIECE, usually short. 2. A rapid repeated FIGURE, either ascending or descending. A SCALE passage is generally called a RUN.

Passamezzo (It., păhs-săh-mĕd'zŏh). An early Italian dance in DUPLE TIME, like the PAVANE, but faster.

Passepied (Fr., păhs-p'yā'). A *Paspy*; an early French dance in 3/8 or 6/8 TIME, with three or four REPRISES; like the MINUET in movement, but quicker.

Passing notes or tones. NOTES or TONES foreign to the CHORDS which they accompany, and passing by a STEP from one to another. They differ from SUSPENSIONS in not being prepared, and in entering (usually) on an unaccented BEAT.

Passion, Passion music. A musical setting of a text descriptive of Christ's sufferings and death (passion).

Passione, con (It., kŏhn păhs-sē-oh'nĕh). Passionately, in an impassioned style, fervently.

Pasticcio (It., păhs-tit'chŏh); **Pastiche** (Fr., păhs-tēsh'). A musical MEDLEY of extracts from different works, pieced together and provided with new words so as to form a "new" COMPOSITION.

Pastoral. 1. A scenic CANTATA representing pastoral life; a pastoral OPERA. 2. An instrumental PIECE imitating in style and instrumentation rural and idyllic scenes. *Also* **Pastorale** (It., păhs-tŏh-**r**ah'leh); **Pastorale** (Fr., păhs-tŏh-răhl').

Patetico,-a (It., păh-tā'tē-kŏh,-kăh). Pathetic.

Patimento (It., păh-tē-men'tŏh). Suffering; grief. *Con espressione di patimento*, with mournful or plaintive expression.

Patter song. A humorous SONG sung in PARLANDO style, usually quite fast.

Pauken (Ger., pow'ken). KETTLEDRUMS.

Pauroso (It., păh-oo-**r**oh'sŏh). Fearful, timid.

Pausa (It., pah'oo-zăh). A REST; a PAUSE. *Pausa lunga*, long pause; *p. generale*, a pause for all performers.

Pause. 1. A full stop. 2. A REST. 3. A FERMATA ⌒.

Pavana (It., păh-vah'năh); **Pavan(e)**. A stately dance of Italian or Spanish origin, in slow TEMPO and ALLA BREVE TIME.

Paventoso (It., păh-ven-toh′sŏh). Fearfully, timidly.

Pearly. A style of PIANO touch producing a clear, round, smooth effect of TONE, especially in SCALE passages.

Ped. Stands for PEDAL; signifies that the right (loud) PIANO pedal is to be pressed; or (in ORGAN music) that NOTES so marked are to be played on the pedals.

Pedal. 1. A foot KEY on the ORGAN or pedal PIANO. 2. A foot lever; as the piano pedals, or the organ swell-pedal. 3. A treadle, like those used for blowing the REED ORGAN. 4. A stop knob or lever worked by the foot (organ). 5. A contraction for PEDAL POINT.

Pedale doppio (It., pĕh-dah′lĕh dô′pē-ŏh). PEDAL-part in OCTAVES.

Pedale ogni battuta (It., pĕh-dah′lĕh ŏhn′yē băht-too′tăh). "Take PEDAL with each measure."

Pedalier. A set of PEDALS, either (1) so adjusted as to play the low OCTAVES of the PIANO, after the manner of ORGAN pedals, or (2) provided with separate strings and action, to be placed underneath the piano.

Pedal organ. The set of STOPS controlled by the ORGAN PEDALS.

Pedal piano. A PIANO provided with a PEDALIER.

Pedal point. An ORGAN point.

Pedal note or **tone**. A sustained or continuously repeated NOTE (TONE).

Pedanteria, con (It., kŏhn pĕh-dăhn-tĕh-rē′ăh). **Pedantisch** (Ger., pĕh-dăhn′tish). Pedantically; in an even, unemotional style.

Peg. A short piece of wood used to tighten or loosen the tension of a STRING, thus raising or lowering its PITCH. Also, tuning peg.

Peghead. Located at the top of the NECK of a STRINGED INSTRU-MENT, a flared extension constructed to hold the tuning PEGS.

Pensiero (It., pen-sē-â′rŏh). A thought. *Pensiero del(la)——*, Souvenir of——, Recollections of——.

Pensoso (It., pen-soh′sōh). Pensive, thoughtful.

Pentatonic scale. A five-TONE SCALE, usually that which avoids SEMITONIC STEPS by skipping the FOURTH and SEVENTH DE-GREES in MAJOR, and the SECOND and SIXTH in MINOR.

Per (It., pĕr). For, by, from, in, through. *Per l'organo*, for the ORGAN; *per il flauto solo*, for solo FLUTE.

Percussion. The striking of one body against another. *Instruments of percussion* are the DRUMS, TAMBOURINE, CYMBALS, BELLS, TRIANGLE, etc., as well as the DULCIMER and PI-ANOFORTE.

Percussion stop. A REED ORGAN STOP that strikes the reed a smart blow when sounding it, to render its vibration prompter and stronger.

Percussive. Sounded by striking.

Perdendosi (It., pâr-den′dŏh-sē). Dying away; MORENDO or DIMINUENDO, together (in modern music) with a slight RAL-LENTANDO.

Perfect pitch. ABSOLUTE PITCH.

Perigordino (It., pĕh-rē-gor-dē′nŏh); **Périgourdine** (Fr., pā-rē-goor-dēn′). An early Flemish dance.

Period. A complete musical thought of eight, twelve, or sixteen MEASURES, ending with an authentic CADENCE.

Perlé (Fr., pâr-lā′); **Perlend** (Ger., pâr′lent). PEARLY.

Perpetual canon. A CANON in which the final CADENCE leads back into the opening MEASURES, like a ROUND.

Perpetuum mobile. Latin for perpetual motion; a type of short and rapid COMPOSITION, usually for a solo instrument.

Pes. HARMONIC support or ACCOMPANIMENT for a ROUND.

Pesante (It., pĕh-sähn'tĕh). Heavy, ponderous; firm, vigorous.

Peu à peu (Fr., pö ăh pö'). Little by little. *Un peu*, a little.

Pezzi (It., pet'sē). PIECES. *Pezzi concertati*, concerted pieces; *p. staccati*, any detached NUMBERS taken from an OPERA, etc.

Pezzo (It., pet'sŏh). A PIECE; a NUMBER (of an OPERA, etc.).

Phantasie (Ger., făhn-tăh-zē). FANCY, imagination.

Phantasiestück (Ger., făhn-tăh-zē'shtük). A FANTASIA; in modern music, a short PIECE of a romantic and intensely subjective cast, with no set FORM.

Phonograph. Sound-reproducing machine that is able to play analog recordings. Using flat, grooved discs, the phonograph "reads" the recording by means of a needle at the end of a tone arm. The pulsations are then electrically amplified so they may be heard through an external AMPLIFIER (on early phonographs, a large horn). Now replaced by CD (COMPACT-DISC) players that play back digital recordings.

Phrase. Half of an eight-MEASURE PERIOD. Also, any short FIGURE or PASSAGE unbroken in continuity and thus complete in itself.

Phrase mark. A curved line connecting the NOTES of a PHRASE.

Phrasing. 1. The bringing out into proper relief the PHRASES (whether MOTIVES, FIGURES, SUBJECTS, or PASSAGES). 2. The signs of NOTATION devised to further the above end.

Phrygian mode. The church MODE corresponding to the SCALE from *E* to *E* on the white KEYS of the PIANO.

Piacevole (It., p'yăh-chā'vŏh-lĕh). Pleasant, agreeable; calls for a smooth, suave delivery, free from strong ACCENTS.

Piangevole (It., p'yăhn-jā'vŏh-lĕh). "Weeping, tearfully"; in a mournful, plaintive style.

Pianino (It., pē-ăh-nē'nŏh). An upright PIANO.

Pianissimo (It., pē-ăh-nēs'sē-mŏh). Very soft; abbreviated *pp*.

Pianississimo (It., pē-ăh-nēs-sēs'sē-mŏh). Very, very soft; abbreviated *ppp*.

Piano (It., pē-ah'nŏh). 1. Soft, softly (abbreviated *p*). *Piano pedal*, the soft (or left) pedal of the PIANOFORTE. 2. Familiar abbreviation of pianoforte.

Piano à queue (Fr., pyăh'noh ah kü). GRAND PIANO; literally, "piano with a tail."

Pianoforte (It., pē-ăh-nŏh-fôr'tĕh; Engl., pī-ăn'oh-fort). A KEYBOARD STRINGED INSTRUMENT OF PERCUSSION, the TONES being produced by hammers striking the strings. The principal parts are the *frame*, the *soundboard*, the *strings*, the *action*, and the *pedals*. The hammer action was first practically developed by Bartolommeo Cristofori of Padua in 1711. Generally, the terms "pianoforte" or "fortepiano" are used to describe instruments built in the 18th century, while the term "piano" describes modern instruments.

Pianola. PLAYER PIANO.

Piano quartet. A COMPOSITION for PIANO, VIOLIN, VIOLA, and CELLO.

Piano quintet. A COMPOSITION for PIANO and STRING QUARTET.

Piano score. An ARRANGEMENT of an ORCHESTRAL work for PIANO.

Piano trio. A COMPOSITION for PIANO, VIOLIN, and CELLO.

Piatti (It., p'yăh'tē). CYMBALS.

Pibroch (pē'brŏh). A COMPOSITION for the Scottish BAGPIPE, consisting of a THEME (or *urlar*) followed by VARIATIONS. Similar to the Indian RAGA.

Picardy third. The frequent practice in BAROQUE MUSIC of ending a PIECE in a MINOR KEY with a MAJOR CHORD; the

Picardy third in this case is the raised (major) THIRD from the TONIC.

Piccanteria, con (It., kŏhn pik-kăhn-tĕh-**r**ē'ăh). With piquant, sprightly expression.

Picchiettato (It., pik-kē-et-tah'tŏh). Detached, STACCATO. See PIQUÉ.

Piccolo (It., pik'kŏh-lŏh, "little"). The octave FLUTE, a small flute pitched an OCTAVE higher than the orchestral flute. (The Italians call it *Flauto piccolo*, or *Ottavino*.)

Pick. 1. (verb) To pluck or twang the STRINGS of a GUITAR, MANDOLIN, etc. 2. (noun) A PLECTRUM.

Piece. 1. A musical COMPOSITION. 2. An instrument, taken as a member of an ORCHESTRA or BAND.

Pièce (Fr., p'yess). A PIECE. *Suite de pièces*, set of pieces.

Pieno (It., p'yâ'nŏh). 1. Full. 2. A mixture STOP on the ORGAN.

Pietoso (It., pē-ĕh-toh'sŏh). "Pitiful, moving"; demands a sympathetic and expressive delivery.

Piffero (It., pif'fĕh-**r**ŏh). 1. A FIFE; also, a primitive kind of OBOE or SHAWM.

Pin. A small metal or wooden anchor to which a STRING is attached.

Pincé (Fr., păn-sā'). 1. Plucked; as the STRINGS of a HARP. 2. PIZZICATO (in VIOLIN playing).

Pipa. A Chinese LUTE.

Pipe. 1. A simple FLAGEOLET or OBOE. 2. An ORGAN pipe; in *flue pipes*, the TONE is produced by the vibration of a column of air within a tube or BODY; they are *open* or *covered (stopped, plugged)*, a stopped pipe yielding a tone an OCTAVE lower than an open pipe of like length; in *reed pipes*, the tone is produced by a REED.

Piqué (Fr., pē-kā'). In VIOLIN playing, the MEZZO-STACCATO called for by a SLUR with STACCATO dots; notes so marked are to be played in one BOW (PICCHIETTATO).

Piston. VALVE.

Pitch. The position of a TONE in the musical SCALE. Pitch is either relative or absolute. The *relative* pitch of a tone is its position (higher or lower) as compared with some other tone (see INTERVAL). Its *absolute* pitch is its fixed position in the entire range of musical tones.

To indicate absolute pitch, the musical scale is divided into a fixed series of OCTAVES, named and lettered as on p. xii, "Table of Clefs."

The number of vibrations made by a tone establishes its absolute pitch; the standard *French pitch* (also called *International,* or *low,* pitch) gives the tone *a*¹ 435 double vibrations per second. The standard of pitch in the United States is *a*¹ = 440 double vibrations per second.

Pitch class. A term denoting a set of all PITCHES with the same name, i.e., pitch class A, inclusive of all possible As, regardless of REGISTER.

Pitch pipe. A small wooden or metal REED PIPE that sounds one or more TONES of fixed PITCH, to give the tone for tuning an instrument, or for a choir.

Più (It., pew). More. When *più* stands alone, as a TEMPO mark, MOSSO is implied; as an *expression* mark, it refers to the next preceding *f* or *p. Più mosso, più moto,* faster; *più mosso ancora,* still faster; *con un poco più di moto,* with a little more movement (that is, somewhat faster).

Piuttosto (It., pew-tos'tŏh). Somewhat, or rather.

Pivot chord. In MODULATION, a CHORD pivotal to both the old KEY and the new; in CHROMATIC modulation, the DIMIN-

ISHED SEVENTH CHORD often functions as such a *passe-partout* device.

Pizzicato (It., pit-sē-kah'tŏh). "Pinched"; plucked with the finger; a direction, in music, to violinists, etc., to play the notes by plucking the STRINGS (abbreviated as *pizz*).

Placidamente (It., plăh-chē-dăh-men'tĕh). Placidly, tranquilly.

Placido (It., plah'chē-dŏh). Placid, smooth.

Plagal mode. A church MODE in which the final KEYNOTE is a FOURTH above the lowest TONE of the mode. See AUTHENTIC MODE.

Plainchant, Plainsong. The UNISON vocal music of the Christian church, probably dating from the first centuries of the Christian era, the style being still obligatory in the Roman Catholic ritual.

Player piano. Trade name of a mechanical PIANO in which the keyboard action is produced by a rotating perforated roll. Stravinsky composed for it, and, more recently, Conlon Nancarrow has written a series of highly original works for the instrument.

Plectrum. A PICK; a small piece of ivory, tortoise shell, metal, or plastic, held between the forefinger and thumb, or fitted to the thumb by a ring, and used to pluck or twang the STRINGS of the MANDOLIN, ZITHER, GUITAR, etc.

Plein (Fr., plăn). Full.

Plein-jeu (Fr., plăn-zhö'). A STOP or combination of stops bringing out the full power of the ORGAN, HARMONIUM, etc.

Pluralism. As in COLLAGE, the use of different styles within a single COMPOSITION, sometimes simultaneously.

Plus (Fr., plü). More.

Po' (It., pô; contraction of *poco*). Little. *Con un po' d'espansione*, with a certain display of emotion; *alzando un po' la* *voce*, raising the voice a little; *ritenendo un po'*, becoming a trifle slower.

Pochette (Fr., pŭ-shĕt'). "Little pocket"; a very small VIOLIN that could be carried in the pocket of a dancing master to accompany his pupils in rehearsal. See KIT.

Pochissimo (It., poh-kee'cee-mŏh). Very little.

Poco (It., pô'kŏh). Little. *A poco a poco*, little by little; *p. allegro*, rather fast; *p. largo*, rather slow; *p. meno*, when standing alone as a tempo mark, MOSSO is implied, i.e., *p. meno mosso*, a little less fast (a little slower); *p. più*, standing alone, also implies *mosso* (a little faster); *p. più lento della prima volta*, somewhat slower than the first time.

Poi (It., pô'ē). Then, thereafter.

Point. An isolated NOTE.

Pointe d'archet. TREMOLO with the point of the VIOLIN BOW.

Point d'orgue (Fr., pwŏhn dôrg). 1. ORGAN POINT. 2. PAUSE. 3. CADENZA.

Pointe (Fr., pwăn't). 1. Point or head of a BOW. 2. Toe (abbrev. *p.*).

Pointillism. Emphasis upon single NOTES in a SERIALLY organized process, brought to extremes of development by Webern.

Polacca (It., poh-lăhk'kăh). A POLONAISE. *Alla polacca*, in the style of a Polonaise (better, *Pollacca*).

Polca (It., pôl'kăh). POLKA.

Polka (pōl'kăh; Bohemian, *pulka*). A lively round dance in 2/4 TIME, originating about 1830 as a peasant dance in Bohemia.

Polka mazurka. A form of MAZURKA accommodated to the steps of the POLKA.

Polo (Sp., poh'loh). A SYNCOPATED Spanish dance in TRIPLE TIME, from Andalusia.

Polonaise (Fr., pŏh-lŏh-näz'). A dance of Polish origin, in 3/4 TIME and moderate TEMPO; formerly in animated processional style, but now merely a slow promenade opening a ball:

RHYTHM:

Last MEASURE:

Polonese (It., pŏh-lŏh-nä'zeh). POLONAISE.

Polymetre. The simultaneous presence of musical lines in different METERS, most common in works of the 14th and 20th centuries.

Polyphonic. 1. Consisting of two or more independently treated MELODIES; CONTRAPUNTAL. 2. Capable of producing two or more TONES simultaneously, like the PIANO, HARP, or ORGAN.

Polyphony. 1. The combination in harmonious progression of two or more independent MELODIES; the independent treatment of the PARTS; COUNTERPOINT, in the widest sense. 2. In a SYNTHESIZER, the ability to play more than one TONE simultaneously. Synthesizers that play up to eight tones at once are said to have eight-voice polyphony.

Polyrhythm. A term encompassing both 1) POLYMETRE and 2) the more frequent use of conflicting transient rhythms (i.e., CROSS-RHYTHMS).

Polytonality. Simultaneous use of two or more different TONALITIES or KEYS. In much modern music, polytonality has become a standard technique.

Pomposo (It., pŏhm-pŏh'sŏh). Pompously, loftily; in a majestic, dignified style.

Ponderoso (It., pŏhn-dĕh-**roh**'sŏh). Ponderous; in a vigorous, impressive style.

Ponticello (It., pŏhn-tē-chel'lŏh). BRIDGE. *Sul ponticello*, near the bridge.

Pop(ular) music. A general term to denote a wide variety of musical styles, generally characterized by their easy accessibility to wide audiences; usually of modest length, with prominent and memorable MELODIES and LYRICS, and a simple, unassuming HARMONIC language.

Portamento (It., por-tăh-men'tŏh). A smooth gliding from one TONE to another, differing from the LEGATO in its more deliberate execution, and in the actual (though very rapid and slurring) sounding of the intermediate TONES.

Portando (It., por-tăhn'dŏh). "Carrying," i.e., the *portamento* effect. *Portando la voce*, vocal PORTAMENTO.

Portale la voce (It., por-tah'tĕh lăh voh'chĕh). "Carry the voice," that is, sing PORTAMENTO.

Portative. A small portable ORGAN that could be used in religious processions.

Posato (It., pŏh-sah'tŏh). Sedate, dignified.

Posaune (Ger., pŏh-zow'nĕ). TROMBONE. Also, a REED STOP in the ORGAN, of 8' (MANUALS) or 16' (PEDAL) PITCH.

Positif (Fr., pah-zē-tēf). CHOIR ORGAN.

Position. 1. The place of the left hand on the FINGERBOARD of the VIOLIN, etc. In the first position, the forefinger stops the TONE (or SEMITONE) above the open string; by shifting up, so that the first finger takes the place previously occupied by the second, the second position is reached, and so on. In the half position, the second, third, and fourth fingers occupy the places taken, in the first position, by the first, second, and third fingers. 2. The arrangement of NOTES in a CHORD, with reference to the lowest PART; in the first, or fundamental position, the lowest part takes the ROOT; in the second, it takes the third, etc. 3. Close (open) position, see HARMONY, *close* and *open*.

Possibile (It., pŏhs-sē'bē-lĕh). Possible. *Pianissimo possibile*, as soft as possible; *il più presto possibile*, as rapid as possible.

Post horn. A HORN without VALVES or KEYS, used on post coaches.

Postlude. 1. A closing VOLUNTARY on the ORGAN. 2. A REFRAIN.

Posto, di (It., dē pôs'tŏh). SLANCIO, DI.

Potpourri (Fr., pŏh-pŏŏ-**r**ē'). A kind of musical MEDLEY, in which all kinds of TUNES, or PARTS of tunes, are connected in an arbitrary manner.

Poussé (Fr., pŏŏs-sā'). UPBOW.

Prächtig (Ger., prĕh**'**tīyh). Grandly, majestically.

Præludium (L., prā-loo'dē-oom). PRELUDE.

Pralltriller (Ger., prähl'trĭl-er). Upper MORDENT.

Precedente (It., prĕh-chĕh-den'tĕh). Preceding. *Moto prece-dente*, in the preceding TEMPO.

Precentor. A director and manager of a CHOIR, and of musical services in general.

Precipitoso (It., prĕh-chē-pē-toh'sŏh). With precipitation, impetuosity, dash.

Preciso (It., prĕh-chē'zŏh). With precision.

Prelude. A musical introduction to a composition or drama.

Preludio (It., preh-loo'dē-oh). PRELUDE.

Preparation. 1. The preparation of a DISSONANCE consists in the presence, in the preceding CHORD and same PART, of the TONE forming the dissonance. 2. The insertion of screws, nuts, bolts, etc., under the strings of a GRAND

PIANO, in accord with instructions contained in the SCORE and in advance of the performance of a work for PREPARED PIANO.

Prepared piano. A modernistic practice initiated by the American composer John Cage, in which the TIMBRE of the GRAND PIANO is altered by systematically placing such objects as screws, bolts, and nuts under its strings.

Pressando (It., pres-săhn'dŏh). Pressing on, accelerating.

Pressez (Fr., pres-sā'). Accelerate; go faster.

Prestamente (It., prĕh-stâh-men'tĕh). Rapidly.

Prestissimo (It., prĕh-stis'sē-mŏh). Very rapidly.

Presto (It., prâ'stŏh). Fast, rapid; faster than ALLEGRO. *Presto assai,* very, extremely rapid; *p. parlante,* a direction in recitatives meaning to "speak rapidly (volubly)."

Primary accent. The DOWNBEAT, or THESIS; the ACCENT beginning the MEASURE, directly following the BAR.

Primary triad. One of the three fundamental TRIADS of a KEY (those on the FIRST, FIFTH, and FOURTH DEGREES).

Prime. The first NOTE of a SCALE.

Primo,-a (It., prē-mŏh,-măh). First. *Prima buffa,* leading lady in comic OPERA; *prima donna,* leading lady in (grand) opera; *prima vista,* at first sight; *prima volta,* the first time (written *Ima volta,* or simply *I,* or *1*), indicates that the MEASURE(S) under its brackets are to be played the first time, before the repeat, whereas, on repeating, those marked *Seconda volta* (or *IIda volta,* or *II,* or *2*) are to be performed instead. Also, a PART marked *primo* is a first or leading part, as in a DUET.

Principal chords. The basic CHORDS of a KEY, i.e., the TRIADS built on the TONIC, DOMINANT, and SUBDOMINANT, with the dominant SEVENTH chord.

Principio (It., prin-chē'pē-ŏh). Beginning, first time. *In principio*, at the beginning; *più marcato del p.*, more marked than the first time.

Processional. A HYMN sung in church during the entrance of choir and clergy.

Process music. MINIMAL MUSIC.

Program music. A class of purely instrumental COMPOSITIONS intended to represent distinct moods or phases of emotion, or to depict actual scenes of events; sometimes called "descriptive music"; as opposed to ABSOLUTE MUSIC.

Progression. The advance from one TONE to another, or from one CHORD to another; the former is MELODIC, the latter HARMONIC PROGRESSION.

Progressive composition. In SONG writing, the setting of each STROPHE to different music, following the changing mood of the text more closely than in the BALLAD or FOLK SONG, wherein MELODY and HARMONY are generally the same for each VERSE.

Progressive tonality. A term used to denote SYMPHONIC works that end in KEYS other than those in which they begin.

Pronto (It., prŏhn'tŏh). Promptly, swiftly.

Pronunziato (It., prŏh-nŏŏn-tsē-ah'tŏh). Pronounced, marked. *Ben pronunziato*, well, clearly enunciated.

Proportion. A term of medieval music THEORY, relating to the proportionate duration of the NOTES of the MELODY, and also the ratio of vibrations of these notes.

Proportional notation. A system of NOTATION developed by Earle Brown in which DURATIONS of NOTES are shown proportionally, relative only to one another and independent of any strict metric system. Also called "time-space notation."

Psalm. A HYMN; a sacred SONG.

Psalmody. Music sung in Protestant churches in England and the U.S. from the 17th to early 19th centuries.

Psaltery (sôl'ter-ī). An ancient instrument, a kind of ZITHER with a varying number of STRINGS plucked by the fingers or with a PLECTRUM, in use to the 17th century; known to the Hebrews as the *Kinnor*, to the Germans as the *Rotta*.

Psaume (Fr., sohm). PSALM.

Pulse. A BEAT or ACCENT.

Pult (Ger., poolt). Music stand.

Punk Rock. A back-to-roots music movement, originating in England in the mid-1970s, featuring simple, repetitive MELODIES, loud, basic CHORD changes, and LYRICS often with a political and/or social message. In the U.S., it merged with NEW WAVE.

Punta (It., pŏŏn'täh'). Point (of the VIOLIN BOW). *Colla punta dell'arco*, at the point of the bow.

Pupitre (Fr., pü'pētr). Music stand.

Q

Qin. An early seven-string Chinese ZITHER, the most honored of all Chinese musical instruments.

Quadrille (kwŏ-drĭl'). A SQUARE DANCE consisting of five (or six) figures named *le Pantalon, l'Été, la Poule, la Pastourelle (la Trenise)*, and *la Finale*. The TIME alternates between 3/8(6/8) and 2/4.

Quadruple counterpoint. See COUNTERPOINT.

Quadruple meter or **time**. That characterized by four BEATS to the MEASURE.

Quadruplet. A group of four equal NOTES, to be executed in the TIME of three or six of the same kind in the established RHYTHM, written:

Quality of tone. That characteristic peculiarity of any vocal or instrumental TONE that distinguishes it from the tone of any other class of voices or instruments. Also called *tone color* or TIMBRE.

Quarter note. A note (♩) equal to one-quarter of the duration of a WHOLE NOTE. In many common METERS (4/4, 3/4, 2/4), the quarter-note is the unit of the MEASURE, or the BEAT. Also called a CROTCHET.

Quarter rest. A REST equal in TIME value to a QUARTER NOTE (𝄽 , or ∤).

Quarter tone. Half a SEMITONE; an INTERVAL which is sometimes used in modern, microtonal compositions. Also used in some non-Western music.

Quartet(te). 1. A concerted instrumental composition for four performers. 2. A COMPOSITION, MOVEMENT, or NUMBER, either vocal or instrumental, in four PARTS. 3. Also, the (four) performers as a group.

Quasi (It., kwah′zē). As if; as it were; nearly; approaching. *Andante quasi allegretto*, ANDANTE approaching ALLEGRETTO.

Quatre (Fr., kăh′tr′); **Quattro** (It., kwăht′trŏh). Four.

Quatour (Fr., kwăh-tü-or′). A vocal or instrumental QUARTET.

Quaver. English term for an EIGHTH NOTE.

Quickstep. A MARCH, usually in 6/8 time.

Quindecima (It., kwin-dā′chē-măh). A FIFTEENTH (either the INTERVAL or the ORGAN STOP). *Alla quindecima* (written simply *15va*), two OCTAVES higher (or lower).

Quint. 1. The INTERVAL of a FIFTH. 2. A 5 1/3' ORGAN STOP, sounding a fifth higher than the normal 8' PITCH. 3. The *E* STRING of the VIOLIN.

Quintet(te). 1. A concerted instrumental composition for five performers. 2. A COMPOSITION, MOVEMENT, or NUMBER, vocal or instrumental, in five PARTS. 3. Also the (five) performers as a group.

Quintole. A QUINTUPLET.

Quotation. In music, the inclusion of musical materials in a composition that allude to other compositions or musics.

Quintuor (Fr., kăn-tü-or'). A QUINTET.

Quintuple rhythm, time. Having five BEATS to the MEASURE.

Quintuplet. A group of five equal NOTES to be executed in the TIME of four of the same kind in the regular RHYTHM, written:

Quitter (Fr., kē-tā'). To quit, leave. *Sans quitter la corde*, without quitting the STRING.

Quodlibet. A musical MEDLEY; POTPOURRI; DUTCH CONCERT. Originally, a PIECE employing several well-known TUNES from various sources, performed either simultaneously or in succession.

R

R. Stands for right (Ger., *rechte*); *r.h.*, right hand (*rechte Hand*). In French ORGAN music, R stands for *clavier de récit* (swell MANUAL).

Rabbia, con (It., kŏhn răhb-bē-ăh). With passion, frenzy; furiously.

Raccoglimento, con (It., kŏhn răhk-kŏhl-yē-men'tŏh). Collectedly, coolly; meditatively.

Raccontando (It., răhk-kŏhn-tăhn'dŏh). Narrating, as if telling a story.

Raddolcente (It., răhd-dōhl-chen'tĕh). Growing calmer and gentler.

Raga. 1. A generic term for Indian SCALES, consisting of five, six, or seven different NOTES and calculated to create a certain mood. Each raga is suited to a particular time of day. The word itself comes from the Sanskrit meaning "color," so that an infinite variety of nuances is possible in the playing of ragas by musicians of India. 2. An instrumental COMPOSITION, as above, usually in three PARTS: an ARHYTHMIC opening section, setting forth the scale TONES; an IMPROVISATORY second part, growing in intensity; and a brief FINALE, where both MELODIC and RHYTHMIC instruments engage in rapidly executed CALL-AND-RESPONSE FIGURES.

Ragtime. A SYNCOPATED American music of black origins, popular from about 1896 to 1918. During this period, the term included vocal and instrumental music, and dance styles associated with the music. As an instrumental genre, it existed as both a popular ballroom style and as the earliest form of JAZZ. In today's usage, the term usually refers to solo works in "ragtime style" for PIANO.

Rallentando (It., răhl-len-tăhn'dŏh). Growing slower and slower.

Rallentare (It., răhl-len-tah'rĕh). To grow slower. *Senza rallentare*, without slackening the pace.

Range. COMPASS.

Rank. A row of ORGAN PIPES. A mixture STOP is said to have two, three, or more ranks, according to the number of pipes sounded by each digital (KEY).

Rant. An early COUNTRY DANCE, or a REEL, commonly performed in Northeast England.

Ranz des vaches (Fr., răns dā văh'sh). One of the AIRS sung, or played on the alpine HORN, in the Swiss Alps as a call to cattle.

Rap. A style of urban black popular music that emerged in the mid-1980s characterized by (often) IMPROVISED rhymes performed to a rhythmic accompaniment; its socially relevant and/or political lyrics are frequently performed A CAPPELLA.

Rapido (It., răh'pē-dŏh). With rapidity; rapidly.

Rasch (Ger., răhsh). Fast, rapid, swift. *Noch rascher*, still faster; *so rasch wie möglich*, as fast as possible.

Ravvivando il tempo (It., răhv-vē-văhn'dŏh). Accelerating the TEMPO.

Ray. Stands for Re, in TONIC SOL-FA.

Re (It., rā); **Ré** (Fr., rā). Second of the ARETINIAN SYLLABLES, and the name of the NOTE *D* in France, Italy, etc.

Realization. The modern practice, responsive to indeterminate compositional procedures, of carrying out instructions, either explicitly or implicitly indicated in a given score, to "realize" a composition.

Rebec. A medieval VIOLIN, shaped like a half pear, with three GUT STRINGS.

Recapitulation. A return of the initial SECTION of a MOVEMENT in SONATA FORM.

Recessional. A HYMN sung in church during the departure of choir and clergy after a service.

Recht (Ger., rěyht). Right. *Recht Hand*, right hand.

Recital. A CONCERT at which either (*a*) all pieces are executed by one performer, or (*b*) all pieces performed are by one composer.

Recitando (It., rěh-chē-tăhn'dŏh). In declamatory style.

Récitatif (Fr., rā-sē-tăh-tēf′); **Recitativ** (Ger., rā-tsē-tăh-tēf′); **Recitative** (res′ĭ-ta-tēv′); **Recitativo** (It., rĕh-chē-tăh-tē′vŏh). 1. Declamatory singing, free in TEMPO and RHYTHM. 2. In PIANO playing, calls for a crisp delivery of the MELODY, free in tempo and rhythm.

Reciting note. The TONE on which most of each verse in a CHANT (PSALM or CANTICLE) is continuously recited; the DOMINANT.

Recorder. Type of FLUTE of the end-blown variety with a WHISTLE MOUTHPIECE.

Redowa. A Bohemian dance, like the MAZURKA, though less strongly accented, in 3/4 TIME and lively TEMPO.

Reduce. In ORGAN music, a direction to decrease the volume of tone by retiring the louder STOPS.

Reduction. Rearrangement of a COMPOSITION for a smaller number of instruments than originally intended, while preserving its FORM as far as possible.

Reed. A thin strip of cane, wood, or metal, so adjusted before an aperture as nearly to close it, fixed at one end, and set by an air current in vibration, which it communicates either to an enclosed column of air (ORGAN PIPE, OBOE), or directly to the free atmosphere, thus producing a musical TONE. A FREE REED vibrates within the aperture without striking the edges; a *beating* or *single reed* strikes on the edges. A *double reed* consists of two beating reeds which strike against each other.

Reed instrument. One whose tone is produced by the vibration of a REED (or reeds) in its MOUTHPIECE.

Reed organ. A KEYBOARD INSTRUMENT whose tones are produced by FREE REEDS; (*a*) in the HARMONIUM (invented 1843 by A. Debain of Paris), the bellows force compressed air *outward* through the reeds; (*b*) in the *American organ*, a suction bellows draws the air *in* through them. Either style has a variety of STOPS of different quality.

Reed pipe. See PIPE.

Reel. A lively dance of Scotland and Ireland, usually in 4/4 (sometimes 6/4) TIME, with REPRISES of eight MEASURES; danced by two couples.

Refrain. A recurring MELODY of a SONG, usually at the end of a STANZA; in popular music, a CHORUS.

Regal. A portable ORGAN with REED PIPES in use during the 16th and 17th centuries.

Reggae. Jamaican POPULAR MUSIC, marked by insistent square RHYTHMS, in the manner of ROCK 'N' ROLL, pioneered by singer/guitarist Bob Marley.

Register. 1. A set of PIPES or REEDS controlled by one draw-stop; a STOP (ORGAN stop). 2. A portion of the vocal COMPASS; as *high* or *low* register; *chest-* or *head-*register. 3. A portion, in the range of certain instruments, differing in quality from the other portions.

Registration. 1. The art of effectively employing and combining the various STOPS of the ORGAN. 2. The combination of stops employed for any given COMPOSITION.

Relation(ship). The degree of affinity between KEYS, CHORDS, and TONES.

Relative key. A MINOR KEY is relative to that MAJOR KEY, the TONIC of which lies a minor THIRD above its own; a major key is relative to that minor key, the tonic of which lies a minor third below its own. *C* major is the relative key to *a* minor.

Relative pitch. The ability to name an INTERVAL, or the exact second NOTE, after hearing an interval and being given the identity of the first note. Compare ABSOLUTE PITCH.

Religioso (It., rĕh-lē-joh'sŏh). In a devotional style.

Remote key. An unrelated KEY.

Renaissance. In music history, the period from 1400 to 1600.

Repeat. 1. The sign: or or , *a* signifying that the music between the double-dotted BARS is to be repeated; *b* and *c*, that the preceding and also the following division is to be repeated. 2. A SECTION or division of music which is repeated.

Repercussion. 1. Repetition of a TONE or CHORD. 2. In a FUGUE, the regular reentrance of SUBJECT and ANSWER after the EPISODES immediately following the EXPOSITION.

Répétiteur (Fr., rĕh-pĕh-tē-tŭhr'). A choral assistant; anyone who conducts rehearsal.

Répétition (Fr., rĕh-pĕh-tē-sē-on'). A rehearsal.

Répétition générale (Fr., -zhĕn-nĕh-rahl'). A dress rehearsal.

Repetizione (It., rĕh-pĕh-tē-tsē-oh'nĕh). RIPETIZIONE.

Replica (It., râ'plē-kăh). A REPEAT or REPRISE. *Da capo senza replica*, play from the beginning without observing the repeats.

Reprise (Fr., rŭ-prēz'). 1. A REPEAT. 2. The revival of a work. 3. BREAK. 4. See REPERCUSSION 2. 5. Reentrance of a PART or THEME after a REST or PAUSE.

Requiem. The first word in the MASS for the dead; hence, the title of the musical setting of that Mass. Its divisions are (1) Requiem, Kyrie, (2) Dies iræ, Requiem, (3) Domine Jesu Christe, (4) Sanctus, Benedictus, and (5) Agnus Dei, Lux æterna.

Resolution. The PROGRESSION of a DISSONANCE, whether a simple INTERVAL or a CHORD, to a CONSONANCE. *Direct resolution*, immediate progression from the dissonance to the consonance; *indirect* (or *delayed*, *deferred*, *retarded*) *r.*, one passing through some intermediate dissonance(s) before reaching the final restful consonance.

Resonance. The resounding of upper PARTIALS over the FUNDAMENTAL.

Resonance-box. A hollow resonant BODY like that of the VIOLIN or ZITHER. Also called SOUNDBOX.

Response. 1. RESPONSORY. 2. ANSWER. 3. The musical reply, by the CHOIR or congregation, to what is said or sung by the priest or officiant.

Responsory. 1. That PSALM, or part of one, sung between the missal lessons. 2. The GRADUAL. 3. A Respond; that is, a part of a psalm (formerly an entire psalm) sung between the lessons at the canonical hours.

Rest. A PAUSE or interval of silence between two TONES; hence, the sign indicating such a pause. See "Notes and Rests," p. ix.

Restez (Fr., res-tā'). "Stay there!" In music for STRINGED INSTRUMENTS, a direction to (*a*) "Play on the same STRING," or (*b*) "Remain in the same POSITION (SHIFT)."

Retardation. 1. A holding-back, decreasing in speed. 2. A SUSPENSION resolving upward.

Retarded progression. A SUSPENSION resolving upward.

Retenu. French for RITENUTO, holding back.

Retrograde. Performing a MELODY backwards; a CRAB MOVEMENT. Also, one of three standard techniques in 12-NOTE COMPOSITION (retrograde, INVERSION, TRANSPOSITION) wherein all NOTES of a SET are played in reverse (i.e., backwards).

Retrograde inversion. A standard technique in 12-NOTE COMPOSITION wherein all NOTES of a SET are played in a reverse succession that also mirrors the original set.

Réveil (or **Reveille**) (Fr., rā-vä'ĕu). The military signal for rising.

Reverse motion. CONTRARY MOTION.

Reversion. RETROGRADE IMITATION.

Rapsodie (Fr., răhp-sŏh-dē'/. A RHAPSODY; generally, an instrumental FANTASIA on FOLK SONGS or on MOTIVES taken from primitive NATIONAL MUSIC.

Rhythm. The measured movement of similar TONE-groups; that is, the effect produced by the systematic grouping of tones with reference to regularity both in their accentuation and in their succession as equal or unequal in TIME VALUE. A *rhythm* is, therefore, a tone-group serving as a pattern for succeeding identical groups.

Rhythm and blues (R & B). A type of black, urban, popular music combining the elements of strong repetitive RHYTHMS, simple MELODIES and HARMONIES, and BLUES. Precursor of early ROCK 'N' ROLL.

Rhythm section. The PERCUSSION section in a JAZZ BAND, consisting of PIANO, BASS, and DRUMS, supplying the main BEAT.

Ribattuta (It., rē-băht-too'tăh). 1. A BEAT 3. 2. A device for beginning a TRILL by dwelling longer on the PRINCIPAL TONE than on the AUXILIARY.

Ribs. The curved sides of the VIOLIN, connecting BELLY and back.

Ricercare (It., rē-chär-käh'rĕh). Instrumental COMPOSITION of the 16th and 17th centuries generally characterized by imitative treatment of the THEME(S).

Ricochet. A DOWN-BOW stroke on the VIOLIN, achieved by throwing the upper third of the BOW on the same STRING, resulting in a bouncing series of rapid NOTES in one stroke.

Riddle canon. A CANON that is not written out so that the performer must find out when the imitating voices must come in.

Riff. A short MELODIC PHRASE, often heard in JAZZ or ROCK music, that is repeated throughout a piece of music. It may also be a characteristic phrase used by an individual musician in various different pieces, as a "musical signature."

Rigadoon. A lively French dance, generally in 4/4 TIME (sometimes 2/2, rarely 6/4), with an UPBEAT of a QUARTER NOTE; it consists of three or four REPRISES. *Also* **Rigaudon** (Fr., rē-goh-dŏhn'); **Rigodone** (It., rē-gŏh-doh'nĕh).

Rigor(e) (It., rē-gohr',-h'rĕh). Rigor, strictness. *Al* (or *con*) *rigore di tempo* (or *a rigor di tempo*), in strict TIME.

Rigoroso (It., rē-gŏh-roh'sŏh). In strict TIME.

Rilasciando (It., rē-lăh-shăhn'dŏh). RALLENTANDO.

Rimettendo (It., rē-met-ten'dŏh). "Resuming" a preceding TEMPO,whether after accelerating or retarding.

Rinforzando (or **-zato**) (It., rin-for-tsăhn'dŏh [or -tsah'tŏh]). With special emphasis; indicates a sudden increase in loudness, either for a TONE or CHORD, or throughout a PHRASE or short PASSAGE.

Rinforzare, senza (It., sen-tsăh rin-for-tsah'rĕh). Without growing louder.

Ring modulator. An electronic device that produces from two inputs of frequencies $(x + x)$ two new, modulated frequencies $(x + y$ and $x - y)$.

Ripetizione (It., rē-pĕh-tē-tsē-oh'nĕh). Repetition.

Ripieno (It., rē-p'yâ'nŏh). "Filling up"; "supplementary." 1. A *ripieno* PART is one reinforcing the leading orchestral parts by doubling them or by filling in the HARMONY. 2. In SCORES, *ripieno* is a direction calling for the entrance of the full string BAND (or, in military music, the CLARINETS, OBOES, etc.). 3. A combination STOP drawing all REGISTERS of any given MANUAL. 4. The full orchestra in a CONCERTO GROSSO, as opposed to the CONCERTINO or soloist.

Ripigliare (It., rē-pēl-yah′rĕh). To resume.

Riposo, con (It., kŏhn rē-pô′sŏh). In a calm, tranquil manner; reposefully.

Riprendendo (It., rē-pren-den′dŏh). Resuming. *Riprendendo pocoa poco il tempo*, gradually regaining the preceding rate of speed.

Risentito (It., rē-sen-tē′tŏh). Energetic, vigorous; expressive.

Risoluto (It., rē-soh-loo′tŏh). In a resolute, vigorous, decided style.

Risvegliato (It., rē-svāl-yah′tŏh). Lively, animated.

Ritardando (It., rē-tar-dăhn′dŏh). Growing slower and slower.

Ritardare, senza (It., sen′tsăh rē-tar-dah′rĕh). Without slackening the pace.

Ritardato (It., rē-tar-dah′tŏh). At a slower pace.

Ritenendo (It., rē-tĕh-nen′dŏh). RALLENTANDO.

Ritenuto (It., rē-tĕh-noo′tŏh). Held back; at a slower rate of speed.

Ritmico (It., rit′mē-kŏh). Rhythmical; MISURATO.

Ritmo (It., rit′mŏh). RHYTHM.

Ritornello (It., rē-tor-nel′lŏh); **Ritornelle** (Fr., rē-toor-nel′). 1. The BURDEN of a SONG. 2. A REPEAT. 3. In accompanied vocal works, an instrumental PRELUDE, INTERLUDE, or POSTLUDE (REFRAIN). 4. In a CONCERTO, the orchestral refrain.

Robusto (It., rŏh-bŏŏ'stŏh). Firmly and boldly.

Rock. A term that covers a variety of popular American styles of ROCK 'N' ROLL music dating from the 1960s, each an outgrowth of the rock 'n' roll of the 1950s, and including ACID ROCK, *folk-r.*, *hard r.*, JAZZ r., *mellow r.*, PUNK R., *soft r.*, etc.

Rockabilly. A 1950s-era music that combined a ROCK 'N' ROLL BEAT with country music sentiments; revived in the 1970s, primarily in England and Europe.

Rock 'n' roll. A popular American style of the 1950s that emerged from black RHYTHM AND BLUES. As opposed to the prevailing popular style of the time, which featured singers with smooth orchestral background, rock 'n' roll featured a percussively heavy reinforcement of the METER (BEAT) played by combos consisting, minimally, of PIANO, BASS, DRUMS, and GUITARS. BLUES harmonic structures were common, but without the characteristic BLUE NOTES or blues mood.

Rococo. An architectural term applied to music, descriptive of the ornamental type of composition current from about 1725 to 1775. As a musical period, it overlaps and joins late BAROQUE and early CLASSICISM.

Roll. 1. A TREMOLO or TRILL on the DRUM. The sign in NOTATION is

Long roll, the prolonged and reiterated drum signal to troops, for attack or rally. 2. In ORGAN playing, a rapid ARPEGGIO. 3. On the TAMBOURINE, the rapid and reiterated hither- and thither-stroke with the knuckles.

Romance. Originally, a BALLAD, or popular tale in verse, in the Romance dialect; now, a title of epico-lyrical SONGS, or of short instrumental pieces of sentimental or romantic cast, and without special FORM. The French romance is a simple love ditty. *Romances sans paroles* (roh-mǎhns' sǎhn pǎh-rohl'), "Songs without Words."

Romanesca. A type of court dance that originated in the Roman countryside in Italy in the 17th century.

Romantic. In music history, the period from about 1815 to c. 1910, overlapping with late CLASSICISM on one end, and IMPRESSIONISM and EXPRESSIONISM on the other.

Romanza. Italian term for a short romantic SONG or a solo instrumental PIECE.

Rondeau. A medieval French SONG with instrumental ACCOMPANIMENT, consisting of an ARIA and a CHORAL REFRAIN.

Rondel. A type of RONDEAU.

Rondo (It., Rondò [rohn'dŏh']). An instrumental PIECE in which the leading THEME (A) is repeated, alternating with the others. A typical pattern, with letters representing thematic sections, would be: A-B-A-C-A-B-A. There are five- and seven-part rondo FORMS.

Root. The lowest NOTE of a chord in the FUNDAMENTAL position.

Rosalia. A type of SEQUENCE modulating a whole TONE higher, popular in semiclassical pieces of the 19th century; named after an Italian song, "Rosalia mia cara."

Rota. A ROUND; also a Latin name for a HURDY-GURDY.

Rotondo (It., rŏh-tŏhn'dŏh). Round, full.

Roulade (Fr., roo-lǎhd'). A GRACE consisting of a RUN or ARPEGGIO from one PRINCIPAL MELODY TONE to another; a vocal or instrumental FLOURISH.

Roulante. French for "rolling." *Caisse roulante*, a TENOR DRUM.

Round. A kind of vocal CANON at the UNISON, without CODA; sometimes with an HARMONIC support or ACCOMPANIMENT, the PES.

Roundelay. A LAY or SONG containing some continued reiteration or REFRAIN.

Rovescio (It., roh-věs'shoh). An inverse motion; *al rovescio* usually means a RETROGRADE or CRAB MOVEMENT, but it may also indicate the INVERSION of INTERVALS in a MELODY, so that upward PROGRESSIONS become downward progressions, and vice versa.

Row. Alternate name of SERIES.

Rubando (It., roo-bähn'doh). Performing in a RUBATO style. *Affretando e rubando il tempo*, perform with increasing speed, and dwell on ACCENTED TONES.

Rubato (It., roo-bäh'tŏh). "Robbed"; meaning, "dwell on, and (often almost insensibly) prolong prominent MELODY TONES or CHORDS." This requires an equivalent acceleration of less prominent tones, which are thus "robbed" of a portion of their time value.

Ruhig (Ger., roo'ĭyh). Quiet, calm, tranquil.

Rührung (Ger., rü'rŏŏng^k). Emotion.

Rumba. A SYNCOPATED Cuban dance music popular in the United States in the 1930s–1950s.

Run. A rapid SCALE PASSAGE; in vocal music, usually such a passage sung to one syllable.

Rustico (It., rŏŏ'stē-kŏh). Rural, pastoral.

Ruvido (It., rŏŏ'vē-dŏh). In a rough, harsh style.

Rhythmé (Fr., rit-mā'). Measured. *Bien rhythmé*, well-balanced and elegant in rhythmical effect.

S

S. Stands for *Segno* in the phrases *al Segno, dal Segno*; for *Senza, Sinistra, Solo, Soprano, Sordini*; and for *Subito* in the phrase *Volti subito* (V.S.).

Sackbut. 1. Early form of TROMBONE. 2. In the Bible, the translation of *sabbek*, a HARP-like instrument.

Saite (Ger., zī'tĕ). A STRING.

Salmo. Italian for PSALM.

Salsa. Modern Latin American dance in a raucous rhythmic manner; *salsa* means "sauce" in Spanish.

Saltarella,-o (It., sähl-tăh-**r**el'läh,-lŏh). A second DIVISION in many 16th-century dance TUNES, in TRIPLE TIME, the skipping step marked in the RHYTHM:

Also, an Italian dance in 3/4 or 6/8 TIME.

Saltato (It., sähl-tah'tŏh). SPRINGING BOW.

Salto (It., sähl'tŏh). Leap; *di salto*, by a leap or leaps. Also, skip or "cut."

Samba. Popular Brazilian dance.

Sampler. An electronic, digital recorder capable of recording a sound and then storing it in the form of digital information. *Sampling*, often used in modern recordings, might involve taking small bits of earlier recordings (such as a GUITAR RIFF) and then adding them to the background of a new work.

Sanctus. See MASS.

Sanft (Ger., zähnft). Soft, low.

Sans (Fr., sähn). Without.

Saraband; Sarabanda (It., säh-**r**äh-bähn'däh); **Sarabande** (Fr., säh-**r**äh-bahn'd); **Sarabande** (Ger., säh-**r**äh-bähn'dĕ). A stately dance of Spanish or Oriental origin. The instrumental form has (usually) two eight-MEASURE REPRISES, in slow TEMPO and TRIPLE TIME; its place in the CLASSICAL SUITE, as the slowest MOVEMENT, is before the GIGUE.

Sarangi. A bowed LUTE of Northern India, with a pinched waist, skin-covered head, and four MELODY strings and as many as twenty-four SYMPATHETIC strings. Tiny nails are used to STOP the strings from the side, enabling the player to imitate the slides and scoops heard in Indian vocal music.

Sardana. A rapid, rustic dance of Catalonia.

Sarod. An unfretted, plucked Indian LUTE, with a skin head, and usually four MELODY, six DRONE, and fifteen SYMPATHETIC STRINGS.

Sarrusphone. A BRASS WIND INSTRUMENT with a double REED, invented (1863) by and named after the bandmaster Sarrus of Paris.

Satz (Ger., sähtz). A MOVEMENT, as of a SONATA or SYMPHONY.

Saudade (Port., săh-oo-dăh′dē). A Brazilian dance characterized by nostalgia or longing.

Sautillé (Fr., soh-tē-yā′). Technique of STRING playing with a bouncing BOW.

Saxhorn. A BRASS WIND INSTRUMENT invented c. 1840 by Adolphe Sax, a Belgian. It is essentially an improved KEY BUGLE or OPHICLEIDE, having from three to five VALVES instead of KEYS.

Saxophone. A metal WIND INSTRUMENT invented c. 1840 by Adolphe Sax of Belgium, having a CLARINET MOUTHPIECE with a SINGLE REED, the KEY mechanism and fingering also resembling those of the CLARINET. It has a mellow, penetrating tone of veiled quality. The two most prominent saxophones used by JAZZ musicians are the TENOR and ALTO instruments, with some players also using the BARITONE.

Saxotromba. A valve TRUMPET invented by Adolphe Sax of Belgium.

Sbalzato (It., zbăhl-tsah'tŏh). Dashingly, impetuously.

Scale. 1. The series of TONES that form (*a*) any MAJOR or MINOR KEY (DIATONIC scale), or (*b*) the CHROMATIC scale of successive SEMITONIC STEPS. 2. The COMPASS of a voice or instrument; also, the series of tones producible on a WIND INSTRUMENT. 3. In the tubes of wind instruments (especially ORGAN PIPES), the ratio between the width of BORE and length.

Scat singing. A type of JAZZ performance in which a singer improvises nonsense words, frequently quite rapidly to imitate the sounds produced by musical instruments.

Scemando (It., shĕh-măhn'dŏh). DIMINUENDO.

Scena (It., shâ'năh). An accompanied dramatic SOLO, consisting of ARIOSO and RECITATIVE passages, and often ending with an ARIA.

Schalkhaft (Ger., shăhlk'hăft). Roguish, sportive, wanton.

Schallplatte (Ger., shăhl'plăht-tĕ). PHONOGRAPH record.

Schaurig (Ger., show'rĭyh). In a style expressive of (or calculated to inspire) mortal dread; weirdly.

Schelmisch (Ger., shĕl'mish). Joking, roguish.

Scherzhaft (Ger., shârts'hähft). Sportive; jocose, BURLESQUE.

Scherzando (It., skâ**r**-tsähn'dŏh). In a playful, sportive, toying manner; lightly, jestingly.

Scherzo (It., skâr'tsŏh). A joke, jest. 1. An instrumental PIECE of a light, piquant, humorous character. 2. A vivacious MOVEMENT in the SYMPHONY, with strongly marked RHYTHM and sharp and unexpected contrasts in both rhythm and HARMONY; usually the third movement.

Schietto (It., skē-et'tŏh). Simply, quietly; neatly, deftly.

Schlag (Ger., shlăyh). A beat or stroke. *Schlaginstrumente*, PERCUSSION instruments.

Schleppen (Ger., shlep'pen). To drag, retard. *Nicht schleppen*, do not drag.

Schluss (Ger., shlŏŏss). Close, CADENCE; end.

Schlüssel (Ger., shl*ü*sel). CLEF.

Schmachtend (Ger., shmah'tent). Languishing(ly); longing(ly).

Schmeichelnd (Ger., shmī'**yh**elnt). Flatteringly; in a coaxing, caressing manner.

Schmelzend (Ger., shmel'tsĕnt). "Melting," lyrical.

Schmerzlich (Ger., shmârts'lĭyh). Painful(ly), sorrowful(ly), plaintive(ly).

Schmetternd (Ger., shmet'ternt). A term calling for BRASS INSTRUMENTS to be played with a blared or "brassy" TONE.

Schnell (Ger., shnel). Fast, quick, rapid. *Schneller*, faster; *nach und nach schneller*, gradually faster.

Schottische (shot'ish). A round dance in 2/4 TIME, a variety of the POLKA.

Schwächer (Ger., shvĕyh'er). Softer, fainter.

Schwebend (Ger., shvā'bent). Floating, soaring; buoyant(ly); in a lofty, elevated style.

Schwellen (Ger., shvel'len). To SWELL, as in an ORGAN.

Schwellwerk (Ger., shvel'verk). Swell ORGAN.

Schwer (Ger., shvār). Heavy, ponderous; difficult.

Schwermüt(h)ig (Ger., shvār'm*ü*'tĭyh). Sad, melancholy.

Schwindend (Ger., shvin'dent). Dying away, MORENDO.

Schwungvoll (Ger., shvŏŏng**ᵏ**'fohl). Swingingly; buoyantly; with sweep and passion.

Scintillante (It., shin-til-lähn'tĕh). Sparkling, brilliant.

Scioltamente (It., shŏl-tăh-men'tĕh). Freely, fluently, nimbly.

Scivolando (It., shē-vŏh-lähn'dŏh). Same as GLISSANDO, in PIANO playing.

Scoop. Vocal TONES are said to be "scooped" when taken, instead of by a firm and just attack, by a rough and imprecise PORTAMENTO from a lower tone.

Scordatura (It., skŏhr-däh-too'răh). A change in the ordinary TUNING of a STRINGED instrument, to obtain special effects or easier execution.

Score. A systematic arrangement of the vocal or instrumental PARTS of a COMPOSITION on separate STAVES one above the other. *Close* or *compressed score*, a short score; *full* or *orchestral s.*, one in which each vocal and instrumental part has a separate staff; *pianoforte s.*, a piano ARRANGE-MENT of an ORCHESTRAL score, the words of any leading vocal parts being inserted *above* the music without their notes; *open s.*, a full score; *organ s.*, like a pianoforte score, sometimes with a third staff for PEDAL BASS; *short s.*, any abridged arrangement or skeleton TRANSCRIPT; also a four-part vocal score on two staves; *supplementary s.*, one appended to the body of the score when all parts cannot be written on one page; *vocal s.*, that of an A CAPPELLA composition; also the vocal parts written out in full, usually on separate staves, the piano accompani-ment being arranged or compressed (from the full instru-mental score) on two staves below the rest.

Scoring. INSTRUMENTATION, ORCHESTRATION.

Scorrendo (It., skŏhr-ren'dŏh). Fluent, flowing, gliding.

Scotch snap or **catch**. The rhythmic MOTIVE ♪♩. found in many Scottish AIRS.

Scozzese, alla (It. ähl'läh skŏht-tsä'zěh). In Scottish style.

Sdegnoso (It., zdäh-yoh'zŏh). In a style expressing scorn, disdain, wrath, or indignation.

Sdrucciolando (It., zdrŏŏt-chŏh-lähn'dŏh) Sliding, GLIS-SANDO.

Se (It., sā). If. *Se biscogna*, if necessary; *se piace*, if you please.

Sea shanty. A SONG originally sung to accompany work at sea, such as hauling up an achor; now, generically any FOLK SONG associated with sailors.

Sec (Fr., sek). Dry, simple.

Secco (It., sek'kŏh). Dry, simple; not dwelt upon. *Recitativo secco*, one with a simple FIGURED-BASS ACCOMPANIMENT. The plural is *secche*.

Sécheresse, avec (Fr., ăh-vĕk sā-shŭ-ress'). Dryly; without dwelling on or embellishing.

Second. 1. The INTERVAL between two CONJUNCT DEGREES. 2. The ALTO PART or voice. 3. Performing a part lower in PITCH than the first, as second BASS, second VIOLINS. 4. Lower in pitch, as second STRING. 5. Higher; as second line of the STAFF.

Secondary chords. SUBORDINATE CHORDS.

Secondary set. A 12-NOTE SET formed from the second half of a set and the first half of a different form of the same set.

Secondo,-a (It., sĕh-kŏhn'dŏh,-dăh). SECOND; also a SECOND PART or performer in a DUET.

Section. A short DIVISION (one or more PERIODS) of a COMPOSITION, having distinct rhythmic and harmonic boundaries; specifically, half a PHRASE.

Secular music. Music other than that intended for worship and devotional purposes.

Seelenvoll (Ger., zeh'len-fol). Soulfully.

Segno (It., sān'yŏh). A sign. *Al segno*, to the sign; *dal segno*, from the sign; directions to the performer to turn back and repeat from the place marked by the sign ℅ to the word *Fine*, or to a double-BAR with FERMATA (⌒).

Segue (It., sā'gwĕh). 1. Follows; *segue l'aria*, the ARIA follows. 2. SIMILE.

Seguendo (It., sĕh-gwen'dŏh). Following. *Seguendo il canto*, same as COL CANTO, COLLA VOCE, i.e., an instrumental PART that follows exactly the vocal line.

Seguidilla (Sp., sā-gwē-dil'yăh). A Spanish dance in TRIPLE TIME, some varieties being slow, others lively; usually in a MINOR KEY, accompanied by GUITAR, voice, and, at times, CASTANETS.

Sehnsüchtig (Ger., zān'züyh'tīyh). Longingly; in a style expressive of yearning.

Sehr (Ger., zār). Very.

Semibiscroma. SIXTY-FOURTH NOTE in Italian.

Semibreve. A WHOLE NOTE.

Semicroma. SIXTEENTH NOTE in Italian.

Semiminima. QUARTER NOTE in Italian.

Semiquaver. SIXTEENTH NOTE.

Semitone. A half tone; the smallest INTERVAL in the Western SCALE.

Semplice (It., sem'plē-chĕh). In a simple, natural, unaffected style.

Sempre (It., sem'prĕh). Always, continually; throughout.

Sensibile (It., sen-sē'bē-lĕh). Audible; sensitive, as in able to be sensed. *Nota sensibile*, leading-note.

Sensibilità, con (It., kŏhn sen-sē-bē-lē-tah'). With feeling.

Sentence. A PASSAGE of symmetrical rhythmic FORM, generally not over sixteen MEASURES long, and usually ending with a full TONIC CADENCE.

Sentimentale (It., sen-tē-men-tah'lĕh). Feelingly.

Sentito (It., sen-tē'tŏh). With feeling, expression, special emphasis.

Senza (It., sen-tsăh). Without. (Abbreviated *S.*) *Senza di slentare*, without retarding; *s. misura*, "without measure," that is, not in strict time; *s. passione*, without passion, quietly; *s. piatti*, "drum alone" (where one performer plays the CYMBALS and BASS DRUM); *s. rallentare*, without retarding; *s. sordini*, see SORDINO; *s. suono*, "without tone," that is, spoken; *s. tempo*, same as *s. misura*.

Sept The INTERVAL of a SEVENTH.

Sept chord. SEVENTH CHORD.

Septet(te). A concerted COMPOSITION for seven voices or instruments.

Septole (Ger., sep-toh'lĕ). A SEPTUPLET.

Septuor (Fr., sep-tü-ohr'). A SEPTET.

Septuplet. A group of seven equal NOTES to be performed in the time of four or six of the same kind in the established RHYTHM.

Sequence. 1. The repetition, at different PITCH levels and more than twice in succession, of a MELODIC MOTIVE. 2. In the Romantic Catholic Church, a kind of HYMN. 3. A string of digital information created by a SEQUENCER.

Sequencer. An electronic device that supplies a sequence of determined voltages in sound synthesis or processing; commonly used to record short melodic or rhythmic patterns, which are then "played back" in a repeating loop through a SYNTHESIZER or other device. DRUM MACHINES often feature built-in sequencers, because RHYTHM patterns tend to repeat through popular SONGS.

Serenade. 1. An "evening SONG"; especially such a song sung by a lover before his lady's window. 2. An instrumental COMPOSITION imitating the above in style.

Serenata (It., sĕh-rĕh-nah'tăh). 1. A species of dramatic CANTATA in vogue during the 18th century. 2. An instrumental COMPOSITION midway between a SUITE and a SYMPHONY, but freer in FORM than either, having five, six, or more MOVEMENTS, and in CHAMBER MUSIC style. 3. See SERENADE.

Sereno (It., seh-rā'nŏh). In a serene, tranquil style.

Serial music. Modern technique of composition in which all thematic materials are derived from a series of twelve different NOTES of the CHROMATIC SCALE, graduated DYNAMICS, a set of different RHYTHMS, and different instrumental TIMBRES. Serial music represents an expansion of the 12-TONE METHOD of composition into the domain of note values, dynamics, and instrumental timbres.

Series. The ordering of PITCH CLASSES or other elements. See SET.

Serietà, con (It., kŏhn seh-rē-ĕh'tah'). Seriously.

Serio,-a (It., sâ'rē-ŏh,-ăh). Serious. *Opera seria*, grand or tragic OPERA; *tenore serio*, dramatic TENOR.

Serioso (It., seh-rē-oh'sŏh). In a serious, grave, impressive style.

Serpent. 1. A BASS WIND INSTRUMENT invented by Canon Guillaume of Auxerre in 1590 (now nearly obsolete). 2. In the ORGAN, a REED STOP.

Serré (Fr., seh-rā', "pressed"). Playing faster and with more excitement.

Sesquialtera (It., sĕs-kwē-ahl'tĕ-rah). In the ORGAN, either a mutation STOP a FIFTH above the FUNDAMENTAL TONE, or (usually) a compound stop of from two to five RANKS.

Sestet; Sestetto (It., ses-tet'tŏh). A SEXTET.

Sestole, Sestolet. A SEXTUPLET.

Set. A term adopted from mathematical set theory to denote a grouping of PITCH CLASSES or other musical elements; normally refers to a 12-NOTE SET containing all pitch classes within the EQUAL TEMPERED system but may also refer to elements indicating DURATION, time points, and/or DYNAMIC levels.

Settimino (It., set-tē-mē'nŏh). A SEPTET.

Seventeenth. 1. INTERVAL of two OCTAVES plus a THIRD. 2. Same as TIERCE (ORGAN STOP).

Seventh chord. A CHORD of the SEVENTH, composed of a ROOT with its THIRD, FIFTH, and seventh.

Severo (It., sĕh-vâ'rŏh). Strictly, with rigid observance of TEMPO and EXPRESSION MARKS.

Sext. 1. The INTERVAL of a SIXTH. 2. The office of the fourth Canonical Hour. 3. A compound ORGAN STOP of two RANKS (a 12th and a 17th) a sixth apart.

Sextet. A concerted COMPOSITION for six voices or instruments, or for six OBBLIGATO voices with instrumental ACCOMPANIMENT.

Sextole, Sextolet. A SEXTUPLET.

Sextuplet. A group of six equal NOTES to be performed in the time of four of the same kind in the established RHYTHM. In the *true* sextuplet, the first, third, and fifth notes are accented; the *false* sextuplet is simply a double TRIPLET.

Sfogato (It., sfŏh-gah'tŏh). "Exhaled"; a direction in vocal music to sing lightly and airily. *Soprano sfogato*, a high soprano voice.

Sforzando, Sforzato (It., sfŏhr-tsăhn'dŏh, sfŏhr-tsah'tŏh). (Written *sfz, sf,* > ∧ 𝆏.) A direction to perform the TONE or CHORD with special stress, or marked and sudden emphasis.

Sfumate, Sfumato (It., sfŏŏ-mah'tĕh, sfŏŏ-mah'tŏh). Very-lightly, like a vanishing smoke-wreath.

Shading. 1. In the interpretation of a COMPOSITION, the combination and alternation of any or all the varying degrees of TONE power between FORTISSIMO and PIANISSIMO, for obtaining artistic effect. 2. The placing of anything so near the top of an ORGAN PIPE as to affect the vibrating column of air within.

Shake. A TRILL. *Shaked graces*, the shaked beat, backfall, ca-
dent, and elevation, and the double relish (all obsolete).

Shakuhachi. A Japanese end-blown bamboo FLUTE, with a
breathy, low tone.

Shamisen. A Japanese long-necked plucked LUTE, with a skin
head and three silk STRINGS.

Shanty. A characteristic SONG of the English working class
in olden times; the word comes from the French *chanter*,
"to sing."

Sharp. The character ♯, which raises the PITCH of the NOTE
before which it is set by a SEMITONE; the *double sharp*, ✕,
raises the note by two semitones.

Sharp (*adjective*). 1. (Of TONES or instruments) Too high in
PITCH. 2. (Of INTERVALS) MAJOR or AUGMENTED. 3. (Of KEYS)
Having a SHARP or sharps in the KEY SIGNATURE. 4. (Of
ORGAN STOPS) Shrill. 5. (Of DIGITALS; *plural*) The black
keys; or any white key a SEMITONE above another (i.e.,
f and *e*).

Shawm. A medieval high-pitched WIND INSTRUMENT, with a
double-REED; an ancestor of the OBOE.

Sheng. A Chinese mouth ORGAN, with several PIPES, each containing a FREE REED, ascending from an air chamber at
the base. The Japanese version of this instrument is called
the SHŌ.

Shift. In playing the VIOLIN, etc., a change by the left hand
from the first POSITION; the second position is called the
half-shift, the third the *whole shift*, and the fourth the
double shift. When out of the first position, the player is
said to be "on the shift," and *shifting up* or *down*, as the
case may be.

Shimmy. An American dance that emphasizes movement of
the upper torso, in quick RAGTIME RHYTHM.

Shō. A Japanese free-reed mouth ORGAN, with continuous sound production possible through both inhalation and exhalation. The Chinese version of this instrument is called the SHENG.

Shofar. An ancient Jewish ritual TRUMPET, made from a ram's HORN.

Si (It., sē). 1. The seventh SOLMISATION syllable. 2. One; it. *Si leva il sordino*, take off the MUTE; *si levano i sordini*, take off the mutes; *si piace*, *si libet*, at pleasure; *si replica*, repeat; *si segue*, proceed; *si tace*, be silent; *si volta*, turn over; *si ha s'immaginar la battuta di 6/8*, imagine the TIME to be 6/8.

Siciliana (It., sē-chē-lē-ah'năh); **Sicilienne** (Fr., sē-sē-l'yen'). Dance of the Sicilian peasants; a kind of PASTORALE in moderately slow TEMPO and 6/8 or 12/8 TIME, frequently in a MINOR KEY. *Alla siciliana*, in the style of the above.

Side drum. The most commonly used DRUM in symphonic BANDS and SCORES; also called SNARE DRUM.

Sight reading. An ability to read unfamiliar music with ease. In singing, it is synonymous with SOLFEGGIO. All professional instrumentalists and vocalists must be able to read at sight as a matter of routine, but there are some extraordinary pianists (in particular) who can play complicated works with great precision and fluency at sight.

Signal horn. A BUGLE.

Signature. The signs set at the head of the STAFF at the beginning of a PIECE or MOVEMENT. *Key signature*, the CHROMATIC SIGN or signs (SHARPS or FLATS); *time s.*, the figures or signs indicating the MEASURE.

Silence. Literally, the absence of sound; in the 20th century, introduced (most conspicuously in Cage's notoriously tacit *4'33''* of 1952) as a viable element of music.

Silenzio (It., sē-len′tsē-ŏh). Silence. *Lurgo silenzio*, a long pause.

Similar motion. Motion of voices in the same direction, as distinguished from CONTRARY MOTION.

Simile (It., sē′mē-lĕh). Similarly; a direction to perform the following MEASURES or PASSAGES in the same style as the preceding. *Simile mark,* 𝄇 or 𝄇 , means that a measure or group of NOTES must be repeated.

Simple. (Of METERS, TONES, or INTERVALS) Not COMPOUND. (Of COUNTERPOINT, IMITATION, RHYTHM, etc.) Not compound or complex; undeveloped, not varied.

Simplement (Fr., sân-pl⁽ᵘ⁾-măhn′). Simply, *semplice*.

Simultaneity. Refers to the simultaneous sounding of multiple TONES, as in a CHORD, but without reference to DIATONIC or HARMONIC function.

Sine tone or **wave**. The sound (and its visual correlate) of one pure FREQUENCY.

Sinfonia (It., sin-fŏh-nē′ăh). 1. A SYMPHONY. 2. An OPERA OVERTURE.

Sinfonie (Ger., sin-fŏh′nē′). SYMPHONY.

Sinfonietta (It., sin-fŏh-nē-ĕt′ah). A small SYMPHONY, sometimes for a CHAMBER ORCHESTRA.

Singbar (Ger., zingᵏ′bar). Singable; CANTABILE. *Sehr singbar vorzutragen*, perform in a very singing style.

Singend (Ger., zing′ent). Singing, melodious, CANTABILE.

Singhiozzando (It., sin-g′yŏht-tsähn′dŏh). Sobbing; catching the breath.

Single reed. A thin piece of cane that beats against the edge of a MOUTHPIECE, as on the CLARINET or SAXOPHONE.

Singspiel (Ger., zing^(k')shpēl). A type of German OPERA established during the 18th century; usually light, and characterized by spoken INTERLUDES.

Singstimme (Ger., zing^(k')shtim'mě). The singing voice; the voice.

Sinistra (It., sĕ-nĭ'sträh). Left. *Mano sinistra (m.s.),* left hand; *colla s.,* with the left hand.

Sino (It., sē'nŏh). To, up to, as far as, until. *Sino* (or *sin'*) *al fine,* to the end.

Sistrum. An ancient instrument that was used in Egyptian religious ritual; it had a semicircular metal frame with CROSSBARS overhung with tinkling rings.

Sitar. A popular Indian STRINGED INSTRUMENT with a gourd bowl BODY and movable metal FRETS, plucked with a PLECTRUM. SYMPATHETIC STRINGS run through the NECK of the instrument, in addition to the MELODY and DRONE (unfretted) strings that are located above the FINGER-BOARD.

Six chord. First INVERSION of a TRIAD.

Sixteenth note. A NOTE with one-half of the TIME VALUE of an EIGHTH NOTE.

Sixth. INTERVAL containing six DIATONIC DEGREES.

Sixty-fourth note. A NOTE with one-half the TIME VALUE of a THIRTY-SECOND NOTE; commonly, the shortest duration in Western music.

Six-four chord. Second INVERSION of a TRIAD.

Skip. MELODIC PROGRESSION by an INTERVAL wider than a SECOND; DISJUNCT progression.

Slam dancing. A PUNK ROCK ritual, in which audience members dance in a spasmodic fashion, slamming or running into each other for added effect. Also called *moshing* (a *mosh pit* being an area where this behavior can occur). See also STAGE DIVING.

Slanciante (It., zlăhn-chăhn'tĕh). "Thrown off," either lightly and deftly or with force and vehemence.

Slancio, con (It., kŏhn zlăhn'chŏh). With dash, vehemence; impetuously. (Often *con islancio*.)

Slancio, di (It.). The direct and "hammer-like" attack of a higher or lower TONE, contrasted with the "carry" of the PORTAMENTO. (Also *di posto*.)

Slargando (It., zlar-găhn'dŏh) or **Slentando** (It., zlen-tăn'-dŏh). Growing slower.

Slide. 1. The movable U-shaped tube in the TROMBONE, etc., used to vary the instrument's PITCH. 2. In the ORGAN, a SLIDER. 3. Three or four swiftly ascending or descending SCALE TONES. 4. On a VIOLIN BOW, that part of the NUT that slides along the stick. 5. To move from one TONE to another as in a GLISSANDO.

Slide horn, trombone, or **trumpet**. One played by the use of a SLIDE instead of KEYS or VALVES.

Slider. A board or plank that lies under a RANK of ORGAN PIPES that is moved sideways by opening a STOP, thus allowing the pipes to sound.

Slur. A curved line under or over two or more NOTES, signifying that they are to be played LEGATO. In vocal music, the slur unites notes to be sung in one breath; the notes so sung are called a *slur*.

Slurred melody. One in which two or more TONES are sung to one syllable; as opposed to *syllabic* melody.

Small octave. See "Table of Clefs," p. xii.

Small orchestra. The usual ORCHESTRA minus the TROMBONES, two HORNS, and perhaps the CLARINETS and KETTLEDRUMS.

Smaniante (It., zmăh-nē-ăhn'tĕh). In an impetuous, passionate style.

Sminuendo (It., zmē-nŏŏ-en'dŏh). DIMINUENDO.

Sminuito (It., zmē-nŏŏ-ē'tŏh). More softly.

Smorendo (It., zmoh-ren'dŏh). Dying away.

Smorfioso (It., zmohr-fē-oh'sŏh). With affected expression.

Smorzando (It., zmohr-tsăhn'dŏh). Dying away.

Snare drum. A SIDE DRUM, across the lower head of which are stretched several METAL STRINGS, the "snares," whose jarring against the head reinforces the tone.

Soave (It., sŏh-ah'vĕh). Suave(ly), sweet(ly), soft(ly), flowing(ly).

Socialist Realism. The official Soviet aesthetic espoused in 1932 addressing the artist's responsibility to emphasize a real world inclined toward a socialist future.

Soffocato (It., sŏhf-fŏh-kah'tŏh). Muffled, damped; choked.

Soft pedal. The left PEDAL on the PIANO reducing the sound by shifting the KEYBOARD so that only two of the three STRINGS in the middle REGISTER of the piano are struck by the HAMMERS.

Soggetto (It., sŏhd-jet'tŏh). SUBJECT; THEME.

Sognando (It., sŏhn-yăhn'dŏh). Dreaming, dreamily.

Soh. Stands for SOL, in TONIC SOL-FA.

Sol (It., sôl). The fifth of the ARETINIAN SYLLABLES; also, the note *G* in France, Italy, etc.

Solenne (It., sŏh-len'nĕh). Solemn, solemnly, with solemnity, in a lofty style.

Sol-fa. 1. To sing SOLFEGGI, especially to the SOLMISATION syllables. 2. Solmisation, and the syllables sung in it.

Solfeggio (It., sŏhl-fed'jŏh; pl. **solfeggi** [-jē]). A vocal exercise either on one vowel, on the SOLMISATION syllables, or to words.

Solito (It., sô'lē-tŏh). Accustomed, habitual. *Al solito*, as usual.

Solmisation. A method of teaching the SCALES and INTERVALS by syllables, ascribed to Guido d'Arezzo. It was based on the HEXACHORD, or SIX-TONE SCALE; the first six tones of the MAJOR scale, *c d e f g a*, were named *ut, re, mi, fa, sol, la*. The seventh syllable *si*, for the LEADING TONE, was added during the 17th century; about the same time, the name *ut* for *C* was changed to *do*, except in France.

Solo (It., soh'loh; pl. **soli** [soh'li]). Alone. A PIECE or PASSAGE for a single voice or instrument, or one in which one voice or instrument predominates. In orchestral scores, it marks a passage where one instrument takes a leading part. In a two-hand arrangement of a PIANO CONCERTO, *Solo* marks the entrances of the solo pianoforte. *Violino solo* means either "VIOLIN alone" or "first violin" (accompanied).

Solo pitch. SCORDATURA.

Solo quartet. 1. A QUARTET consisting of four singers (four "solo voices"). 2. A PIECE or PASSAGE in four parts for four singers. 3. A nonconcerted piece for four instruments, one of which has a leading PART.

Sombre (Fr., sŏhn'br). Dark, veiled, obscure.

Sommesso,-a (It., sŏhm-mes'sŏh,-säh). Subdued.

Sommo,-a (It., sŏhm'mŏh,-mäh). Utmost, highest, greatest, extreme. *Con sommo espressione*, with intense feeling.

Son (Fr., sŏhn). Sound; TONE.

Sonabile (It., sŏh-nah'bē-lĕh). Sounding, resounding, sonorous, resonant.

Sonata (It., sŏh-nah'tăh). An instrumental COMPOSITION in three or four extended MOVEMENTS contrasted in THEME, TEMPO, and mood; usually for a solo instrument or CHAMBER ENSEMBLE.

Sonata-concerto form. A combination of the SONATA FORM with the RITORNELLO procedure.

Sonata form. This is the procedure usually used for first movements of classical SYMPHONIES, SONATAS, and CHAMBER works; it may be used for other movements as well; a TERNARY FORM, with EXPOSITION, DEVELOPMENT, and RECAPITULATION. Also known as *sonata allegro form* and *first movement form*.

Sonatina (It., sŏh-năh-tē'năh); **Sonatine** (Fr., sŏh-năh-tēn'); **Sonatine** (Ger., sŏh-năh-tē'nĕ). A short SONATA in two or three (rarely four) MOVEMENTS, the first in the characteristic first-movement, i.e., sonata, form, abbreviated.

Sonevole (It., sŏh-nā'vŏh-lĕh). Sonorous, resounding.

Song. A short poem with a musical setting characterized by a structure in simple PERIODS. There are FOLK SONGS and ART SONGS; the latter may be either *strophic* (each strophe sung to the same tune, with a change at most in the final one), or *progressively* (or *through*) *composed* (each strophe sung to different music).

Song form. A form of COMPOSITION, either vocal or instrumental, that has three SECTIONS and two THEMES, the second (contrasting) occupying the second section.

Sono (It., sô'nŏh). Sound; TONE.

Sonoro,-a (It., sŏh-nô'rŏh,-răh; plural, *sonore* [-rĕh]). Sonorously, resoundingly, resonantly, ringingly.

Sopra (It., soh'prah). On, upon; above, over; higher. In PIANO music, *sopra* written in the PART for either hand means that that hand is to play (reach) *over* the other. *Sopra una corda*, on one STRING; *come s.*, as above; *nella parte di s.*, in the higher (or highest) part.

Sopran (Ger., sŏh-**prahn**'). SOPRANO.

Sopranino (It., sŏh-prah-nee'nŏh). "Little SOPRANO"; the highest PITCH of the soprano REGISTER, as in sopranino SAXOPHONES and RECORDERS.

Soprano (It., sŏh-**prah**'nŏh). The highest class of the human voice; the female soprano, or *treble*, has a normal COMPASS from c^1 to a^2; solo voices often reach above c^3, some as high as c^4. *Soprano clef*, the C CLEF on the first line; *s. drammatico*, *s. giusto*, a female soprano of dramatic power; *s. leggiero*, a light soprano; *s. sfogato*, see SFOGATO; *s. string*, the E STRING on the VIOLIN.

Sordamente (It., sŏh**r**-dăh-men'tĕh). With a veiled, muffled tone.

Sordino (It., sŏh**r**-dē'nŏh; plural, *sordini*). 1. A MUTE; *con sordini*, with the mutes; *senza sordini*, without the mutes; *si levano i sordini*, take off the mutes. 2. DAMPER (of the PIANO); *senza sordini*, with damper pedal; so used by Beethoven, who wrote *con sordini* to express the release (raising) of the damper pedal, instead of ✻.

Sortita (It., sŏh**r**-tē'tăh). 1. A closing VOLUNTARY. 2. The first NUMBER sung by any leading character in an OPERA. An *Aria di sortita* is, however, also an AIR at the conclusion of which the singer makes his or her exit.

Sospirando (It., sŏh-spē-**r**ăhn'dŏh). Sighing, sobbing; catching the breath.

Sospiroso (It., sŏh-spē-**r**oh'sŏh). Sighing deeply; plaintive, mournful.

Sostenuto (It., sŏh-stĕh-noo'tŏh). Sustained, prolonged. Standing alone, as a TEMPO-mark, it is much the same as ANDANTE CANTABILE; it may also imply A TENUTO, or a uniform rate of decreased speed. *Più sostenuto* is much the same as MENO MOSSO. *Sostenuto pedal*, sustaining PEDAL.

Sotto (It., sŏht'tŏh). Below, under. In PIANO music, *sotto* written in the PART for either hand means that that hand is to play (reach) *under* the other. *Sottovoce* (or *sotto voce*), in an undertone, aside, under the breath.

Soubrette (Fr., soo-bret'). In comedy and comedy OPERA, a maidservant or lady's maid of an intriguing and coquettish character; also applied to various light roles of similar type.

Soul. A style of black RHYTHM AND BLUES, featuring intense gospel-influenced singing.

Sound. A noise of any kind. The word is often inexactly used instead of TONE (musical tone).

Soundboard. The thin plate of wood placed below or behind the STRINGS of various instruments to reinforce and prolong their TONES. In the ORGAN, the cover of the windchest.

Sound bow. The thick rim of a BELL, against which the clapper strikes.

Soundbox. The BODY of a STRINGED INSTRUMENT that amplifies its sound.

Sound hole. A hole cut in the BELLY of a STRINGED INSTRUMENT, believed to improve the projection and quality of the instrument's tone.

Soundpost. In the VIOLIN, etc., the small cylindrical wooden prop set inside the BODY, between BELLY and back, just behind (nearly beneath) the treble foot of the BRIDGE.

Sourdine (Fr., soor-dēn'). An HARMONIUM STOP which partially cuts off the wind supply, so that full CHORDS can be played softly. Also, see SORDINO.

Sousaphone. A spiral type of BASS TUBA, which is coiled around the player, with a large bell turned forwards; named after Sousa, the "March King," who used it often in his bands.

Soutenu (Fr., soo-tĕh-nü'). Held or sustained.

Space. In the STAFF, the INTERVAL between two lines or LEDGER lines.

Space (or **Spatial**) **music**. A modern development of performance, in which the placement of musicians and singers is considered as essential to the composition itself; in some modern works, the players are positioned at far distances from one another.

Spasshaft (Ger., shpahs'hähft). SCHERZANDO.

Spianato,-a (It., sp'yăh-nah'tŏh,-täh). Smooth, even, tranquil.

Spiccato (It., spik-kah'toh). Sharp STACCATO. See SPRINGING BOW.

Spigliatezza (It., spēl-yăh-tet'säh). Agility, dexterity.

Spinet (spin'et or spī-net'). An obsolete KEYBOARD stringed instrument like a HARPSICHORD, but smaller.

Spinto (It., spin'toh). Compelled, intense; applied to a high voice in expressive, emotional OPERA parts.

Spirito, con (It., kŏhn spē'rē-tŏh). Spiritedly; with spirit, animation, energy.

Spiritual. A religious SONG, originally cultivated by black slaves in the South. Generically, a folk HYMN from the African-American tradition.

Spitze (Ger., shpit-sĕ). 1. Point (of the BOW). 2. Toe (in ORGAN playing).

Spitzig (Ger., shpit-ziyh). Sharp, pointed.

Sprechgesang (Ger., shpreh'gĕsang^k). SPRECHSTIMME.

Sprechstimme (Ger., shpreh'shtim-meh). Literally, "speech song"; a type of inflected vocal delivery, with PITCHES indicated only approximately on the music STAFF. This is a modern technique often used in contemporary OPERA and SONG CYCLES.

Springing bow. In VIOLIN playing, a style of bowing in which the BOW is allowed to drop on the STRING, making it rebound and quit the string between each two NOTES. There are two varieties: (1) the *Spiccato*, indicated by dots over the notes, and played near the middle of the bow with a loose wrist, for rapid PASSAGES in equal notes, employing the wrist stroke throughout for each detached note; and (2) the *Saltato*, with a longer fall and higher rebound, generally employed when several equal STAC-CATO notes are to be taken in one bow.

Square dance. A parlor or COUNTRY DANCE, such as a QUAD-RILLE, performed by several couples in a square formation.

Square time. A popular term for 4/4 time; MARCH TIME.

Squillante (It., skwil-lähn'tĕh). Ringing, tinkling; piercing.

Stabat Mater (L., stäh'bäht mäh'tĕr). A Latin SEQUENCE on the Crucifixion sung in the Roman Catholic liturgy.

Stabile (It., stah'bē-lĕh). Steady, firm.

Staccato (It., stăhk-kah'tŏh). Detached, separated; a style in which the NOTES played or sung are more or less abruptly disconnected. See also SPRINGING BOW.

Staccato mark. A dot ( ) or wedge-shaped stroke ( ) over a NOTE, the former indicating a less abrupt *staccato* than the latter; the *mezzo-staccato* is indicated by dotted notes under a SLUR.

Staff. The five parallel lines used in modern NOTATION; PLAINCHANT uses only four. *Staff notation*, the staff and all musical signs connected with it; *grand* or *great s.*, comprised of eleven lines, with middle *C* occupying the (middle) sixth. The plural form is *staves*.

Stage diving. Associated with PUNK ROCK, this practice involves audience members jumping onto the edge of the stage, and then diving back into the assembled throng. See also SLAM DANCING.

Stanchezza, con (It., kŏhn stăhn-ket'săh). Wearily, draggingly.

Ständchen (Ger., shtän'yhĕn). SERENADE.

Stanza. A symmetric unit of a SONG.

Stark (Ger., shtark). Loud, forcible; FORTE.

Stärker (Ger., shtâr'ker). Louder, stronger; *più FORTE*.

Steam organ. The CALLIOPE.

Steel drums. Popular in the Caribbean islands, these PERCUSSION INSTRUMENTS are made out of the tops of large oil drums. Indentations made in the drums allow the player to play different NOTES, and by striking in more than one spot at once, HARMONIES. Commonly heard on streetcorners in major, urban American cities, as well as on the concert stage.

Steg (Ger., shteg). The BRIDGE on STRINGED INSTRUMENTS. *Am steg*, bowing near the BRIDGE.

Stem. The vertical line attached to a NOTE head.

Stendando (It., sten-tăhn'dŏh). Delaying, retarding, dragging.

Step. A MELODIC PROGRESSION of a SECOND; also, a DEGREE. *Chromatic step*, progression of a CHROMATIC second; *diatonic s.*, progression between neighboring tones of any DIATONIC SCALE; *half s.*, step of a SEMITONE; *whole s.*, step of a WHOLE TONE.

Sterbend (Ger., shtâr'bent). Dying; MORENDO.

Stereophonic. Two-channel sound reproduction to create a more "realistic" sound. Compare MONOPHONIC.

Stesso (It., stes'sŏh). The same. *Lo stesso* (or *l'istesso*) *movimento*, the same movement.

Stil (Ger., shtēl); **Stile** (It., stē'lĕh). Style. *Stile osservato*, strict style, especially of pure vocal music; *s. rappresentativo*, dramatic MONODIC SONG with instrumental accompaniment in CHORDS; the kind of operatic RECITATIVE originating towards the close of the 16th century.

Stillgedackt (Ger., shtil'gĕ-dähkt'). A soft-toned stopped ORGAN REGISTER.

Stimme (Ger., shtim'mĕ). 1. VOICE. 2. PART; *mit der Stimme*, COLLA PARTE. 3. ORGAN STOP. 4. SOUNDPOST.

Stimmung (Ger., shtim'mŏŏng^k). 1. TUNING, ACCORDATURA. *Stimmung halten*, to keep in tune. 2. PITCH; a mood, frame of mind. *Stimmungsbild*, a "mood-picture," a short, characteristic PIECE.

Stinguendo (It., stin-gwen'dŏh). Dying away.

Stirato (It., stē-**r**ah'tŏh). Dragging, delaying.

Stiriana (It., stē-rē-ah'näh). STYRIENNE.

Stochastic (From Greek "stochos" = goal). A term borrowed from probability theory and denoting a modern compositional process that is governed by rules of probability.

Stop. 1. That part of the ORGAN mechanism that admits and "stops" the flow of wind to the grooves beneath the PIPES. 2. A set or row of organ pipes of like character, arranged in graduated succession. These are called *speaking* or *sounding* stops, classed as *flue* (having flue pipes) and *reed* (having reed pipes) work. 3. (*a*) On the VIOLIN, etc., the pressure of a finger on a STRING, to vary the latter's PITCH; a *double stop* is when two or more strings are so pressed and sounded simultaneously; (*b*) on WIND INSTRU-

MENTS with finger-holes, the closing of a hole by finger or key to alter the pitch; (*c*) on wind instruments of the TRUMPET family, the partial closing of the BELL by inserting the hand.

Stopped notes. 1. On STRINGED INSTRUMENTS, pressing a finger down on the STRING to shorten its vibrating length, thus raising its PITCH. 2. TONES obtained by stopping; opposed to *open*.

Stopped pipes. ORGAN PIPES closed (plugged or covered) at the top; opposed to *open*.

Straccicalando (It., străht-chē-căh-lăhn'dŏh). Babbling, prattling.

Strain. In general, a SONG, TUNE, AIR, MELODY; also, some well-defined PASSAGE in, or part of, a PIECE. Technically, a PERIOD, SENTENCE, or short DIVISION of a COMPOSITION; a MOTIVE or THEME.

Strappare (It., străhp-pah'rĕh). To pluck off; in PIANO playing, to throw off a NOTE or CHORD by a rapid, light turn of the wrist.

Strascinando (It., străh-shē-năhn'dŏh). Dragging, drawling. *Strascinando l'arco*, drawing the BOW so as to bind the NOTES.

Strascinare la voce (It., străh-shē-nah'rĕh lăh voh'chĕh). To sing a PORTAMENTO with exaggerated dragging or drawling.

Strathspey (strath-spay'). A lively Scottish dance, somewhat slower than the REEL, and also in 4/4 TIME, but progressing in dotted EIGHTH NOTES alternating with SIXTEENTH NOTES, the latter often preceding the former (see SCOTCH SNAP).

Stravagante (It., străh-văh-găhn'tĕh). Extravagant, fantastic, whimsical.

Streichinstrumente (Ger., shtriyh'in-stroo-men'tĕ). Bowed instruments.

Streng (Ger., shtreng^k). Severe(ly), strict(ly).

Strepitoso (It., strĕh-pē-toh'sŏh). In a noisy, boisterous, impetuous style.

Stretch. On a KEYBOARD instrument, a wide INTERVAL or spread CHORD whose TONES are to be taken simultaneously by the fingers of one hand.

Stretta (It., stret'tăh). A closing PASSAGE (CODA) in swifter TEMPO than the one preceding. *Alla stretta*, in the style of a stretta.

Strette (Fr., stret). A STRETTO.

Stresttissimo (It., stret-tis'sē-mŏh). Very hurriedly.

Stretto (It., stret'tŏh). A division of a FUGUE (usually a final DEVELOPMENT, for the sake of effect) in which SUBJECT and ANSWER follow in such close succession as to overlap.

Stretto,-a (It., stret'tŏh,-tăh). Pressed together, narrowed; hurried. *Andante stretto*, same as ANDANTE AGITATO; *stretto pedale*, the quick, deft shifting of the loud PIANO PEDAL, in a strongly marked CHORD PASSAGE, so that the HARMONIES may be at once forcible and distinct.

Strict style. A style of COMPOSITION in which DISSONANCES are regularly prepared and resolved.

Stridente (It., strē-den'tĕh). Strident; rough, harsh; MARTELLATO.

String. A tone-producing cord. *First string*, the highest of a set; *open s.*, one not stopped or shortened; *silver s.*, one covered with silver wire; *soprano s.*, the E string of the VIOLIN; *the Strings*, the string group in the ORCHESTRA.

String drum. An instrument more familiarly known as a "lion's roar" (Ger., *Löwenebrull*; It., *rugghio di leone*;

Fr., *tambour à cordes*); a friction DRUM with a cylindrical-shaped bucket through which a length of cord or GUT STRING is pulled to produce a distinct "roaring" sound.

Stringed instruments. All instruments whose tones are produced by strings, whether struck, plucked, or bowed. See also CHORDOPHONE.

Stringendo (It., strin-jen'dŏh). Hastening, accelerating the movement, usually suddenly and rapidly, with a CRESCENDO.

Stringere (It., strin'jĕh'rĕh). To hasten. *Senza stringere*, without hastening.

String piano. A traditional PIANO which is sounded by the player's acting directly upon the strings, i.e., strumming, plucking, hammering, etc.

String trio. A COMPOSITION for three STRINGED INSTRUMENTS; in the CLASSICAL period, usually (*a*) two VIOLINS and CELLO, or (*b*) VIOLIN, VIOLA, and CELLO; in the RENAISSANCE and BAROQUE periods, this INSTRUMENTATION might also include a CONTINUO PART.

String quartet. A COMPOSITION for four STRINGED INSTRUMENTS, usually first and second VIOLINS, VIOLA, and CELLO. Also, the string group in the ORCHESTRA.

String quintet. A COMPOSITION for five STRINGED INSTRUMENTS; INSTRUMENTATION may be (*a*) two VIOLINS, two VIOLAS, and CELLO, (*b*) two violins, one viola, and two celli, or (*c*) two violins, viola, cello, and DOUBLE BASS. Also, the string group in the ORCHESTRA.

Stringy. Having the quality of TONE peculiar to bowed instruments.

Strisciando (It., strē-shăhn'dŏh). Gliding, smooth, LEGATO.

Strophe. Literally, a "turn" in Greek; a break in the continuity of a SONG, leading to a new SECTION, but preserving the unity of RHYTHM and musical setting.

Strophic composition. See SONG.

Structure. Denoting the methods and mechanisms, often forming a system, giving rise to the ultimate structural integrity of a work; indication, particularly noticeable in the 20th century, of the composer's concern for rational control and structural "meaning" in a given piece.

Strumento (It., stru-mĕn'tŏh). Italian word for instruments.

Stück (Ger., shtük). A PIECE; a NUMBER.

Study. An ÉTUDE, a teaching piece.

Stürmisch (Ger., shtür'mish). Stormy, passionate, impetuous.

Sturm und Drang (Ger., shtoorm ŏŏnt drahng). Literally, "storm and stress"; a literary term borrowed by music theorists and critics to describe a highly emotional MINOR KEY style of composition that emerged during the early CLASSICAL period, in the 1770s, particularly in Germany.

Style galant (Fr., stēl ga-lähn'). "Elegant" style of composition, emphasizing entertainment value, popular in the second half of the 18th century in France and elsewhere.

Styrienne (Fr., stē-rē-enn'). An AIR in slow movement and 2/4 TIME, often in a MINOR KEY, with a Jodler (YODEL) after each verse; for vocal or instrumental solo.

Su (It., soo). On, upon, by, near. *Arco in su*, UP-BOW.

Suave (It., sŏŏ-ah'vĕh). SOAVE.

Subbass, Subbourdon. An ORGAN STOP of 16' or 32' PITCH, generally on the PEDAL, and STOPPED.

Subdominant. The TONE just below the DOMINANT in a DIATONIC SCALE; the FOURTH DEGREE.

Subito (It., soo'bē-tŏh). Suddenly, without pause. *Volti subito*, turn over (the page) quickly; *p subito* (after *f*), an abrupt change to PIANO, without gradation.

Subject. A MELODIC MOTIVE or PHRASE upon which a COMPOSITION or MOVEMENT is founded; a THEME.

Submediant. The third SCALE TONE below the TONIC; the sixth DEGREE.

Suboctave. 1. The OCTAVE below a given NOTE. 2. The double CONTRA-OCTAVE.

Subordinate chords. CHORDS not FUNDAMENTAL or PRINCIPAL; the TRIADS built on the second, third, sixth, and seventh SCALE DEGREES, and all seventh chords but the DOMINANT SEVENTH.

Subprincipal. A subbass ORGAN PEDAL STOP of 32′ PITCH.

Substitution. In CONTRAPUNTAL PROGRESSION, the RESOLUTION or PREPARATION of a DISSONANCE by substituting, for the regular TONE of resolution or preparation, its higher or lower OCTAVE in some other part.

Subtonic. The LEADING TONE.

Suffocato (It., sŏŏf-fŏh-kah′tŏh). SOFFOCATO.

Sugli, Sui (It., sool′yē, soo′ē). On the; near the.

Suite (Fr., süē′t′). A set or series of PIECES in various (idealized) dance forms. The earlier suites have four chief divisions: ALLEMANDE, COURANTE, SARABAND, and GIGUE; other forms introduced at will (*intermezzi*) are the BOURRÉE, BRANLE, GAVOTTE, MINUET, MUSETTE, PASSEPIED, LOURE, PAVANE, etc., often before the concluding *Gigue*. Also referred to as CLASSICAL SUITE, or BAROQUE SUITE; the modern orchestral suite is more like a DIVERTIMENTO.

Suivez (Fr., süē-vā′). 1. Same as COLLA PARTE. 2. "Continue," "go on."

Sul, sull', sulla, sulle (It.). On the, near the. *Sulla corda La*, on the A STRING; *Sulla tastiera*, near or by the FINGERBOARD; *sul ponticello*, near the BRIDGE.

Suonare (It., sŏŏ-ô-näh′rĕh). Early form of the verb *sonare*, "to sound," "to play."

Superbamente (It., sŏŏ-pâr′bäh-men′tĕh). Proudly, loftily.

Superdominant. The sixth DEGREE of a DIATONIC SCALE.

Superfluous. AUGMENTED.

Superoctave. 1. An ORGAN STOP of 2′ PITCH. 2. A COUPLER bringing into action KEYS an OCTAVE above those struck, either on the same MANUAL or another. 3. The octave above a given TONE.

Supertonic. The second DEGREE of a DIATONIC SCALE.

Supplicando (It., sŏŏp-plē-kähn′dōh). In a style expressive of supplication, entreaty, pleading.

Surf music. California-born instrumental and vocal music, especially popular in the 1960s and 1970s, associated with the teenage sport of surfing. Twangy guitar solos were popularized by instrumental groups like The Ventures, while sunny harmonies and teenage themes were promoted by *surfmeisters*, The Beach Boys.

Suspension. A DISSONANCE caused by suspending (holding back) a TONE or tones of a CHORD while the other tones progress.

Süss (Ger., züss). Sweet(ly).

Sustain. To hold during the full TIME VALUE (of NOTES); also to perform in SOSTENUTO or LEGATO style.

Sustaining pedal. A PIANO PEDAL which holds up DAMPERS already raised by depressed KEYS, thus prolonging the TONES of strings affected.

Susurrante (It., sŏŏ-sŏŏ-rähn′tĕh). In a whispering, murmurous tone.

Suzuki Method. A process of musical education for young children based upon the repetition of (and adaptation to) external stimuli; founded by Shin'ichi Suzuki of Japan, and particularly popular for teaching the VIOLIN.

Svanirando (It., zvăh-nē-**răhn**'dŏh). Vanishing; fainter and fainter.

Svegliato (It., zvĕhl-yah'tŏh). Lively, animated, brisk.

Svelto (It., zvel'tŏh). Light, nimble.

Swell. 1. In the ORGAN, a set of PIPES enclosed in a box with movable shutters that may be opened and closed by a PEDAL. 2. The swell organ (the pipes enclosed, and their KEYBOARD). 3. A CRESCENDO ⟨ , or crescendo and DIMINUENDO ⟨ ⟩.

Swing. A smooth, sophisticated style of JAZZ playing, popular in the 1930s, characterized by a light, regular ACCENT on all four BEATS, usually emphasized by GUITAR, BASS, and DRUMS. Swing bands were usually large, well-rehearsed ensembles, featuring sections of SAXOPHONES, TRUMPETS, and TROMBONES, playing melodic RIFFS in HARMONY, often in a CALL-AND-RESPONSE pattern. Popular swing bands were led by Count Basie, Benny Goodman, The Dorsey Brothers, and Glenn Miller.

Syllabic melody. One each TONE of which is sung to a separate syllable.

Syllable name. A syllable taken as the name of a NOTE or TONE; as *Do* for C.

Symbolism. Denoting compositions of the late 19th and early 20th centuries that, like their counterparts in the visual arts, are characterized by intensely emotional characters, themes, and/or situations.

Sympathetic strings. STRINGS stretched below or above the principal strings of LUTES and other instruments to provide sympathetic resonance and thus enhance the sounds. These strings are not PLUCKED or FRETTED, but are set into vibration when another string of similar frequency is plucked or struck. This effect is called SYMPATHETIC VIBRATION.

Symphonic. Resembling, or relating or pertaining to, a SYMPHONY. *Symphonic ode*, a symphonic COMPOSITION combining CHORUS and ORCHESTRA; *s. poem*, an extended orchestral composition which follows in its development the thread of a story or the ideas of a poem, repeating and interweaving its THEMES appropriately; it has no fixed FORM, nor has it set divisions like those of a symphony.

Symphonie (Fr., sahn-fŏh'nē). SYMPHONY.

Symphony. An ORCHESTRAL COMPOSITION of from three to five distinct MOVEMENTS or divisions, each with its own THEME(S) and its own DEVELOPMENT. Usual plan: I. ALLEGRO (often SONATA FORM, usually with a slow introduction); II. ADAGIO; III. MINUET or SCHERZO; and, IV. ALLEGRO or PRESTO.

Syncopate. To efface or shift the ACCENT of a TONE or CHORD falling on a naturally strong BEAT by tying it over from the preceding weak beat; the latter then (generally) takes the accent. *Syncopation*, the regular shift of every beat in a measure by the same amount ahead of or beyond its usual position, creating both rhythmic tension and repeatedly unaccented strong beats.

Syncopated pedal. The release of the DAMPER pedal on striking a CHORD, followed by immediate depression of the pedal.

Synklavier. Trade name of the Yamaha Corporation for an ACOUSTIC PIANO that has been modified to include electronic sensors under each key, so that it may also operate as a SYNTHESIZER. Through a CD-ROM DRIVE, the piano can also be played automatically, like an old-fashioned PLAYER PIANO, although it is controlled via digital recording rather than mechanically.

Synthesizer. A class of electronic devices that make possible the creation of any sound via electronic synthesis; pioneer achievements were introduced in the 1960s by Moog and Buchla. Early synthesizers were MONOPHONIC (only capable of playing a single TONE at one time); more modern instruments are POLYPHONIC (able to play two, three, four, or more NOTES at the same time, depending on their built-in level of polyphony). Modern synthesizers usually have built-in sounds as well as some means of storing and recording new sounds (i.e., SEQUENCING and SAMPLING capabilities).

Syrinx. PANPIPES.

System. Generally referring to compositional practices based on the systematic treatment of some organizing aspect(s) of music.

T

T. Stands for TASTO, TEMPO, TENOR, Toe (in ORGAN music), *Tre* (T.C. = *tre corde*), and TUTTI.

Tabla. A pair of single-headed tunable Indian DRUMS. The *baya* is the larger drum, featuring an earthenware or copper body, and is played by the left hand. The daya is smaller with a wooden shell. Both are tuned by means of a black paste that is applied in layers to the skin head. A wide variety of TONES can be played by varying the position and shape of the hands as they strike the drum heads.

Tablature. 1. The rules and regulations for the poetry and song of the MEISTERSINGER. 2. Early musical NOTATION for the LUTE, VIOL, and ORGAN. 3. A method of showing the finger-positions on STRINGED INSTRUMENTS, especially popular for teaching GUITAR and BANJO.

Tabor. A small DRUM, tapped with only one hand or a short stick, often used to accompany the FIFE.

Tacet. Latin for "it is silent"; a common usage in ORCHESTRAL PARTS to mark a MOVEMENT in which an instrument in question is not playing.

Tafelmusik (Ger., tăh'fel-moo-zik). "Table music"; that is, music performed informally at a dinner gathering.

Tail. STEM.

Tailpiece. An anchor for the STRINGS, located at the lower end of the BODY of a VIOLIN, GUITAR, etc.

Takt (Ger., tăhkt). A BEAT; a MEASURE; TIME. *Ein Takt wie vorher zwei*, one measure like two before (same as DOPPIO MOVIMENTO); *streng im Takt*, strictly in time.

Talea (L., tăh-lā-ŭ). See ISORHYTHM.

Talon (Fr., tah-lohn'). The end of the BOW of the VIOLIN; literally, "heel."

Tambour (Fr., tahn-bŏŏr). DRUM.

Tambour de basque (Fr., -duh băhsk). A TAMBOURINE.

Tambourine. A small, shallow DRUM with one head of parchment; held in one hand and struck by the other. Around the hoop are several pairs of loose metallic plates called *jingles*.

Tambour militaire (Fr., -mē-lē-tarh'). A military DRUM; a SIDE DRUM.

Tambura. A long-necked Indian LUTE, usually used as a DRONE.

Tam-tam. A GONG.

Tändelnd (Ger., ten'delnt). In a toying, bantering style.

Tangent (from L., *tangere*, "to touch"). A small brass wedge used to strike the strings of a CLAVICHORD, located on the upperside of the back of each of the clavichord's KEYS.

Tango. An Argentine dance, characterized by strongly marked SYNCOPATION; became popular in ballrooms in the U.S. and Europe around 1912.

Tanto (It., tähn'tŏh). As much, so much, too (much). *Allegro non tanto*, not too fast; *a tanto possibile*, as much as possible.

Tanz (Ger., tähnts). A dance.

Tarantella (It., täh-**rä**hn-tel'läh); **Tarantelle** (Ger., täh-**rä**hn-tel'lĕ). A dance of southern Italy, in 6/8 TIME, the rate of speed gradually increasing, and the mode alternating between MAJOR and MINOR. Also, an instrumental piece in 3/8 or 6/8 time, very rapid TEMPO, and bold and brilliant style.

Tardamente (It., tăr-dăh-men'tĕh). Slowly, lingeringly.

Tardando (It., tăr-dähn'dŏh). Delaying, retarding.

Tardato (It., tăr-dăh'tŏh). Delayed, slower; retarded.

Tardo (It., tăr'dŏh). Slow, lingering.

Tarentelle (Fr., täh-**rä**hn-tel'). TARANTELLA.

Tastiera (It., täh-stē-â'**rä**h). KEYBOARD; FINGERBOARD. *Sulla tastiera*, on (near) the fingerboard.

Tasto (It., täh'stŏh). KEY; FRET; touch; FINGERBOARD. *Sul tasto*, on (near) the fingerboard; *tasto solo* means that the BASS PART is to be played, either as written or in OCTAVES, without CHORDS.

Te. Stands for SI, in TONIC SOL-FA.

Technic (tek'nik); **Technique** (Fr., tek-nēk'). All that relates to the purely mechanical part of an instrumental or vocal performance; mechanical training, skill, dexterity.

Tedesco,-a (It., tĕh-dĕh'skŏh,-skäh). German. *Alla tedesca*, in the German style (in WALTZ RHYTHMS, with changing TEMPO).

Teil (Ger., tile). A PART or section; a MOVEMENT.

Tema (It., tâ′măh). THEME.

Tema con variazioni (It., târ′māh kŏhn vâr-ē-āh-tsē′ŏh-nē). THEME AND VARIATIONS.

Temperament. A system of TUNING in which TONES of very nearly the same PITCH, like *C* sharp and *D* flat, are made to sound alike by slightly "tempering" them (that is, slightly raising or lowering them). When applied to all the tones of an instrument (as the PIANO), this system is called "equal temperament"; when only the keys most used are tuned (as was done formerly), the temperament is said to be "unequal."

Tempestoso (It., tem-pĕh-stŏh′sŏh). Stormily, passionately, impetuously.

Temple block. A hollow block of resonant wood, struck with a drumstick; also called CHINESE BLOCK, or Korean temple block.

Tempo (It., tem′pŏh). 1. Rate of speed, movement. 2. TIME, MEASURE. *A tempo*, return to the preceding pace; *in t.*, same as *a t.*; *sempre in t.*, always at the same pace; *in t. misurato*, in strict time (after A PIACERE); *t. com(m)odo*, at a convenient pace; *t. di Ballo, Minuetto*, etc., in the movement of a Ball, MINUET, etc.; *t. giusto*, at a proper, appropriate pace; *t. rubato*, see RUBATO; *l'istesso t.*, or *lo stesso t.*, the same tempo (indicates, at a change of RHYTHM, that the pace remains the same); *senza t.*, same as A PIACERE; *t. primo*, at the original pace.

Tempo mark. A word or phrase indicating the rate of speed at which a piece should be performed. Thus, "Adagio, M.M. = 56," signifies a tranquil movement in which a QUARTER NOTE has the TIME VALUE of one BEAT of the METRONOME set at 56.

Tenero (It., tâ'nĕh-rŏh). Tenderly, with tender emotion; delicately, softly.

Tenor. The high natural male VOICE; the *dramatic tenor*, of full and powerful quality, has a range from *c* to *b*^{1}♭; the *lyric tenor*, sweeter and less powerful, from *d* to *c*^{2} (or *c*^{2}♯). 2. The VIOLA. 3. A prefix to the names of instruments of similar compass, as *tenor* TROMBONE.

Tenor C. Small *c*:

Tenor clef. The *C* CLEF on the fourth line of the STAFF.

Tenore (It., tĕh-noh'rĕh). TENOR.

Tenth. 1. The DIATONIC INTERVAL of an OCTAVE plus two DEGREES. 2. Same as DECIMA 2.

Tenuto (It., tĕh-noo'tŏh). "Held"; means (*a*) generally, that a TONE so marked is to be sustained for its full time value; (*b*) occasionally, LEGATO. *Forte tenuto (f ten.)*, FORTE throughout; *t. mark*, a short stroke over a NOTE.

Tepidamente (It., tĕh-pē-dăh-men'tĕh). Lukewarmly; in an even, unimpassioned style.

Ternary. Composed of, or progressing by, threes. *Ternary form*, RONDO form; *t. measure*, simple TRIPLE TIME.

Terz (Ger., târts); **Terza** (It., târ-tsăh). The INTERVAL of a THIRD.

Terzett (Ger., târ-tset'); **Terzetto** (It., târ-tset'tŏh). Properly, a vocal TRIO (seldom an instrumental one).

Tessitura (It., tes-sē-too'răh). The range covered by the main body of the TONES of a given PART, not including infrequent high or low tones. In English, we say that the part "lies" high or low.

Tetrachord. 1. The INTERVAL of a PERFECT FOURTH; the four SCALE-TONES contained in a perfect fourth. 2. A set of four PITCH CLASSES, usually associated with a 12-NOTE SET.

Tetralogy. A connected series of four related stage works or ORATORIOS.

Text. Words to which music is set.

Texture music. Music in which timbral concerns in the form of atmospheric sound masses (characterized by their loudness, density, and/or instrumentation) is the primary feature.

Thematic composition. A style based on the CONTRAPUNTAL treatment or DEVELOPMENT of one or more THEMES (INVENTION, FUGUE, CANON).

Theme. A SUBJECT. Specifically, an extended and rounded off SUBJECT with ACCOMPANIMENT, in PERIOD FORM, proposed as a groundwork for elaborate VARIATIONS.

Theme and variations. A form of COMPOSITION in which the principal THEME is clearly and explicitly stated at the beginning, and is then followed by a number of VARIATIONS.

Theme song. The most prominent SONG in a MUSICAL, or a movie, calculated to express the abiding sentiment of the entire production.

Theorbo. A large, double-necked BASS LUTE.

Theory. The systematic study of basic musical principles, particularly as these relate to composition.

Theremin. An early electronic MELODY instrument, invented by the Franco-Russian physicist, Leon Theremin. The *Theremin* has two poles, one vertical and one horizontal, that react to movements around them. Each pole produces an electrical field, which, when disturbed, changes either the VOLUME or PITCH of the sound that is produced.

Thesis. DOWNBEAT, strong beat.

Third. An INTERVAL embracing three DEGREES. Also, the third degree of the SCALE; the MEDIANT.

Third Stream. A term introduced in the 1950s to denote music exhibiting both JAZZ and CLASSICAL roots.

Thirteenth. An INTERVAL embracing an OCTAVE and a SIXTH; a compound sixth.

Thirty-second note. A NOTE with one-half the TIME VALUE of a SIXTEENTH NOTE.

Thoroughbass. FIGURED BASS.

Three step. The ordinary (Vienna) WALTZ.

Through-composed. This term is applied to SONGS with different musical settings for each STANZA of the poem; as opposed to STROPHIC.

Thumb position. The high positions in CELLO playing, where the thumb quits the neck of the instrument.

Tie. A curved line joining two NOTES of like PITCH that are to be sounded as one note equal to their united time value.

Tied notes. 1. NOTES joined by a TIE. 2. Notes whose HOOKS are run together in one or more thick strokes.

Tierce (tērs). 1. Third. 2. In the ORGAN, a mutation STOP pitched two and one-third OCTAVES above the DIAPASON. 3. One of the Canonical Hours.

Tierce de Picardi (Fr., t'yĕrs duh pē-kar'dē). A PICARDY THIRD.

Timbale (Fr., tăn-băhl'); **Timballo** (It., tim-băhl'lŏh). KETTLEDRUM.

Timbre (Fr., tăn'br). TONE COLOR or quality.

Timbrel (Hebrew). A TAMBOURINE or TABOR.

Time. 1. The division of the MEASURE into equal fractional parts of a WHOLE NOTE (**o**), thus regulating the ACCENTS and rhythmic flow of music. The sign for time is the *time signature*. There are two classes of time: *duple* and *triple*. In *duple time*, the *number of beats* to the measure is divisible by two; in *triple time*, by three. There are also two subclasses, *compound duple time* and *compound triple time*; in the former, *each beat* contains a dotted note (or its equivalent in other notes or RESTS) divisible by three; in the latter, not only the number of beats in each measure is divisible by three, but also each beat, as above.

Time-bracket notation. A type of highly flexible musical NOTATION developed by Cage in his mature works whereby time lengths are left, to large degree, to the discretion of the performer. In the following example

00'00''-00'15''   00'30''-01'00'',

the performer is instructed to (1) begin playing the excerpt at any time between the first pair of bracketed times, and to (2) end playing the exerpt at any time between the second pair of bracketed times.

Time-Space Notation. PROPORTIONAL NOTATION.

Time value. The length of TIME a given NOTE is held.

Timoroso (It., tē-mŏh-**r**oh'sŏh). In a style expressive of timidity, hesitation, or fear.

Timpani (It., tim'păh-nē). KETTLEDRUMS. *Timpani coperti*, muffled DRUMS.

Tin whistle. A small, high-pitched, end-blown WHISTLE FLUTE, made of metal; also called *Pennywhistle*.

Tinto, con (It., kŏhn tin'tŏh). With shading; expressively.

Toccata (It., tŏhk-kah'tăh). Literally, a COMPOSITION for ORGAN or HARPSICHORD (PIANO), free and bold in style, consisting of RUNS and PASSAGES alternating with FUGUED or CONTRAPUNTAL work, generally in equal NOTES, with a flowing, animated, and rapid movement.

Todesgesang or **Todeslied** (Ger., tŏh'des-gĕsang[k] or tŏh'des-lēt). A DIRGE; a musical COMPOSITION commemorating the dead. Also *Totenlied* (Ger., to'ten-lēt).

Tom-tom. 1. Indian DRUM producing a dull but incisive tone. 2. In modern ORCHESTRAS, a tunable, deep-bodied, double-headed drum producing a hollow but sharp sound.

Ton (Ger., tohn). A TONE; KEY; MODE; PITCH; OCTAVE-SCALE.

Tonada (Sp., tŏh-nah'tăh). A generic name for a Spanish SONG or dance, also adopted in Latin America.

Tonadilla (Sp., tŏh-nah-dē'ya). A Spanish theater piece of a light genre.

Tonal. Pertaining to TONES, or to a tone, MODE, or KEY. *Tonal imitation*, IMITATION within the key of a COMPOSITION; non-modulating imitation.

Tonal answer. An ANSWER to the SUBJECT in a FUGUE, in which the TONIC is answered by the DOMINANT and the dominant is answered by the tonic, thus altering the intervallic content of the THEME.

Tonality. See KEY.

Tonante (It., tŏh-năhn'tĕh). Thundering, thunderous.

Tonart (Ger., tohn'art). KEY (TONALITY).

Tondichtung (Ger., tohn'dihyh-tŏŏng^k). SYMPHONIC POEM.

Tone. See ACOUSTICS. *Half tone*, a MINOR or CHROMATIC SECOND; *whole t.*, a MAJOR second.

Tone cluster. Several consecutive NOTES, of the DIATONIC, PENTATONIC, or CHROMATIC SCALE, played simultaneously in a "cluster." Diatonic PIANO *tone clusters*, executed with the hands, forearms, or specially designed depressing sticks, were introduced by the American composer Henry Cowell.

Tone color. Quality of tone; TIMBRE.

Tone poem. SYMPHONIC POEM.

Tone row. The fundamental SUBJECT in a 12-TONE COMPOSITION.

Tongue. 1. (*noun*) A REED. 2. (*verb*) To employ the tongue in producing, modifying, or interrupting the tones of certain wind instruments. See TONGUING.

Tonguing. The production of tone effects on WIND INSTRU-MENTS by the aid of the tongue. *Single tonguing*, the effect obtained by the repeated tongue thrust to the nearly in-audible consonant *t* or *d*; *double t.*, that obtained by the repetition of *t k*; *triple t.*, by *t k t*; etc.

Tonic. 1. The KEYNOTE of a SCALE. 2. The TRIAD on the keynote (tonic CHORD). *Tonic pedal*, ORGAN-POINT on the keynote; *t. section*, a SECTION or sentence in the key in which the COMPOSITION began, with a CADENCE to the tonic of that KEY.

Tonic Sol-fa. A method of teaching vocal music, invented by Sarah Ann Glover of Norwich, England, about 1812, wherein pupils are taught to recognize the TONES of the SCALE by observing the mental impressions peculiar to each tone. It is based on the MOVABLE DO system, and uses the syllables *doh*, *ray*, *me*, *fah*, *soh*, *lah*, and *te*.

Tonkunst (Ger., tohn'kŭnst). The art of music. *Tonkünstler*, COMPOSER.

Tonleiter (Ger., tohn'līter). SCALE.

Tonsatz (Ger., tohn'sähtz). A COMPOSITION.

Tonus peregrinus. Latin for "wandering MODE"; an excerpt of PLAINCHANT used in a CHORAL work.

Torch song. A highly emotional American popular SONG sung by a female who "carries a torch" for an unresponsive male.

Tornando (It., tohr-nähn'dōh). Returning. *Tornando al primo tempo*, or *tornando come prima*, returning to (resuming) the original TEMPO.

Tostamente (It., tŏh-stäh-men'tĕh). Rapidly and boldly.

Tostissimo (It., tŏh-stis's̄e-mŏh). Extremely fast.

Tosto (It., tô'stŏh). Swift, bold; soon. *Allegro molto, più tosto presto*, very fast, nearly PRESTO.

Total serialism. SERIAL MUSIC.

Touch. 1. The method and manner of applying the fingers to the KEYS of KEYBOARD instruments. 2. The amount and kind of resistance overcome by the fingers in depressing the keys of an ORGAN or PIANO; as a *heavy*, *light*, or *elastic* touch. This resistance can be varied on electronic instruments, such as keyboard SYNTHESIZERS, through a *touch-control* setting.

Touche (Fr., toosh). FINGERBOARD. *Sur la touche*, an instruction for string players to BOW on the FINGERBOARD.

Toye. Short PIECE for the VIRGINAL composed during the 16th and 17th centuries.

Tragicamente (It., trăh-jē-kăh-men'těh). Tragically.

Tranquillo (It., trăhn-kwil'lōh). Tranquilly, quietly, calmly.

Transcendental. The PIANO style of Liszt and his followers; so called because it surpasses the playing of former pianists, and exceeds the limits of the piano by imitating the ORCHESTRA.

Transcription. The ARRANGEMENT or adaptation of a PIECE for some voice or instrument other than that for which it was originally intended.

Transient. PASSING; not PRINCIPAL; intermediate. *Transient chord*, an intermediate CHORD foreign both to the KEY left and that reached; *t. modulation*, a temporary MODULATION, soon followed by a return to the original key.

Transition. 1. MODULATION, especially a TRANSIENT one. 2. In TONIC SOL-FA, a modulation without change of MODE.

Transpose. To perform or write out a COMPOSITION in a KEY other than that in which it was originally written.

Transposing instruments. 1. Instruments whose natural SCALE is always written in *C* major, regardless of the actual PITCH. 2. Instruments having some device by which the action or STRINGS can be shifted so that higher or lower TONES are produced than when they are in the normal position.

Transposition. 1. NOTATION or performance of a composition in a different KEY from the one in which it was originally written. 2. One of three standard techniques in 12-NOTE COMPOSITION (RETROGRADE, INVERSION, transposition).

Transverse flute. CROSS-FLUTE.

Traps. Colloquial term for the DRUM set in a JAZZ BAND.

Trascinando (It., trăh-shē-nähn'dŏh). Dragging, delayed.

Trasporto, con (It., kŏhn trăh-spôr'tŏh). With transport, ecstatically.

Trattenuto (It., trăht-tĕh-noo'tŏh). Held back, retarded.

Trauermusik (Ger., trow'er-moo-zĭk). Funeral music.

Träumerisch (Ger., troy'mĕrish). Dreamy.

Traurig (Ger., trow'rĭyh). Sad, melancholy.

Trautonium. An electronic musical instrumental introduced by the German electrical engineer Trautwein.

Traversflöte (Ger., trăh-vârs'flö'tĕ). The CROSS-FLUTE; or, a 4' ORGAN STOP resembling it in TIMBRE.

Tre (It., trā). Three. *A tre,* for three voices or instruments; *a tre voci,* for (in) three parts; *tre corde,* see UNO, *Una corda.*

Treble. SOPRANO. *Treble clef,* the G CLEF:

Treibend (Ger., trī'bent). Urging, hastening.

Tremolo (It., trâ'mŏh-lŏh). A quivering, fluttering. 1. In singing, a tremulous, unsteady TONE. 2. On bowed instruments, an effect produced by the very rapid alternation of DOWN-BOW and UP-BOW, written:

3. On the PIANO, the rapid alternation of the tones of a CHORD. 4. The effect produced by the *tremolo stop*, or *tremulant* (ORGAN). 5. The TREMULANT.

Tremoloso (It., trĕh-mŏh-loh'sŏh). With a tremulous, fluttering effect.

Tremulant. The TREMOLO STOP in an ORGAN.

Trepak (trĕh-pahk'). A Russian dance in fast DUPLE TIME.

Très (Fr., trä). Very; MOLTO.

Triad. A three-note CHORD composed of a given TONE (the ROOT), with its THIRD and FIFTH in ascending order in the SCALE.

Triangle. A steel rod bent into triangular shape, with one corner left slightly open; it is struck with a metal wand.

Trichord. A set of three PITCH CLASSES, usually a fragment of a 12-NOTE SET.

Trichord piano. One having three STRINGS (UNISONS) to each TONE throughout the greater part of its COMPASS.

Trill, Triller (Ger., tril'ler); **Trillo** (It., tril'lŏh). The even and rapid alternation of two TONES a MAJOR or MINOR SECOND apart; the lower tone is the *principal note*, the higher tone the *auxiliary*. Sign *tr* or *tr*⁓⁓⁓⁓.

Trio (It., trē'ŏh). 1. A piece for three voices or in three parts. 2. In MINUETS, MARCHES, etc., the *trio* or *alternativo* is a second dance or march, after which the first is repeated.

Trio sonata. A type of BAROQUE CHAMBER MUSIC written in three PARTS, the upper two supported by a FIGURED BASS.

Triole (Ger., trē-oh'lĕ); **Triolet** (Fr., trē-oh-lā). TRIPLET.

Trionfale (It., trē-ŏhn'fah'lĕh). Triumphal.

Trionfante (It., trē-ŏhn-fähn'tĕh). Triumphant.

Triple concerto. CONCERTO for three solo instruments and OR-CHESTRA.

Triple counterpoint. See COUNTERPOINT.

Triple-croche (Fr., trĕp'l krōsh). THIRTY-SECOND NOTE.

Triplet. A group of three equal NOTES to be performed in the time of two of like value in the established RHYTHM; written:

Triple time. METER containing three units, as in 3/4 or 3/8.

Tristo,-a (It., trī'stōh,-stäh). In a style expressive of sadness or melancholy.

Tritone. The INTERVAL of three WHOLE TONES; the AUGMENTED FOURTH (DIMINISHED FIFTH):

Trochee (tro'kē). A metrical foot of two syllables, long and short, with the accent on the first: ⌣⌣ .

Tromba marina (It., trŏm-bäh'-mah-rī'näh). Literally, a "marine TRUMPET"; a MONOCHORD, with a single STRING stretched over a very long wooden box, used in the Middle Ages for acoustical experiments, and which could easily produce a long series of HARMONICS. There is no reasonable explanation for the origin of the name.

Trombone. The middle instrument of the BRASS group, pitched below the TRUMPET and the HORN and above the TUBA. The name itself is the augmentative form of the Italian word *tromba*, trumpet, and therefore means "big trumpet." The common trombone is characterized by a long, U-shaped SLIDE, which enables the player to vary the PITCH of the instrument.

Trommel (Ger., trôm'mel). DRUM.

Trompette (Fr., trŏhm-pet'). TRUMPET.

Trompette à pistons (Fr., -pēs-ton'). A regular TRUMPET with pistons (or VALVES).

Tronco,-a (It., trŏhn'kŏh,-käh). Cut off short; stopped abruptly.

Trope. In medieval Roman liturgy, as an insertion of a musical section, usually a HYMN. Also, an introduction to a Gregorian CHANT.

Troppo (It., trŏp'pŏh). Too, too much. *Allegro, ma non troppo*, rapid, but not too fast.

Troubadours. A class of traveling poet-musicians originating in Provence, and flourishing in France, Spain, and Italy from the 11th century until toward the close of the 13th; their language was *langue d'oc*.

Trouvères. A class of traveling poet-musicians originating in the north of France and flourishing in France, Spain, and Italy from the 12th century until toward the close of the 13th; their language was *langue d'oil*.

Trüb(e) (Ger., trüp, trü'bĕ). Gloomy, dismal; sad, melancholy.

Trumpet. 1. A metal WIND INSTRUMENT with cupped MOUTH-PIECE and small BELL; the tone is brilliant, penetrating, and of great carrying power. The modern trumpet has VALVES, enabling the player to change the instrument's PITCH. It is a TRANSPOSING INSTRUMENT, with an ordinary COMPASS of about two OCTAVES. Also *tromba* (It., trŏm-bäh); *trompette* (Fr., trŏm-pět'). 2. In the ORGAN, an 8' REED STOP of powerful tone.

Tuba. 1. A name applied to the three lowest members of the SAXHORN family; they are metal WIND INSTRUMENTS of ponderous tone, with a COMPASS of some four OCTAVES, and with VALVES to enable the player to play in a variety of KEYS. 2. The straight TRUMPET of the Romans. 3. In the

ORGAN, a REED STOP (*tuba mirabilis*) on a heavy pressure of wind, of very powerful and thrilling tone.

Tubular chimes. Metal BELLS made of long, hollow cylindrical tubes, suspended from a bar.

Tumultuoso (It., too-mŏŏl-too-oh'sŏh). Vehement, impetuous; agitated.

Tune. 1. (noun) An AIR, MELODY; a term chiefly applied to short, simple pieces or familiar MELODIES. 2. (verb) To adjust the PITCH of a TONE to an external standard, such as CONCERT PITCH.

Tuning. 1. The process of bringing an instrument into TUNE. 2. The ACCORDATURA of a STRINGED INSTRUMENT. *Tuning cone, t. horn,* a hollow cone of metal, for tuning metal flue PIPES in the ORGAN; *t. crook,* a CROOK; *t. fork,* a two-pronged instrument of metal, yielding one fixed TONE (usually a^1 or c^2); *t. hammer, t. key,* a hand wrench for tuning PIANOS; *t. slide,* a sliding U-shaped section of the tube in certain BRASS INSTRUMENTS, used to adjust their PITCH to that of other instruments.

Turco,-a (It., toor'kŏh,-kăh). Turkish. *Alla turca,* in Turkish style, i.e., with a noisy and somewhat monotonous HARMONIC ACCOMPANIMENT.

Turn. A melodic GRACE consisting (usually) of four notes, a PRINCIPAL NOTE (struck twice) with its higher and lower AUXILIARY. Sign ∾.

Tusch (Ger., toosh). In German usage, a complimentary FANFARE played by orchestral musicians for an honored conductor or soloist.

Tutti (It., too'tē). The indication in an orchestral or choral SCORE that the entire ORCHESTRA or CHORUS is to enter; usually placed after an extended SOLO PASSAGE.

Twelfth. 1. The INTERVAL of an OCTAVE plus a FIFTH; a compound fifth. 2. A mutation STOP in the ORGAN, pitched a TWELFTH higher than the DIAPASON.

Twelve-note composition. An historically significant, a hierarchical method of musical organization, most profoundly developed by Schoenberg, wherein all twelve NOTES of the CHROMATIC SCALE are ordered and treated without undue concern for TONAL and/or HARMONIC functions. The term is generally interchangeable with DODECAPHONY.

Two step. Quick American ballroom dance popular in the 1900s and 1910s.

Tympani. An incorrect, but frequently encountered spelling of TIMPANI.

Tyrolienne (Fr., tē-rŏh-l'yen′). A Tyrolese dance or dance SONG, a peculiar feature of the latter being the YODEL, especially as a REFRAIN. Hence, a modern round dance in 3/4 TIME and easy movement.

U

Üben (Ger., *ü*′ben). To practice.

Über (Ger., *ü*′ber). Over, above.

Übermässig (Ger., *ü*-ber′mä′sīyh). AUGMENTED.

Übung (Ger., *ü*′bŏŏng^k). EXERCISE; practice.

Uguale (It., oo-gwäh′lĕh). Equal, like, similar.

Ugualmente (It., oo-gwähl-mĕn′tĕh). Equally, similarly; evenly, smoothly, tranquilly.

Ukulele. Popular GUITAR-type instrument.

Umano,-a (It., oo-mah′nŏh,-näh). Human. *Voce umana*, Vox humana, an ORGAN STOP.

Umore, con (It., kŏhn oo-moh′rĕh). With humor.

Un or **Une** (Fr., ön or ün). One; a or an. *Un peu plus lent*, a little slower.

Un or **Uno,-a** (It., oon or oo′nŏh,-năh). One; a or an. *Una corda*, with the soft PEDAL; *tre corde*, release the soft pedal.

Und (Ger., oont). And.

Unda maris (L., "wave of the sea"). In the ORGAN, an 8′ flue STOP pitched a trifle lower than the surrounding foundation stops, the interference of its TONE with theirs producing BEATS and a wavy, undulatory effect of tone.

Undecuplet. A group of eleven equal NOTES to be performed in the time of eight (or six) of like value in the established RHYTHM.

Undulazione (It., ŏŏn-doo-lăh-tsē-oh′nĕh). On bowed instruments, the VIBRATO effect.

Unequal voices. Voices different in COMPASS and QUALITY; mixed voices.

Ungebunden (Ger., ŏŏn′gĕ-bŏŏn′den). Unconstrained. *Mit ungebundenem Humor*, with unconstrained humor, *burlando*.

Ungeduldig (Ger., ŏŏn′gĕ-dŏŏl′dīyh). Impatient(ly).

Ungestüm (Ger., ŏŏn′gĕ-shtüm′). Impetuous(ly).

Ungherese (It., ŏŏn-gā-rā′sĕh). Hungarian.

Unison. A TONE of the same PITCH as a given tone; also, a higher or lower OCTAVE of the given tone. In the PIANO, a group of two or three STRINGS tuned to the same pitch and struck by one hammer; a string in such a group is called a *unison string*.

Unisono (It., oo-nē′sŏh-nŏh). UNISON. *All′ unisono*, progressing in unison with or in OCTAVES.

Unitamente (It., oo-nē-tăh-mĕn′tĕh). Unitedly, together.

Uniti (It., oo-nē′tē). This signifies, after a section marked "DIVISI," that the instruments or voices are to again perform their parts in UNISON.

Unito,-a (It., oo-nē′tŏh,-tāh). United, joined.

Un poco (It., oon pô′kŏh). "A little," as in *poco più lento*, a little more slowly.

Unruhig (Ger., ŏŏn′roo′ĭyh). Restless(ly), unquiet(ly).

Unter (Ger., ŏŏn′ter). Under, below, sub-.

Unvocal. 1. Not suitable for singing. 2. Not vibrating with TONE; *unvocal air* is breath escaping with a more or less audible sigh or hiss, due to unskillful management of the voice.

Upbeat. 1. The raising of the hand in beating TIME. 2. An unaccented part of a MEASURE (see AUFTAKT).

Up-bow. The stroke of the BOW in the direction from POINT to NUT; the *up-bow mark* is ᴠ or ʌ.

Upright piano. A PIANO standing up, with its STRINGS arranged cross-wise (diagonally) along the vertical SOUNDBOARD, as distinguished from a GRAND PIANO in which the strings and the soundboard are horizontal.

Ut. 1. The first of the SOLMISATION syllables. 2. The NOTE *C* in France (pronounced üt).

V

V. Stands for VIDE, VIOLINO, *Volti*, and VOCE; *Vv.*, for *Violini*.

Va (It., vah). Go on, continue. *Va crescendo*, go on increasing (in loudness).

Vacillando (It., văh-chē-lähn′dŏh). Vacillating; means that the PASSAGE is to be performed in a wavering, hesitating style.

Vaghezza, con (It., kŏhn văh-gĕt'tsăh). With charm.

Vago (It., văh'gŏh). Vague, dreamy.

Valse (Fr., văhls). WALTZ. *Valse chantée*, waltz-song; *Valse de salon*, a salon PIECE in waltz TIME for the PIANO.

Value. The value (better TIME VALUE) of a NOTE or REST is its length or DURATION as compared (*a*) with other notes in the same movement, or (*b*) with the standard WHOLE NOTE or any fractional note.

Valve. In BRASS WIND INSTRUMENTS, a device for diverting the air current from the main tube into an additional side tube, thus lengthening the air column and lowering the PITCH of the instrument's entire SCALE. There are *piston* valves and *rotary* valves.

Valzer (It., văhl'tser). WALTZ.

Vamp. Expression in POPULAR MUSIC meaning to IMPROVISE an introduction or an ACCOMPANIMENT.

Variable metres. Systematic oscillation of changing METERS in consecutive MEASURES.

Variamente (It., văh-rē-ăh-men'těh). Variously, differently.

Variante (It., văh-rē-ăhn'těh); **Variante** (Fr., văh-rē-ăhn't). A variant; a different (optional) reading. See OSSIA.

Variation. One of a set or series of transformations of a THEME by means of HARMONIC, RHYTHMIC, and MELODIC changes and embellishments.

Variazioni (It., văh-rē-ăh-tsē-oh'nē). VARIATIONS.

Varié (Fr., văh-rē-ā'). Varied. *Air* or *thème varié*, same as TEMA CON VARIAZIONI.

Varsoviana (It., var-sŏh-vē-ah'năh); **Varsovienne** (Fr., var-sŏh-v'yen'). A dance in moderate TEMPO and 3/4 TIME, with an AUFTAKT of a QUARTER NOTE, the DOWNBEAT of every second MEASURE being strongly marked.

Vaudeville (Fr., voh-d′-vēl′). A light comedy, often a parody, in which dialogue and pantomime alternate with witty and satirical couplets generally set to well-known popular AIRS.

Veemente (It., vĕh-ĕh-men′tĕh); **Veemenza, con** (It., kŏhn vĕh-ĕh-men′tsăh). Vehemently, passionately.

Veil. A voice the TONE of which is not quite clear and bell-like, but somewhat obscured, is said to have a "veil," or to be "veiled."

Velato,-a (It., vĕh-lah′tŏh,-tăh). Veiled.

Vellutato (It., vel-loo-tah′tŏh). Velvety.

Veloce (It., vĕh-loh′chĕh). Rapid, swift; often means that a PASSAGE is to be performed faster than those before and after, then being the opposite of RITENUTO.

Velocità, con (It., kŏhn vĕh-lŏh-chē-tah′). Rapidly, swiftly.

Velocissimo (It., vĕh-lŏh-chis′sē-mŏh). Very fast, with extreme rapidity.

Vent (Fr., vahn). "Wind." *Instruments à vent*, WIND INSTRUMENTS.

Ventil. A VALVE.

Venusto (It., vĕh-nŏŏ′stŏh). Graceful, elegant.

Vergnügt (Ger., fâr-gnüyht′). Cheerful(ly), cheery (cheerily).

Vergrösserung (Ger., fâr-grös′serŏŏng^k). AUGMENTATION.

Verhallend (Ger., fâr-hăhl′lent). Dying away.

Verismo (It., vĕr-ēz′mŏh). A realistic type of OPERA that emerged in Italy in the 1890s; its stories are based on contemporary fiction or actual dramatic events.

Verkleinerung (Ger., fâr-klīn′erŏŏng^k). DIMINUTION.

Verlöschend (Ger., fâr-lö′shent). Dying away.

Vermindert (Ger., fâr-min′dert). DIMINISHED (INTERVAL).

Verschiebung, mit (Ger., mit fâr-shē'bŏŏng^k). With shifting (soft) PEDAL. *Ohne Verschiebung*, release soft pedal. See UNO, *una corda, tre corde*.

Verschwindend (Ger., fâr-shvin'dent). Vanishing, dying away.

Verse. 1. In sacred vocal music, a portion of an ANTHEM or service for solo voice(s). 2. A STANZA.

Verse-anthem. One in which the verses (SOLI, DUETS, TRIOS, QUARTETS) predominate over the CHORUSES. *Verse-service*, a choral service for solo voices.

Verset. 1. A short verse, usually forming but one sentence with its response, for example:
> *Vers.* O Lord, save Thy people,
> *Resp.* And bless Thine inheritance.

2. A short PRELUDE or INTERLUDE for ORGAN.

Versetzung (Ger., fâr-set'zŏŏng^k). TRANSPOSITION.

Versicle. See VERSET 1.

Verstimmt (Ger., fâr-shtimt'). Out of TUNE; out of humor, depressed.

Verweilend (Ger., fâr-vī'lent). Delaying.

Vespers. EVENSONG; the sixth of the CANONICAL HOURS.

Vezzosamente (It., vet-tsŏh-säh-men'teh). In a graceful, elegant style.

Vibraharp. A common name for the VIBRAPHONE.

Vibrante (It., vē-brăhn'tĕh). With a vibrating, agitated effect or tone.

Vibraphone. A PERCUSSION instrument consisting of suspended metal bars in KEYBOARD arrangement, which, when struck with mallets, produce TONES that are amplified by resonator tubes below the bars. A motor-driven mechanism causes the VIBRATO that gives the instrument its name.

Vibration. Rapid oscillations of a sounding body, such as a STRING, or a column of air in WIND INSTRUMENTS, which result in the production of definite TONES. The human ear is capable of perceiving vibrations from about sixteen to several thousand per second. The lowest *A* on the PIANO KEYBOARD has 27 1/2 vibrations per second, and the high *C* on the keyboard vibrates at 4,224 per second.

Vibrato (It., vē-brăh′tŏh). 1. On bowed instruments, the wavering effect of TONE obtained by rapidly shaking the finger on the STRING that it is stopping. 2. In singing, (*a*) a tremulous effect caused by very rapid partial interruptions of the tone; (*b*) strongly accented, and diminishing in intensity: ♩ (also instrumental effect).

Vicendevole (It., vē-chen-dā′vŏh-lĕh). Changeably, inconstantly.

Vicino (It., vē-chē′nŏh). Near. *Più vicino*, nearer (as of sounds coming nearer and growing louder).

Victrola. Trademark for PHONOGRAPH.

Vide (L., vē′deh); **Vedi** (It., vē′dē). See. *Vi — de*, written in SCORES, means that a "cut" is to be made, and directs the performers to skip from *Vi-* over to *de*.

Viel (Ger., fēl). Much, great. *Mit vielem Nachdruck*, with strong emphasis.

Vielle à roue (Fr., vē-ĕh′lĕh ăh roo). A medieval VIOL with a mechanical wheel attachment: a HURDY-GURDY.

Vielstimmung (Ger., fēl′shtim-miyh). POLYPHONIC, many-voiced.

Viennese School. Refers to various styles of COMPOSITION centered around Austria. The *Classical Viennese School* includes Haydn, Mozart, Beethoven, Schubert, and others. Some observers perceive a continuity leading to the

Strauss family in the later 19th century. The *20th Century Viennese School* refers to the group of modern composers, mainly Schoenberg and his disciples, who write in the DODECAPHONIC style.

Viertelnote (Ger., fēr'tĕhl-noh-tĕh). A QUARTER NOTE.

Vif (Fr., vēf). Lively.

Vigoroso (It., vē-gŏh-roh'sŏh). With vigor, energy.

Vihuela (Sp., bē-wĕh'lah). An old Spanish LUTE.

Villancico (Sp., bĕl-yăhn-sē'cŏh). A Spanish CHORAL SONG of the RENAISSANCE.

Villanella (It., vĕl-lăh-nel'lăh). Type of 16th-century vocal music originating in Naples and of a rather light-hearted nature, less refined than the MADRIGAL; used by some modern composers as a kind of instrumental rustic dance.

Viol. An early type of bowed instrument, differing from the VIOLIN family by having a *fretted* FINGERBOARD, a variable number of STRINGS (usually six), and in the shape of its BODY. It was made in four sizes, like the violin, by which it was superseded in the ORCHESTRA, etc.

Viola (It., vē-ô'lah). The tenor VIOLIN. A bowed STRING INSTRUMENT with its four strings tuned a FIFTH lower than the violin: *C, G, D, A.*

Viola da braccio (It., -brah'chŏh). Literally, "viol for the arm"; an early bowed STRINGED INSTRUMENT held in the arm like the VIOLIN or VIOLA.

Viola da gamba (It., -gahm'băh). Literally, "viol for the leg"; an early bowed STRINGED INSTRUMENT of the size approximating the CELLO, and held between the knees.

Viola d'amore (It., -dăh-moh'rĕh). Literally, "viola of love"; an early STRINGED INSTRUMENT in the middle RANGE, supplied with SYMPATHETIC STRINGS.

Viole (Fr., v'yohl'). A VIOL; a VIOLA.

Violento (It., vē-ŏh-len'tŏh). In a violent, impetuous style.

Violin family. The familiar four-stringed bowed instruments, constructed in four sizes, tuned as follows:

Violina. A metal flue STOP in the ORGAN, of stringy TIMBRE, usually of 4' PITCH.

Violinata (It., vē-ŏh-lē-nah'tăh). 1. A piece for VIOLIN. 2. A PIECE for an instrument (other than the violin) that imitates the violin style.

Violin clef. The G CLEF . *French violin clef,* the G clef set on the lowest line of the STAFF.

Violin diapason. A DIAPASON ORGAN STOP of stringy TONE.

Violino (It., vē-ŏh-lē'nŏh). VIOLIN.

Violon (Fr., v'yŏh-lŏhn'). 1. VIOLIN. 2. VIOLIN DIAPASON.

Violoncello (It., vē-ŏh-lŏhn-chel'lŏh). A four-stringed bowed instrument of VIOLIN type, held, while playing, between the knees; familiarly called the 'CELLO.

Violone (It., vē-ŏh-loh'nĕh). 1. The BASS VIOL. 2. An ORGAN STOP on the PEDAL, of 16' PITCH and violoncello-like TIMBRE.

Virelai (Fr., vēr-eh-lā'). A medieval French SONG or BALLAD; the name comes from *Vire,* in Normandy.

Virginal. A small kind of HARPSICHORD.

Virtuoso,-a (It., vēr-too-oh'sŏh,-säh). A highly proficient instrumentalist or vocalist.

Vista (It., vĭ'stäh). Sight. *A (prima) vista*, at (first) sight.

Vistamente (It., vĭ'stäh-men'tĕh). Briskly, animatedly.

Vite (Fr., veet). Fast.

Vivace (It., vē-vah'chĕh). Lively, animated, brisk. As a TEMPO MARK standing by itself, *vivace* calls for a movement equalling or exceeding ALLEGRO in rapidity.

Vivacetto (It., vē-väh-chet'tŏh). Less lively than VIVACE, about ALLEGRETTO.

Vivacemente (It., vē-väh-chĕh-men'tĕh). Lively, spirited, animated, brisk; VIVACE.

Vivacissimo (It., vē-väh-chis'sē-mŏh). Very lively, PRESTO.

Vivo (It., vē'vŏh). Lively, spiritedly, briskly.

Vocal. Pertaining to the voice; suitable for the singing voice. *Vocal cords*, the two opposed ligaments set in the larynx, whose vibration, caused by expelling air from the lungs, produces vocal tones; *v. glottis*, the aperture between the vocal cords.

Vocal score. An OPERA SCORE arranged for voices and PIANO.

Vocalise (Fr., vŏh-cäh-lēz'). A vocal EXERCISE or ETUDE, sung to vowels or SOLMISATION syllables.

Voce (It., voh'chĕh; pl., **Voci** [voh'chē]). VOICE; PART. *A due (tre) voci*, for two (three) parts or voices, in two (three) parts; *mezza v., sotta v.*, see MEZZA; SOTTO.

Voce di petto (It., -dē pet'tŏh). Chest voice.

Voce di testa (It., -dē tĕs'täh). Head voice.

Voice. 1. The singing voice, divided into six principal classes: SOPRANO, MEZZO-SOPRANO, CONTRALTO (ALTO), TENOR, BARITONE, and BASS. 2. The word *voice* is often used instead of "PART," in imitation of foreign usage.

Voice leading. The art of arranging the voices in a POLYPHONIC COMPOSITION so that each PART has a logical continuation.

Voicing. TUNING.

Voix (Fr., v'wăh). VOICE; PART. *À deux (trois) voix*, for two (three) voices, in two (three) parts.

Volante (It., vŏh-lăhn'tĕh). Flying; light, swift.

Volata (It., vŏh-lah'tăh); **Volate** (Ger., vŏh-lah'tĕ); **Volatine** (Fr., vŏh-lăh-tēn'). A short vocal RUN or TRILL; a run or DIVISION; a light, rapid series of NOTES.

Volatina (It., vŏh-lăh-tē'năh). A short VOLATA.

Volkslied (Ger., fŏhlks'lēt). FOLK SONG.

Volkstümlich (Ger., fohlks'tǖm'lǐyh). Like a German FOLK SONG, or POPULAR MUSIC. Also seen as **im Volkston** (im-fŏhlks'tohn).

Voll (Ger., fŏhl). Full. *Volles Orchester*, full ORCHESTRA; *volles Werk*, full ORGAN; *mit vollem Chore*, with full CHORUS.

Volltönend (Ger., fŏhl-tön'ent). Sonorous, resonant.

Volta (It., vŏhl'tăh). A turn or time. *Prime volta* (or *Ima volta*, *Ima*, *Ia*, *I.*, *1.*), first time; *secunda v.* (or *IIda v.*, etc.), second time; *una v.*, once; *due v.*, twice.

Volteggiando (It., vŏhl-ted-jăhn'dŏh). Crossing hands on a KEYBOARD.

Volti subito (It., vŏhl'tē soo'bē-tŏh). Turn over instantly.

Volubilmente (It., vŏh-loo-bēl-men'tĕh). Fluently, flowingly.

Voluntary. An ORGAN solo before, during, or after divine service; or, a CHORAL PIECE opening the service.

Voluttuoso (It., vŏhl-lŏŏt-too-oh'sŏh). Voluptuous.

Vom (Ger., fŏhm). From the. *Vom Anfang*, DA CAPO.

Vorausnahme (Ger., fohr-ows-năhme). ANTICIPATION.

Vorhalt (Ger., fohr'hălt). A SUSPENSION.

Vorher (Ger., fohr-hăr'). Before; previous(ly).

Vorig (Ger., fohr'ĭyh). Preceding; previous; as *voriges Zeitmass (tempo precedente).*

Vorschlag (Ger., fohr'shlăyh). APPOGGIATURA.

Vorspiel (Ger., fohr'shpēl). PRELUDE, INTRODUCTION; OVERTURE.

Vortrag (Ger., fohr-trah). Rendering, INTERPRETATION, PERFORMANCE, STYLE, delivery, EXECUTION.

Vortragzeichen (Ger., fohr'trah-tsihen). EXPRESSION MARK.

Vorwärts (Ger., fohr'vârts). Forwards. *Etwas vorwärts gehend,* somewhat faster, POCO PIÙ MOSSO.

Vox (L., vōx). VOICE. *Vox angelica* (angelic voice), a 4' STOP corresponding to the 8' Vox humana; *Vox humana* (human voice), an 8' REED stop, the tone of which has a (fancied) resemblance to the human voice.

Vuoto (It., voo-oh'toh). "Empty"; used in the indication *corda vuoto,* open string.

W

Wachsend (Ger., văh'sent). CRESCENDO, "growing."

Wagner tuba. A BRASS INSTRUMENT introduced by Wagner in his MUSIC DRAMAS, in two sizes, TENOR and BASS.

Wah Wah Pedal. A foot-operated switch connected to an ELECTRIC GUITAR that activates a crying effect. Eric Clapton popularized this effect while playing lead guitar with the group Cream.

Waits (also **Waytes, Wayghtes,** etc.). Originally, English street watchmen, who gave notice of their coming by sounding HORNS, etc.; later, town musicians; and, still later, various irregular BANDS of indifferent music makers.

Waldflöte (Ger., văhlt'flö'tĕ). An open metal flue STOP in the ORGAN, of 2' or 4' PITCH and suave, full tone.

Waldhorn (Ger., vălht'horn). The FRENCH HORN without VALVES.

Waltz. A round dance in 3/4 TIME, varying in TEMPO from slow to moderately fast. *Waltzsong*, a SONG in WALTZ RHYTHM.

Walzer (Ger., vähl'tser). WALTZ.

Warble. YODEL.

Wärme, mit (Ger., mit vârmĕ). With warmth, warmly. *Mit grosser Wärme*, with great warmth.

Wehmüt(h)ig (Ger., mit vā'mü'tĭyh). In a style expressive of sadness or melancholy.

Weich (Ger., vīyh). Soft, tender; mellow, suave.

Weihnachtmusik (Ger., vī'nahts-moo-zīk). Christmas music.

Well tempered. In EQUAL TEMPERAMENT, as in Bach's *Well Tempered Clavier*.

Wenig (Ger., vā'nĭyh). Little. *Ein klein wenig langsamer*, a very little slower.

Whipping bow. A form of VIOLIN technique in which the BOW is made to fall with a certain vehemence on the STRINGS. Chiefly employed to mark sharply single TONES in rapid TEMPO, as

Whistle. A simple end-blown FLUTE, with or without holes.

White note. One with an open head: (o ♩).

Whole consort. Used in RENAISSANCE times to indicate an instrumental ensemble with all instruments drawn from the same family. Compare BROKEN CONSORT.

Whole note. The NOTE o. In COMMON (4/4) TIME, a note held for four BEATS.

Whole shift. SHIFT.

Whole step. 1. The STEP of a WHOLE TONE. 2. A whole tone.

Whole tone. A MAJOR SECOND.

Whole-tone scale. A SCALE consisting only of WHOLE TONES, and therefore lacking the DOMINANT and either MAJOR or MINOR TRIADS; popularized by Debussy and his followers.

Wie (Ger., vē). As. *Wie oben*, as above; *w. vorher*, as before, as first; *w. aus der Ferne*, as from a distance.

Wiegend (Ger., vē'ghent). Swaying, rocking.

Wiegenlied (Ger., vee'ghen-leed). A lullaby.

Wind band. 1. A company of performers on WIND INSTRU-MENTS. 2. The wind instruments in the ORCHESTRA; also, the players on, or parts written for, the same.

Wind instruments. Instruments whose TONES are produced by wind (that is, compressed air).

Wolf. 1. The DISCORD produced when playing, in certain KEYS, on an ORGAN tuned in unequal TEMPERAMENT. 2. In bowed instruments, an imperfect or jarring vibration caused by sounding some particular TONE(S). See DIFFERENTIAL TONE.

Woodblocks. Another name for *Chinese blocks*.

Woodwind. Wind instruments that use REEDS (CLARINET, OBOE, SAXOPHONE, etc.) and the FLUTE (which was formerly made of wood).

Working-out. DEVELOPMENT SECTION in SONATA FORM.

Wuchtig (Ger., vooh'tīyh). Weighty, weightily; ponderous(ly), with strong emphasis.

Würdevoll (Ger., vür'de-fohl'). With dignity; loftily.

Wüt(h)end (Ger., vü'tent). Furious(ly), frantic(ally).

X

Xylophone. An instrument consisting of a row of flat wooden bars fastened horizontally to two stretched boards, tuned to the TONES of the SCALE, and struck with two mallets. Some xylophones also have resonating chambers placed below each bar to amplify the tone.

Y

Yodel. A type of singing in Switzerland, and generally in the Alps, characterized by the frequent alternation of FALSETTO TONES with chest tones; a kind of warble. The original German spelling is *Jodel*.

Z

Zamacueca (Sp., thăh-măh-kwěh'kăh). The national dance of Chile, in rapid TRIPLE TIME.

Zapateado (Sp., thăh-păh-tā-ăh'dō). Spanish dance in TRIPLE TIME, characterized by heel stamping to emphasize the strong SYNCOPATION.

Zart (Ger., tsährt). Tender, soft, delicate, DOLCE; slender. *Mit zarten Stimmen*, with soft-toned STOPS.

Zartflöte (Ger. tsărt'flö'tě). In the ORGAN, a 4' FLUTE STOP of very delicate tone.

Zärtlich (Ger., tsâhrt'lĭyh). Tender(ly), caressing(ly).

Zarzuela (Sp., thăhr-thoo-āl'ăh). Type of Spanish OPERA with spoken dialogue.

Zeffiroso (Ir., dzef-fě-roh'sŏh). Zephyr-like.

Zeitmas (Ger., tzīt-măhs). TEMPO.

Zeitoper (Ger. tzīt'oh-per). Literally, "OPERA of the time" or "age"; German operas of the 1920s and early 1930s with distinct sociopolitical themes, driven by a generalized tendency of artists toward the creation of socially relevant art.

Zeloso (It., dzeh-loh'sŏh). Zealously, enthusiastically, with energy and fire.

Zheng. A Chinese half-tube ZITHER, commonly with sixteen to eighteen STRINGS.

Ziemlich (Ger., tsĕm'lĭyh). Somewhat, rather. *Ziemlich bewegt und frei in Vortrag*, quite animated and free in delivery (style).

Zierlich (Ger., tsĕr'lĭyh). Neat(ly), delicate(ly); graceful(ly).

Zigeunermusik (Ger., tsĭ-goy'ner-moo-zĭk). Gypsy music.

Zimbalon. CIMBALOM.

Zingara, alla (It., ăhl'lăh tsin'găh-răh). In Gypsy style.

Zither (Ger., tsit'ter). 1. The modern ZITHER has thirty-two or more STRINGS stretched over a shallow wooden SOUNDBOX, which has a fretted FINGERBOARD on the side next to the player; above the fingerboard are five MELODY strings, plucked with a metal "ring" worn on the thumb. 2. Generally, any instrument whose strings run parallel to and along the full length of the SOUNDBOX.

Zitternd (Ger., tsit'ternt). Trembling, tremulous.

Zögernd (Ger., tsö'gernt). Hesitating, retarding.

Zu (Ger., tsoo). Too; to.

Zunehmend (Ger., tsoo'nă'ment). Increasing, CRESCENDO.

Züruckgehend (Ger., tsoo-rŭk'gă'ent). Returning (to a preceding slower TEMPO).

Züruckhaltend (Ger., tsoo-rŭk'hăl'tent). Holding back, RITARDANDO.

Zwei (Ger., tsvī). Two.

Zweihändig (Ger., tsvī'hen'dĭyh). For two hands.

Zweistimmig (Ger., tsvī′shtim′mīyh). For two voices; in or for two PARTS.

Zwischensatz (Ger., tsvish′en-zăhts′). EPISODE.

Zwischenspiel (Ger., tsvish′en-shpēl′). INTERLUDE, INTERMEZZO.

Noteworthy Musicians

A

Abbado, Claudio (1933–   ), outstanding Italian conductor.

Absil, Jean (1893–1974), eminent Belgian composer.

Adam, Adolphe (1803–1856), celebrated French opera composer.

Adam de la Halle (c.1237–c.1287), foremost French trouvère, known also as "Le Bossu d'Arras" ("Hunchback of Arras").

Adams, John (1947–   ), prominent American composer.

Adderley, Julian "Cannonball" (1928–1975), black American bebop alto saxophonist.

Addinsell, Richard (1904–1977), English composer of theater and film music.

Adorno, Theodor (1903–1969), significant German philosopher.

Albéniz, Isaac (1860–1909), eminent Spanish composer.

Albert, Eugène d' (1864–1932), Scottish-born German composer.

Alberti, Domenico (1710–c.1740), Italian harpsichordist and composer, inventor of the "Alberti bass."

Albinoni, Tomaso (1671–1751), Italian violinist and composer.

Albright, William (1944–   ), talented American composer.

Alkan, Charles-Valentin (1813–1888), eccentric French pianist and composer.

Althouse, Paul (1889–1954), talented American tenor.

Amati, Nicola (or **Niccolò**) (1596–1684), illustrious Italian violin builder and teacher of Guarneri and Stradivari.

Amirkhanian, Charles (1945–   ), American avant-garde composer and influential radio producer.

Amram, David (1930–   ), American composer.

Anderson, Laurie (1947–   ), imaginative American composer and performance artist.

Anderson, Leroy (1908–1975), American composer of light instrumental music.

Anderson, Marian (1899–1993), celebrated black American contralto; the first black American member of the Metropolitan Opera.

Anderson, T.J. (b. Thomas Jefferson Anderson, Jr., 1928–1993), inventive black American composer.

Andriessen, Louis (1939–   ), prominent Dutch composer.

Angeles, Victoria de los (1923–   ), famous Spanish soprano.

Ansermet, Ernest (1883–1969), celebrated Swiss conductor.

Antes, John (1740–1811), American-Moravian composer, the first known American-born composer to write chamber music.

Antheil, George (1900–1959), remarkable American composer of the avant-garde.

Apel, Willi (1893–1988), eminent German music scholar.

Arcadelt, Jacob (c.1505–1568), great Flemish composer.

Arel, Bülent (1918–1990), Turkish-born American composer.

Arensky, Anton (1861–1906), Russian composer.

Argento, Dominick (1927–   ), esteemed American opera composer.

Arlen, Harold (b. Hyman Arluck, 1905–1986), American composer of popular songs, Broadway musicals, and Hollywood film scores.

Armstrong, Louis (1901–1971), also known as "Satchmo" (for "Satchel Mouth"), famous black American jazz trumpeter, singer, bandleader, and entertainer.

Arne, Thomas (1710–1778), famous English dramatic composer.

Arnold, Malcolm (1921–), versatile English composer.

Arnold, Samuel (1740–1802), celebrated English dramatic composer.

Arrau, Claudio (1903–1991), eminent Chilean-born American pianist.

Arriaga, Juan (1806–1826), precocious and short-lived Spanish composer.

Arroyo, Martina (1936–), American soprano.

Asafiev, Boris (1884–1949), Russian composer and writer on music.

Ashkenazy, Vladimir (1937–), greatly gifted Russian pianist.

Ashley, Robert (1930–), American composer of the avantgarde, known particularly for his highly original video operas.

Atterberg, Kurt (1887–1974), eminent Swedish composer.

Auber, Daniel-François-Esprit (1782–1871), French opera composer.

Aubert, Louis-François-Marie (1877–1968), French opera composer.

Audran, Edmond (1840–1904), French operetta composer.

Auer, Leopold (1845–1930), celebrated Hungarian violinist and teacher of Heifetz, Zimbalist, and Elman.

Augér, Arleen (1939–1993), esteemed American soprano.

Auric, Georges (1899–1983), notable French composer.

Austin, Larry (1930–   ), American composer of the avant-garde.

Avison, Charles (1709–1770), English organist and composer.

Ax, Emmanuel (1949–   ), talented Polish-born American pianist.

B

Babbitt, Milton (1916–   ), prominent American composer and noted theoretician.

Bach, Carl Philipp Emanuel (1714–1788), noted German composer, third son of Johann Sebastian Bach.

Bach, Johann Christian (1735–1782), noted German composer, eleventh and youngest surviving son of Johann Sebastian Bach; known also as the "London Bach" because of his long residence in London.

Bach, Johann Sebastian (1685–1750), outstanding German composer, organist, and pedagogue, a giant of Baroque polyphony.

Bach, Wilhelm Friedemann (1710–1784), notable German composer, eldest son of Johann Sebastian Bach.

Bachauer, Gina (1913–1976), eminent Greek pianist.

Backhaus, Wilhelm (1884–1969), eminent German pianist.

Bacon, Ernst (1898–1990), remarkable American composer.

Badings, Henk (1907–1987), prominent Dutch composer.

Badura-Skoda, Paul (1927–   ), eminent Austrian pianist.

Baez, Joan (1941–   ), popular American folksinger.

Baird, Tadeusz (1928–1981), prominent Polish composer.

Baker, David (1931–   ), American jazz composer and educator.

Baker, Dame Janet (1933–), celebrated English mezzo-soprano.

Baker, Josephine (1906–1975), colorful black American-born French dancer, singer, and actress.

Baker, Theodore (1851–1934), significant American musicologist, and original author of this dictionary.

Balakirev, Mily (1837–1910), significant Russian composer, one of the "Mighty Five."

Balfe, Michael William (1808–1870), notable Irish opera composer.

Bantock, Sir Granville (1868–1946), eminent English composer.

Barati, George (1913–), Hungarian-born American cellist and composer.

Barber, Samuel (1910–1981), outstanding American composer.

Barbirolli, Sir John (1899–1970), prominent English conductor.

Barenboim, Daniel (1942–), greatly talented Israeli pianist and conductor.

Barraqué, Jean (1928–1973), eccentric French composer.

Barraud, Henry (1900–), French composer.

Bartók, Béla (1881–1945), great Hungarian composer, whose style was intimately welded to his pioneering folk music research.

Basie, William "Count" (1904–1984), great American jazz pianist and bandleader.

Bassett, Leslie (1923–), distinguished American composer.

Battistini, Mattia (1856–1928), celebrated Italian baritone.

Bauer, Harold (1873–1951), distinguished English pianist.

Bauer, Marion (1887–1955), American composer and writer.

Bax, Sir Arnold (1883–1953), outstanding English composer.

Beach, Mrs. H.H.A. (Amy Marcy Cheney) (1867–1944), American composer.

Beardslee, Bethany (1927–), American soprano, specialist in modern music.

Bechet, Sidney (1897–1961), famous black American jazz clarinetist and soprano saxophonist.

Becker, John (1886–1961), remarkable American composer.

Beckwith, John (1927–), prominent Canadian composer.

Beecham, Sir Thomas (1879–1961), significant English conductor.

Beeson, Jack (1921–), American composer.

Beethoven, Ludwig van (1770–1827), great German composer, master of the symphony, string quartet, and piano sonata, who bridged the Classic and Romantic periods.

Beiderbecke, Bix (1903–1931), American jazz cornetist.

Beinum, Eduard van (1900–1959), Dutch conductor.

Beissel, Johann Conrad (1690–1768), German-American composer of sacred music.

Belafonte, Harry (1927–), popular American folksinger and actor.

Bellini, Vincenzo (1801–1835), celebrated Italian composer of *bel canto* opera.

Benedict, Sir Julius (1804–1885), German-English conductor and composer.

Benjamin, Arthur (1893–1960), Australian composer.

Bennett, Richard Rodney (1936–), prolific English composer.

Bennett, Robert Russell (1894–1981), American composer and arranger.

Bennett, Sir William Sterndale (1816–1875), English composer.

Benoit, Peter (1834–1901), Flemish composer.

Berberian, Cathy (1925–1983), versatile American mezzosoprano, specialist in modern music; first wife of **Luciano Berio.**

Berg, Alban (1885–1935), leading Austrian twelve-tone composer; celebrated pupil of Arnold Schoenberg.

Berger, Arthur (1912–), American composer and writer on music.

Bergsma, William (1921–1994), notable American composer.

Berio, Luciano (1925–), outstanding Italian composer; married, to her death in 1983, to **Cathy Berberian.**

Bériot, Charles de (1802–1870), Belgian violinist and composer.

Berkeley, Sir Lennox (1903–1989), notable English composer, father of **Michael Berkeley.**

Berkeley, Michael (1948–), English composer.

Berlin, Irving (b. Israel Baline, 1888–1989), American composer of enormously popular songs and Broadway shows.

Berlioz, Hector (1803–1869), outstanding French composer, a master of orchestration.

Berman, Lazar (1930–), Russian pianist.

Bernstein, Elmer (1922–), significant American film composer.

Bernstein, Leonard (1918–1990), widely celebrated American conductor, composer of popular and art music, and commentator on music.

Berry, Chuck (1926–), American rock 'n' roll singer, guitarist, and songwriter.

Berwald, Franz Adolf (1796–1868), Swedish composer.

Biggs, E. Power (1906–1977), eminent English-American organist.

Billings, William (1746–1800), American composer of ingenious "fuguing tunes."

Binchois, Gilles (c.1400–1460), important Franco-Flemish composer.

Bing, Sir Rudolf (1902–), Austrian-born English opera impressario; general manager of New York's Metropolitan Opera from 1950 to 1972.

Birtwistle, Sir Harrison (1934–), outstanding English composer.

Bishop, Sir Henry Rowley (1786–1855), noted English composer, whose most popular songs include "Home Sweet Home."

Bizet, Georges (1838–1875), great French opera composer, most famous for *Carmen*.

Björling, Jussi (1911–1960), eminent Swedish tenor.

Blacher, Boris (1903–1975), remarkable German composer.

Blake, Eubie (b. James Hubert Blake, 1883–1983), black American jazz piano player, vaudevillian, and composer of popular music.

Bland, James A. (1854–1911), American minstrel and composer, whose songs include "Carry Me Back to Old Virginy."

Bliss, Sir Arthur (1891–1975), prominent English composer.

Blitzstein, Marc (1905–1964), important American composer of socially conscious theater music.

Bloch, Ernest (1880–1959), important Swiss-born American composer.

Blom, Eric (1888–1959), eminent English writer on music.

Blomdahl, Karl-Birger (1916–1968), significant Swedish composer.

Blow, John (1649–1708), great English composer and organist.

Boccherini, Luigi (1743–1805), famous Italian composer and cellist.

Böhm, Karl (1894–1981), Austrian conductor of great renown.

Boieldieu, François-Adrien (1775–1834), celebrated French opera composer.

Boito, Arrigo (1842–1918), important Italian poet and opera composer.

Bolet, Jorge (1914–1990), brilliant Cuban-born American pianist.

Bolcom, William (1938–   ), American composer and pianist.

Bonaventura, Mario di (1924–   ), American conductor, educator, and music publisher.

Bond, Carrie Jacobs (1862–1946), American song composer.

Bonnet, Joseph (1884–1944), eminent French organist.

Bononcini, Giovanni (1670–1747), Italian composer.

Borge, Victor (real name **Borge Rosenbaum**) (1909–   ), popular Danish pianist and musical humorist.

Borodin, Alexander (1833–1887), celebrated Russian composer, one of the "Mighty Five."

Boulanger, Lili (1893–1918), French composer, sister of **Nadia Boulanger.**

Boulanger, Nadia (1887–1979), renowned French composition teacher.

Boulez, Pierre (1925–   ), celebrated French composer, conductor, and theorist.

Boult, Sir Adrian (1889–1983), eminent English conductor.

Bowie, David (1947–), popular British rock musician.

Brahms, Johannes (1833–1897), great German composer and master symphonist of the late Romantic era.

Brailowsky, Alexander (1896–1976), Russian pianist.

Brain, Dennis (1921–1957), English horn virtuoso.

Brant, Henry (1913–), Canadian-born American composer, pioneer of spatial music.

Brendel, Alfred (1931–), eminent Austrian pianist.

Brian, Havergal (1876–1972), prolific English symphonic composer.

Bridge, Frank (1879–1941), distinguished English composer and teacher of Benjamin Britten.

Bristow, George Frederick (1825–1898), patriotic American composer.

Britten, Benjamin (1913–1976), outstanding English composer, one of the most important opera composers of the 20th century.

Brooks, Garth (1961–), very popular country singer and guitarist.

Brouwer, Leo (1939–), Cuban guitarist and composer.

Brown, Earle (1926–), American composer of the avant-garde.

Brown, James (1928–), black American soul singer, dancer, and entertainer.

Browning, John (1933–), brilliant American pianist.

Brownlee, John (1900–1969), talented American baritone.

Brubeck, Dave (1920–), prominent American jazz pianist, bandleader, and composer.

Bruch, Max (1838–1920), celebrated German composer.

Bruckner, Anton (1824–1896), imposing Austrian symphonic composer.

Brumel, Antoine (1460–c.1520), Flemish composer.

Bryars, Gavin (1943–), innovative English composer.

Bryn-Julson, Phyllis (1945–), esteemed American soprano.

Buck, Dudley (1839–1909), noted American organist, composer, and pedagogue.

Buchla, Donald (1937–), American electronic instrument designer and builder, composer, and performer.

Bull, John (c.1562–1628), famous English composer and organist.

Bull, Ole (1810–1880), eccentric Norwegian violinist.

Bülow, Hans von (1830–1894), celebrated German pianist and conductor.

Bumbry, Grace (1937–), American soprano.

Burkhard, Willy (1900–1955), significant Swiss composer.

Burney, Charles (1726–1814), important English music historian.

Busoni, Ferruccio (1866–1924), influential Italian-German composer, pianist, and writer on modern aesthetics.

Bussotti, Sylvano (1931–), significant Italian composer of the avant-garde.

Buxtehude, Dietrich (c. 1637–1707), significant Danish-born German organist and composer.

Byrd, Donald (1932–), inspired black American jazz trumpeter, flugelhornist, and teacher.

Byrd, William (1543–1623), great English composer and organist.

Byrne, David (1952–), popular Scottish-born American musician, leader of the popular alternative group, Talking Heads.

C

Caballé, Montserrat (1933–), celebrated Spanish soprano.

Cabezón, Antonio de (1510–1566), great Spanish organist and composer.

Caccini, Giulio (1551–1618), important Italian composer, one of the originators of opera.

Cadman, Charles Wakefield (1881–1946), American composer and early researcher into the music of native Americans.

Cage, John (1912–1992), outstanding American composer, writer, philosopher, and visual artist of the experimental school, who radically changed the course of 20th-century music.

Caldwell, Sarah (1924–), American conductor and opera director.

Callas, Maria (1923–1977), celebrated American soprano.

Calvé, Emma (1858–1942), French soprano.

Cardew, Cornelius (1936–1981), important English composer of the avant-garde.

Carissimi, Giacomo (1605–1674), important Italian composer.

Carmichael, Hoagy (1899–1981), American pianist and composer of popular music.

Carpenter, John Alden (1876–1951), significant American composer.

Carr, Benjamin (1768–1831), English-American composer and publisher.

Carrillo, Julián (1875–1965), significant Mexican composer.

Carter, Benny (1907–), outstanding black American jazz instrumentalist, bandleader, arranger, and composer.

Carter, Elliott (1908–), highly respected American composer, innovator of "metric modulation."

Caruso, Enrico (1873–1921), legendary Italian tenor.

Casadesus, Gaby (1901–), French pianist and teacher, wife of Robert and mother of **Jean Casadesus.**

Casadesus, Jean (1927–1972), French pianist.

Casadesus, Robert (1899–1972), French pianist and composer.

Casals, Pablo (1876–1973), outstanding Spanish cellist.

Casella, Alfredo (1883–1947), significant Italian composer.

Cash, Johnny (1932–), popular American country singer, guitarist, and songwriter.

Castelnuovo-Tedesco, Mario (1895–1968), greatly significant Italian composer.

Castro, Juan José (1895–1968), eminent Argentine composer and conductor.

Cavalli, Pier Francesco (1602–1676), historically significant Italian opera composer.

Celibidache, Sergiu (1912–), prominent Rumanian conductor.

Cesti, Antonio (1623–1669), renowned Italian composer.

Chabrier, Emmanuel (1841–1894), famous French composer.

Chadwick, George Whitefield (1854–1931), eminent American composer.

Chaliapin, Feodor (1873–1938), legendary Russian bass.

Chaminade, Cécile (1857–1944), stylish French composer and pianist.

Charles, Ray (b. Ray Charles Robinson, 1930–), outstanding black American rhythm and blues and soul singer, pianist, arranger, and songwriter.

Charpentier, Gustave (1860–1956), French composer and organist.

Charpentier, Marc-Antoine (c.1645–50–1704), French composer.

Chasins, Abram (1903–1987), American pianist and composer.

Chausson, Ernest (1855–1899), distinguished French composer.

Chávez, Carlos (1899–1978), leading Mexican composer.

Checker, Chubby (b. Ernest Evans) (1941–), American rock 'n' roll singer who launched a dance craze with his recording of Hank Ballard's song, "The Twist."

Cherkassky, Shura (1911–), remarkable Russian-born American pianist.

Cherubini, Luigi (1760–1842), famous Italian composer.

Childs, Barney (1926–), American avant-garde composer.

Chopin, Frédéric (1810–1849), incomparable Polish composer and genius of the piano who created a unique romantic style of keyboard music.

Chou Wen-chung (1923–), remarkable Chinese-born American composer.

Cimarosa, Domenico (1749–1801), famous Italian composer.

Clapton, Eric (1945–), virtuoso English guitarist and singer.

Clementi, Aldo (1925–), Italian composer of the avant-garde.

Clementi, Muzio (1752–1832), celebrated Italian pianist and composer.

Cliburn, Van (b. Harvey Lavan, Jr., 1934–), brilliant American pianist.

Cline, Patsy (b. Virginia Patterson Hensley, 1932–1963), legendary American country vocalist.

Cohan, George M(ichael) (1878–1965), celebrated American composer of popular songs.

Cole, Nat "King" (b. Nathaniel Adams Coles, 1917–1965), beloved black American pianist and singer.

Coleman, Ornette (1930–), black American jazz alto saxophonist and composer, innovator of a radically new freestyle form of improvisation.

Coleridge-Taylor, Samuel (1875–1912), esteemed English composer of African descent.

Colgrass, Michael (1932–), American composer.

Coltrane, John (1926–1967), remarkable black American jazz musician, virtuoso on the tenor saxophone.

Consoli, Marc-Antonio (1941–), Italian-born American composer.

Converse, Frederick Shepherd (1871–1940), distinguished American composer.

Copland, Aaron (1900–1990), greatly distinguished and exceptionally gifted American composer.

Corea, Chick (b. Armando Anthony Corea, 1941–), American jazz pianist and composer.

Corelli, Arcangelo (1653–1713), famous Italian violinist and composer.

Corigliano, John (1938–), gifted American composer.

Cornelius, Peter (1824–1874), important German composer and writer.

Cortot, Alfred (1877–1962), famous French pianist.

Couperin, François (1668–1733), great French keyboard composer and organist.

Cowell, Henry (1897–1965), remarkable American composer, innovator of "tone clusters."

Craft, Robert (1923–), American conductor and writer; Stravinsky's amanuensis and literary collaborator.

Crawford-Seeger, Ruth (1901–1953), significant American composer and folklorist, wife of **Charles Seeger.**

Crécquillon, Thomas (c.1480–c.1500), Franco-Flemish composer.

Creston, Paul (1906–1989), American composer.

Crosby, Bing (b. Harry Lillis Crosby, 1901–1977), extremely popular American singer and actor.

Crumb, George (1929–), inventive American composer.

Cugat, Xavier (1900–1990), popular Spanish-American bandleader.

Cui, Cesar (1835–1918), significant Russian composer, one of the "Mighty Five."

Curran, Alvin (1938–), important American composer of the experimental school.

Curtis-Smith, Curtis (1941–), American composer and pianist.

Czerny, Carl (1791–1857), celebrated Austrian pianist, pedagogue, and composer of piano exercises.

D

Dahl, Ingolf (1912–1970), distinguished Swedish-born American composer, conductor, and teacher.

Dallapiccola, Luigi (1904–1975), important Italian serial composer.

Damrosch, Frank (1859–1937), German-American conductor and teacher.

Damrosch, Leopold (1832–1885), German-American conductor, father of **Frank** and **Walter Damrosch.**

Damrosch, Walter (1862–1950), famous German-American conductor, composer, and educator.

Da Ponte, Lorenzo (1749–1838), famous Italian librettist, particularly known for his collaborations with Mozart.

Daquin, Louis-Claude (1694–1772), French organist and composer.

Dargomyzhsky, Alexander (1813–1869), outstanding Russian composer.

David, Ferdinand (1810–1873), noted German violinist and composer.

David, Johann Nepomuk (1895–1977), outstanding Austrian composer.

Davidovsky, Mario (1934–   ), Argentine composer.

Davies, Sir Peter Maxwell (1934–   ), remarkable English composer and conductor.

Davis, Anthony (1951–   ), black American composer and pianist.

Davis, Sir Colin (1927–   ), eminent English conductor.

Davis, Miles (b. Miles Dewey Davis, III, 1926–1991), outstanding black American jazz trumpeter and bandleader.

Debussy, Claude (1862–1918), great modern French composer; originator of musical Impressionism.

DeGaetani, Jan (1933–1989), remarkable American mezzo-soprano, specializing in modern music.

De Koven, Reginald (1859–1920), American composer of light operas and songs.

Delden, Lex van (1919–1988), prominent Dutch composer.

Delibes, Léo (1836–1891), famous French composer.

Delius, Frederick (b. Fritz Theodor Albert Delius, 1862–1934), important English composer of German parentage.

Dello Joio, Norman (1913–), American composer.

Del Tredici, David (1937–), whimsical American composer.

Denisov, Edison (1929–), innovative Russian composer.

De Reszke, Jean (1850–1925), celebrated Polish tenor.

Des Prez, Josquin (c. 1440–1521), also known as simply **Josquin**, masterful Flemish polyphonic composer.

Dessau, Paul (1894–1979), German composer.

Diabelli, Anton (1781–1858), Austrian composer and music publisher, known chiefly through a set of variations Beethoven wrote on one of his themes.

Diamond, David (1915–), prolific American composer.

Dichter, Misha (1945–), talented American pianist.

Dickinson, Peter (1934–), English composer.

Diddley, Bo (b. Ellas Bates McDaniel, 1928–), black American rock 'n' roll singer and guitarist.

Dittersdorf, Karl Ditters von (1739–1799), Austrian violinist and composer.

Dodge, Charles (1942–), important American composer of avant-garde tendencies.

Dohnányi, Ernst von (1877–1960), significant Hungarian composer, pianist, and pedagogue.

Dolmetsch, Arnold (1858–1940), French-born English music scholar and instrumentalist.

Domingo, Plácido (1941–), famous Spanish tenor.

Domino, "Fats" (b. Antoine Domino, Jr., 1928–), early black American rock 'n' roll singer and pianist.

Donizetti, Gaetano (1797–1848), prolific Italian composer of operas in the *bel canto* tradition.

Dorati, Antal (1906–1988), distiguished Hungarian-born American conductor.

Dorsey, Jimmy (1904–1957), popular American jazz clarinetist, saxophonist, and dance-band leader, brother of **Tommy Dorsey.**

Dorsey, Tommy (1905–1956), popular American jazz trombonist and dance-band leader.

Dowland, John (1563–1626), great English lutenist and composer.

Dragonetti, Domenico (1763–1846), Italian double-bass virtuoso.

Dresden, Sem (1881–1957), notable Dutch composer and pedagogue.

Druckman, Jacob (1928–), outstanding American composer.

Dubois, Théodore (1837–1924), French organist and pedagogue.

Duckworth, William (1943–), American composer, teacher, and writer on music.

Dufallo, Richard (1933–), American clarinetist and conductor.

Dufay, Guillaume (c.1400–1474), great French composer.

Dukas, Paul (1865–1935), famous French composer and pedagogue.

Duke, Vernon. See **Dukelsky, Vladimir.**

Dukelsky, Vladimir (1903–1969), versatile Russian-American composer of serious and popular music, the latter under the pseudonym "Vernon Duke."

Dunstable (or **Dunstaple**), **John** (c. 1390–1453), great English composer.

Duparc, Henri (1848–1933), French song composer.

DuPré, Jacqueline (1945–1987), renowned English cellist.

DuPré, Marcel (1886–1971), remarkable French organist.

Durey, Louis (1888–1979), French composer.

Dushkin, Samuel (1891–1976), Polish-American violinist.

Dussek, Johann Ladislav (1760–1812), notable Bohemian pianist and conductor.

Dvořák, Antonín (1841–1904), famous Czech composer.

Dylan, Bob (b. Robert Allen Zimmerman, 1941–   ), American folksinger and songwriter; a beacon of 1960s socially conscious folk-rock.

E

Egge, Klaus (1906–1979), prominent Norwegian composer.

Egk, Werner (1901–1983), significant German composer.

Ehrling, Sixten (1918–   ), noted Swedish conductor.

Einem, Gottfried von (1918–   ), American composer.

Einstein, Alfred (1880–1952), eminent German-born American musicologist.

Eisler, Hanns (1898–1962), remarkable German composer of politically oriented works.

El-Dabh, Halim (1921–   ), Egyptian-born American composer.

Elgar, Sir Edward (1857–1934), great English composer.

Ellington, Edward Kennedy "Duke" (1899–1974), famous black American pianist, bandleader, and composer.

Elman, Mischa (1891–1967), remarkable Russian-born American violinist.

Emmett, Daniel Decatur (1815–1904), American composer of popular songs, including "Dixie."

Enesco, Georges (1881–1955), famous Rumanian violinist, conductor, composer, and educator.

Engelmann, Hans Ulrich (1921–   ), German composer.

Eno, Brian (1948–), English composer, musician, and producer.

Entremont, Philippe (1934–), eminent French pianist and conductor.

Erb, Donald (1927–), significant American composer.

Erickson, Robert (1917–), important American composer.

Evans, Bill (1929–1980), American jazz pianist and composer.

Ewen, David (1907–1985), prolific Polish-born American writer on music.

F

Falla, Manuel de (1876–1946), great Spanish composer.

Farinelli (1705–1782), Italian castrato of legendary virtuosity.

Farkas, Ferenc (1905–), prominent Hungarian composer.

Farrar, Geraldine (1882–1967), celebrated American soprano.

Farrell, Eileen (1920–), brilliant American soprano.

Farwell, Arthur (1872–1952), American composer and pedagogue.

Fauré, Gabriel (1845–1924), important French composer and pedagogue.

Faure, Jean-Baptiste (1830–1914), famous French baritone.

Fayrfax, Robert (1464–1521), English composer.

Feinstein, Michael (1956–), remarkably facile American singer and pianist of popular music.

Feldman, Morton (1926–1987), important American composer of the experimental school.

Feltsman, Vladimir (1952–), prominent Russian pianist.

Ferguson, Maynard (1928–), Canadian jazz trumpeter.

Ferneyhough, Brian (1943–), remarkable English composer.

Ferrero, Willy (1906–1954), American-born Italian conductor.

Ferrier, Kathleen (1912–1953), remarkable English contralto.

Fiedler, Arthur (1894–1979), popular American conductor.

Field, John (1782–1837), remarkable Irish pianist and composer.

Fine, Irving (1914–1962), American composer.

Fine, Vivian (1913–), American composer, teacher, and pianist.

Finney, Ross Lee (1906–), distinguished American composer.

Firkušný, Rudolf (1912–), eminent Czech-born American pianist.

Fischer-Dieskau, Dietrich (1925–), celebrated German baritone.

Fitzgerald, Ella (1918–), remarkable black American jazz vocalist.

Flagstad, Kirsten (1895–1962), celebrated Norwegian soprano.

Fleisher, Leon (1928–), distinguished American pianist and conductor.

Flothius, Marius (1914–), eminent Dutch composer.

Flotow, Friedrich von (1813–1883), famous German opera composer.

Floyd, Carlisle (1926–), American composer.

Foote, Arthur (1853–1937), distinguished American composer.

Fortner, Wolfgang (1907–1987), important German composer.

Foss, Lukas (1922–), brilliant German-born American pianist, conductor, and composer.

Foster, Stephen (1826–1864), famous American song composer.

Fox, Virgil (1912–1980), famous American organist.

Francescatti, Zino (1905–1991), brilliant French violinist.

Franck, César (1822–1890), great Belgian composer and organist.

Franklin, Aretha (1942–), outstanding black American soul singer.

Franz, Robert (1815–1892), famous German lieder composer.

Freeman, Harry (1869–1954), famous black American composer.

Frescobaldi, Girolamo (1583–1643), great Italian organist and composer.

Friml, Rudolf (1881–1972), famous Bohemian-American operetta composer.

Froberger, Johann Jakob (1616–1667), eminent German organist and composer.

Fry, William Henry (1813–1864), American composer and journalist.

Furtwängler, Wilhelm (1886–1954), celebrated German conductor.

Fux, Johann Joseph (1660–1741), renowned Austrian organist, music theorist, pedagogue, and composer.

G

Gabrieli, Andrea (c.1510–1586), eminent Italian organist and composer.

Gabrieli, Giovanni (c.1556–1612), celebrated Italian organist, composer, and teacher.

Gabrilowitsch, Ossip (1878–1936), notable Russian-American pianist.

Gade, Niels (1817–1890), significant Danish composer and conductor.

Galilei, Vincenzo (c. 1520–1591), celebrated Italian lutenist, composer, and music theorist, father of the great astronomer Galileo Galilei.

Galli-Curci, Amelita (1882–1963), brilliant Italian soprano.

Galuppi, Baldassare (1706–1785), celebrated Italian composer.

Galway, James (1939–), famous Irish flute virtuoso.

Garden, Mary (1874–1967), celebrated Scottish soprano.

Garland, Judy (1922–1969), famous American pop singer and actress.

Gatti-Casazza, Giulio (1868–1940), famous Italian impresario.

Gedda, Nicolai (1925–), noted Swedish tenor.

Geminiani, Francesco (1687–1762), Italian violinist and composer.

Gerhard, Roberto (1896–1970), great Spanish-born English composer.

German, Sir Edward (1862–1936), English composer.

Gershwin, George (b. Jacob Gershvin, 1898–1937), immensely gifted American songwriter and composer, brother of **Ira Gershwin.**

Gershwin, Ira (1896–1983), talented American librettist and lyricist.

Gesualdo, Don Carlo (c. 1560–1613), influential Italian composer of highly chromatic works that anticipated future styles.

Getz, Stan (1927–1991), famous American jazz tenor saxophonist.

Giannini, Vittorio (1903–1966), American composer.

Gibbons, Orlando (1583–1625), celebrated English composer and organist.

Gideon, Miriam (1906–), American composer and pedagogue.

Gieseking, Walter (1895–1956), distinguished German pianist.

Gigli, Beniamino (1890–1957), celebrated Italian tenor.

Gilbert, Henry Franklin (1868–1928), remarkable American composer.

Gilbert, Sir William (1836–1911), English playwright, most famous for his stage collaborations with Sir Arthur Sullivan.

Gilels, Emil (1916–1985), eminent Russian pianist.

Gillespie, John Birks "Dizzy" (1917–1993), famous black American jazz trumpeter and bandleader; with Charlie "Bird" Parker, established the bebop style.

Gilmore, Patrick (1829–1892), Irish-American bandmaster.

Ginastera, Alberto (1916–1983), outstanding Argentine composer.

Giulini, Carlo Maria (1914–), eminent Italian conductor.

Glanville-Hicks, Peggy (1912–1990), important Australian-born American composer and music critic.

Glass, Philip (1937–), remarkable American composer, early proponent of musical Minimalism.

Glazunov, Alexander (1865–1936), eminent Russian composer.

Glière, Reinhold (1875–1956), eminent Russian composer.

Glinka, Mikhail (1804–1857), great Russian composer, called "the father of Russian music" for his pioneering cultivation of Russian folk modalities.

Gluck, Christoph Willibald, Ritter von (1714–1787), renowned German composer.

Godowsky, Leopold (1870–1838), famous Polish-born American pianist and composer of virtuoso etudes.

Goldmark, Karl (1830–1915), eminent Hungarian composer.

Goldmark, Rubin (1872–1936), important American composer and teacher.

Golschmann, Vladimir (1893–1972), French-born American conductor.

Goodman, Benny (b. Benjamin David Goodman, 1909–1986), famous American clarinetist and swing band leader.

Goossens, Sir Eugene (1893–1962), distinguished English conductor and composer.

Górecki, Henryk (1933–), significant Polish composer.

Gossec, François (1734–1829), significant South Netherlands composer.

Gottschalk, Louis Moreau (1829–1869), celebrated American pianist and composer.

Goudimel, Claude (c.1510–1572), celebrated French composer and music theorist.

Gould, Glenn (1932–1982), remarkable and individualistic Canadian pianist, noted for his unorthodox interpretations.

Gould, Morton (1913–), extraordinarily talented and versatile American conductor and composer.

Gounod, Charles (1818–1893), famous French composer.

Grainger, Percy (1882–1961), celebrated Australian-born American pianist and composer.

Gramm, Donald (1927–1983), American bass-baritone.

Granados, Enrique (1867–1916), outstanding Spanish composer.

Grandjany, Marcel (1891–1975), French-born American harpist.

Grappelli, Stéphane (1908–), outstanding French jazz violinist.

Greenberg, Noah (1919–1966), noted American conductor and musicologist, specialist in early music.

Gretchaninoff, Alexander (1864–1956), Russian-born American composer.

Grétry, André (1741–1813), significant French composer.

Grieg, Edvard (1843–1907), lyrical Norwegian composer.

Griffes, Charles Tomlinson (1884–1920), outstanding American composer.

Grofé, Ferde (1892–1972), American composer, pianist, and arranger.

Grove, Sir George (1820–1900), eminent English musicologist.

Gruenberg, Louis (1884–1964), Russian-born American composer.

Guarneri, Giuseppe (1698–1744), celebrated Italian violin maker.

Gubaidulina, Sofia (1931–), remarkable Russian composer.

Guido d'Arezzo (c.991–after 1033), famous Italian reformer of musical notation and vocal instruction.

Guilmant, Alexandre (1837–1911), French organist and composer.

Gulda, Friedrich (1930–), remarkable Austrian pianist.

Guthrie, Arlo (1947–), socially conscious American folksinger, guitarist, and songwriter, son of **Woody Guthrie.**

Guthrie, Woody (1912–1967), legendary American folksinger and songwriter, famous for "This Land Is Your Land" and other songs.

H

Hába, Alois (1893–1973), notable Czech composer and pedagogue, brother of **Karel Hába.**

Hába, Karel (1898–1972), important Czech composer.

Hadley, Henry (1871–1937), noted American composer and conductor.

Hageman, Richard (1882–1966), distinguished Dutch-American pianist, conductor, and composer.

Haieff, Alexei (1914–1994), Russian-American composer.

Hale, Philip (1854–1934), noted American music critic.

Halévy, Fromental (1799–1862), celebrated French composer.

Hamilton, Iain (1922–), remarkable Scottish composer.

Hammerstein, Oscar, II (1895–1960), outstanding American lyricist, most famous for his stage collaborations with Richard Rodgers.

Hampton, Lionel (1909–), noted black American jazz vibraphonist, drummer, pianist, and bandleader.

Handel, George Frideric (1685–1759), outstanding German organist and composer, innovator of England's oratorio and a giant of the late Baroque.

Handy, W(illiam) C(hristopher) (1873–1958), noted black American composer, known as the "father of the blues."

Hanon, Charles-Louis (1819–1900), French pianist, pedagogue, and composer of keyboard exercises.

Hanslick, Eduard (1825–1904), eminent and polemic Austrian music critic.

Hanson, Howard (1896–1981), important American composer, conductor, and educator.

Harbison, John (1938–   ), significant American composer.

Harris, Roy (1896–1979), significant American composer.

Harrison, George (1943–   ), English rock singer and guitarist; member of the fantastically popular rock group The Beatles.

Harrison, Lou (1917–   ), inventive American composer, innovator with Western applications of the Indonesian gamelan.

Hart, Lorenz (1895–1943), outstanding American lyricist, most famous for his stage collaborations with Richard Rodgers.

Harty, Sir Hamilton (1879–1941), Irish composer and conductor.

Hasse, Johann Adolph (1699–1783), celebrated German composer.

Hassler, Hans Leo (1564–1612), important German organist and composer.

Haubenstock-Ramati, Roman (1919–1994), Polish composer of experimental music.

Hauer, Josef Matthias (1883–1959), influential Austrian music theorist and composer.

Hauptmann, Moritz (1792–1868), eminent German music theorist, pedagogue, and composer.

Hawkins, Coleman (1904–1969), also known as "Hawk," outstanding black American jazz tenor saxophonist.

Hawkins, Sir John (1719–1789), eminent English music historian.

Haydn, Franz Joseph (1732–1809), illustrious Austrian composer, the first master of Viennese Classicism and the "Father of the Symphony"; brother of **Michael Haydn.**

Haydn, Michael (1737–1806), eminent Austrian composer.

Hayes, Roland (1887–1977), distinguished black American tenor.

Heifetz, Jascha (1899–1987), celebrated Russian-born American violinist.

Heller, Stephen (1813–1888), noted Hungarian pianist and composer.

Henderson, Skitch (1918–), popular English-born American pianist, conductor, composer, and arranger.

Hendrix, Jimi (1942–1970), influential black American rock guitarist, singer, and songwriter.

Henry, Pierre (1927–), important French composer and acoustic inventor; developer of *musique concrète.*

Henschel, Sir George (1850–1934), German-born English conductor, composer, and baritone.

Hensel, Fanny Cäcilia (1805–1847), German pianist and composer, sister of Felix Mendelssohn.

Henselt, Adolf von (1814–1889), German pianist and composer.

Henze, Hans Werner (1926–), outstanding German composer of the modern school.

Herbert, Victor (1859–1924), famous Irish-born American composer.

Herbst, Johannes (1735–1812), German-American Moravian minister and composer.

Herman, Woody (1913–1987), noted American clarinetist, saxophonist, and bandleader.

Hérold, Louis (1791–1833), French composer.

Herrmann, Bernard (1911–1975), outstanding American film composer and conductor.

Herz, Henri (1803–1888), Austrian pianist and composer.

Heseltine, Philip (1894–1930), brilliant English composer and writer under the pen name Peter Warlock.

Hess, Dame Myra (1890–1965), distinguished English pianist.

Hewitt, James (1770–1827), English-born American composer.

Hildegard van Bingen (1098–1179), remarkable German composer, poet, and mystic.

Hill, Edward Burlingame (1872–1960), eminent American composer and teacher.

Hiller, Ferdinand von (1811–1885), noted German conductor, composer, and writer on music.

Hiller, Lejaren (1924–1994), American composer and computer-music theorist.

Hindemith, Paul (1895–1963), significant German-born American composer, a leading master of the 20th century and originator of *Gebrauchmusik* ("music for use").

Hines, Earl "Fatha" (1905–1983), remarkable black American jazz pianist.

Hogwood, Christopher (1941–), prominent harpsichordist, conductor, and musicologist.

Holiday, Billie (b. Eleanora Holiday, 1915–1959), also known as "Lady Day," outstanding black American jazz singer.

Hollander, Lorin (1944–), talented American pianist.

Holliger, Heinz (1939–   ), noted Swiss oboist and composer.

Holmboe, Vagn (1909–   ), eminent Danish composer.

Holmès, Augusta (b. Mary Anne Holmes, 1847–1903), French composer.

Holst, Gustav (1874–1934), important English composer.

Honegger, Arthur (1892–1955), remarkable French composer.

Hopkinson, Francis (1737–1791), American statesman and composer.

Horne, Lena (b. Lena Calhoun, 1917–   ), remarkable black American singer of popular music.

Horne, Marilyn (1934–   ), outstanding American mezzo-soprano.

Horowitz, Vladimir (1903–1989), outstanding Russian-born American pianist of legendary fame.

Houston, Whitney (1963–   ), enormously successful black American singer of popular music.

Hovhaness, Alan (1911–   ), prolific and proficient American composer of Armenian-Scottish descent.

Howard, John Tasker (1890–1964), American writer on music.

Hubay, Jenö (1858–1937), noted Hungarian violinist.

Huberman, Bronislaw (1882–1947), famous Polish violinist.

Hummel, Johann Nepomuk (1778–1837), celebrated Austrian pianist, composer, and pedagogue.

Humperdinck, Engelbert (1854–1921), famous German composer.

Husa, Karel (1921–   ), distinguished Czech-born American composer and conductor.

Huss, Henry Holden (1862–1953), American pianist and composer.

Hutcheson, Ernest (1871–1951), Australian pianist, writer on music, teacher, and composer.

I

Ibert, Jacques (1890–1962), distinguished French composer.

Imbrie, Andrew (1921–   ), notable American composer.

Indy, Vincent d' (1851–1931), eminent French composer.

Ippolitov-Ivanov, Mikhail (1859–1935), important Russian composer and pedagogue.

Ireland, John (1879–1962), eminent English composer.

Isaac, Heinrich (c. 1450–1517), important Flemish composer.

Iturbi, José (1895–1980), celebrated Spanish pianist and conductor.

Ives, Burl (1909–1995), popular American folksinger.

Ives, Charles (1874–1954), outstanding American composer whose music, extraordinarily original and yet deeply national in its sources of inspiration, profoundly changed the direction of American music.

J

Jackson, Mahalia (1911–1972), remarkable black American gospel singer.

Jackson, Michael (1958–   ), black American rock superstar.

Jadassohn, Salomon (1831–1902), German pedagogue, conductor, and composer.

Jagger, Mick (1943–   ), English rock singer and songwriter; member of the enduring rock group The Rolling Stones.

James, Harry (1916–1983), popular American jazz trumpeter and bandleader.

James, Philip (1890–1975), important American composer and conductor.

Janáček, Leoš (1854–1928), greatly significant Czech composer.

Janequin, Clément (c.1485–1558), important French composer.

Jaques-Dalcroze, Émile (1865–1950), Swiss music educator and composer, creator of "Eurhythmics."

Jarrett, Keith (1945–), versatile American jazz pianist.

Joachim, Joseph (1831–1907), renowned Hungarian-born violinist and composer.

Johannesen, Grant (1921–), American pianist and pedagogue.

Johansen, Gunnar (1906–1991), Danish-American pianist and composer.

John, Elton (b. Reginald Kenneth Dwight, 1947–), phenomenally successful English rock pianist, singer, and songwriter.

Johnson, James P(rice) (1891–1955), black American jazz pianist and composer.

Johnson, J(ohn) Rosamond (1873–1954), significant black American composer and bass, brother of James Weldon Johnson, who composed the lyrics to many of his songs.

Johnson, Thor (1913–1975), American conductor.

Jolivet, André (1905–1974), significant French composer.

Jolson, Al (b. Asa Yoelson, 1886–1950), popular Lithuanian-born American singer and actor.

Jommelli, Niccolò (1714–1774), significant Italian composer.

Jones, Quincy (1933–), versatile black American pianist, trumpeter, bandleader, recording executive, composer, and producer.

Joplin, Janis (1943–1970), plaintive American rock and blues singer.

Joplin, Scott (1868–1917), remarkable black American pianist and composer, best known for his piano rags.

Joseffy, Rafael (1852–1915), eminent Hungarian-American pianist and composer.

Josquin. See **De Prez, Josquin**.

Josten, Werner (1885–1929), German-born American conductor and composer.

Joubert, John (1927–), significant South African-born English composer.

Juilliard, Augustus D. (1836–1919), important American music patron, founder of The Juilliard School of Music in New York.

K

Kabalevsky, Dmitri (1904–1987), noted Russian composer.

Kagel, Mauricio (1931–), remarkable Argentine composer.

Kalkbrenner, Frédéric (1785–1849), celebrated French pianist of German descent.

Karajan, Herbert von (1908–1989), preeminent Austrian conductor in the grand Germanic tradition.

Karg-Elert, Sigfrid (1877–1933), distinguished German organist and composer.

Kay, Ulysses (1917–1995), eminent black American composer.

Keiser, Reinhard (1674–1739), German opera composer.

Kelley, Edgar Stillman (1857–1944), American composer.

Kenton, Stan (1911–1979), American jazz bandleader.

Kern, Jerome (1885–1945), famous American composer for stage and screen.

Khachaturian, Aram (1903–1978), brilliant Russian composer of Armenian descent.

Khrennikov, Tikhon (1913–   ), important Russian music administrator and composer.

Kindler, Hans (1892–1949), Dutch-born American cellist and conductor, founder of the National Symphony Orchestra in Washington, D.C.

King, B. B. (b. Riley Bo King, 1925–   ), soulful black American blues singer and guitarist.

Kinkeldey, Otto (1878–1966), eminent American musicologist.

Kipnis, Alexander (1891–1978), eminent Russian-born American bass, father of **Igor Kipnis.**

Kipnis, Igor (1930–   ), distinguished American harpsichordist and fortepianist.

Kirchner, Leon (1919–   ), significant American composer.

Kirk, Rahsaan (b. Roland Kirk, 1936–1977), black American jazz instrumentalist and composer.

Kirkpatrick, John (1905–1991), eminent American pianist.

Kirkpatrick, Ralph (1911–1984), talented American keyboardist and scholar.

Kirnberger, Johann Philipp (1721–1783), noted German music theorist.

Kissin, Evgeny (1971–   ), precocious Russian pianist.

Klebe, Giselher (1925–   ), German composer.

Kleiber, Erich (1890–1956), eminent Austrian conductor.

Klemperer, Otto (1885–1973), celebrated German conductor.

Klindworth, Karl (1830–1916), German pianist and teacher.

Knussen, Oliver (1952–   ), significant English composer.

Köchel, Ludwig, Ritter von (1800–1877), Austrian botanist, mineralogist, and music bibliographer, famous for his monumental catalog of Mozart's work.

Kodály, Zoltán (1882–1967), renowned Hungarian composer, ethnomusicologist, and music educator.

Koechlin, Charles (1867–1950), noted French composer.

Köhler, Louis (1820–1886), German pianist and composer.

Korngold, Erich Wolfgang (1897–1957), remarkable Austrian-born American composer.

Kostelanetz, André (1901–1980), highly successful Russian-born American conductor.

Koussevitzky, Serge (1874–1951), celebrated Russian-born American conductor and double-bass virtuoso.

Kraft, William (1923–   ), American composer and percussionist.

Krauss, Clemens (1893–1954), eminent Austrian conductor.

Krehbiel, Henry (1854–1923), notable American music critic.

Kreisler, Fritz (1875–1962), great Austrian-born American violinist.

Krenek, Ernst (1900–1991), remarkable Austrian-born American composer.

Kreutzer, Rodolphe (1766–1831), famous French violinist, dedicatee of Beethoven's *Kreutzer Sonata.*

Krips, Josef (1902–1974), eminent Austrian conductor.

Krupa, Gene (1909–1973), successful American jazz drummer.

Kubelík, Jan (1880–1940), famous Czech-born Hungarian violinist, father of **Rafael Kubelík.**

Kubelík, Rafael (1914–   ), eminent Czech-born Swiss conductor.

Kubik, Gail (1914–1984), American composer.

Kuhnau, Johann (1660–1722), erudite German organist and composer.

Kullack, Theodor (1818–1882), famous German pianist.

Kupferman, Meyer (1926–), notable American composer.

Kurtág, György (1926–), significant Rumanian-born Hungarian composer.

L

La Barbara, Joan (1947–), American composer and outstanding experimental vocalist; wife of **Morton Subotnick.**

Lachenmann, Helmut Friedrich (1935–), German composer.

Laderman, Ezra (1924–), noted American composer.

Lalo, Édouard (1823–1892), distinguished French composer of Spanish descent.

Lambert, Constant (1905–1951), remarkable English conductor, composer, and writer on music.

La Montaine, John (1920–), American composer and pianist.

Lamoureux, Charles (1834–1899), noted French conductor and violinist.

Landowska, Wanda (1879–1959), celebrated Polish-born French harpsichordist, pianist, and pedagogue.

Landowski, Marcel (1915–), significant French composer.

Landré, Guillaume (1905–1968), important Dutch composer.

Lanner, Joseph (1801–1843), historically significant Austrian violinist, conductor, and composer.

Lanza, Mario (b. Alfredo Arnold Cocozza, 1921–1959), popular American tenor and actor.

Larrocha, Alicia de (1923–), brilliant Spanish pianist.

Lassen, Eduard (1830–1904), Danish conductor and composer.

Lassus, Orlando di (1532–1594), great Franco-Flemish composer, also known (in Latin) as Orlandus Lassus and (in French) as Roland de Lassus.

Lavry, Marc (1903–1967), significant Latvian-born Israel composer.

Law, Andrew (1749–1821), American singing teacher and composer.

Leadbelly (b. Huddie Ledbetter, 1885–1949), influential black American folksinger, guitarist, and songwriter.

Lear, Evelyn (1926–), outstanding American soprano.

Le Caine, Hugh (1914–1977), Canadian physicist, acoustician, and creator of prototypical electronic musical instruments.

LeClair, Jean-Marie (1697–1764), celebrated French violinist and composer.

Lecuona, Ernesto (1896–1963), Cuban composer of popular music.

Lee, Peggy (b. Norma Dolores Egstrom, 1920–), popular American singer, songwriter, and actress.

Lees, Benjamin (1924–), outstanding American composer.

Leeuw, Ton de (1926–), important Dutch composer.

Leginska, Ethel (1886–1970), English-born American pianist, teacher, and composer.

Lehár, Franz (1870–1948), celebrated Austrian operetta composer of Hungarian descent.

Lehmann, Lilli (1848–1929), celebrated German soprano.

Lehmann, Liza (1862–1918), English soprano and composer.

Lehmann, Lotte (1888–1976), celebrated German-born American soprano.

Leibowitz, René (1913–1972), noted Polish-born French conductor, composer, writer on music, music theorist, and pedagogue.

Leinsdorf, Erich (1912–1993), eminent Austrian-born American conductor.

Le Jeune, Claude (c. 1528–1600), important French composer.

Lennon, John (1940–1980), English rock singer, guitarist, and songwriter; member of the fantastically popular rock group The Beatles.

Lentz, Daniel (1941–), important American composer.

Lenya, Lotte (1898–1981), sultry Austrian-American singer and actress, wife of **Kurt Weill.**

Leoncavallo, Ruggero (1857–1919), noted Italian composer, among his works the beloved opera *Pagliacci*.

Leoninus (c. 1135–c. 1201), celebrated French composer and poet, master of the Notre Dame School of Paris.

Leppard, Raymond (1927–), eminent English conductor.

Lerner, Alan Jay (1918–1986), distinguished American lyricist and playwright, most famous for his collaborations with Frederick Loewe.

Leschetizky, Theodor (1830–1915), renowned Polish pianist.

Levant, Oscar (1905–1972), colorful American pianist and composer.

Levine, James (1943–), brilliant American pianist and conductor.

Lewenthal, Raymond (1926–1988), American pianist.

Lewis, Henry (1932–), black American conductor.

Lewis, Jerry Lee (1935–), rollicking American rock 'n' roll and country pianist and singer.

Lhévinne, Josef (1874–1944), distinguished Russian pianist, husband of **Rosina Lhévinne.**

Lhévinne, Rosina (1880–1976), distinguished Russian pianist.

Liadov, Anatoli (1855–1914), prominent Russian conductor and composer.

Liberace (b. Wladziu Valentino, 1919–1987), flamboyant American pianist and showman.

Liebermann, Rolf (1910–   ), esteemed Swiss opera impresario and composer.

Lieberson, Goddard (1911–1977), English-American recording executive and composer, father of **Peter Lieberson.**

Lieberson, Peter (1946–   ), gifted American composer.

Ligeti, György (1923–   ), eminent Hungarian-born Austrian composer and pedagogue.

Lind, Jenny (1820–1887), celebrated Swedish soprano, nicknamed the "Swedish nightingale."

Lipatti, Dinu (1917–1950), outstanding Rumanian pianist and composer.

Liszt, Franz (1811–1886), greatly celebrated Hungarian pianist and composer, creator of the modern form of the symphonic poem and innovating genius of modern piano technique.

Lloyd Webber, Andrew (1948–   ), tremendously successful English stage composer.

Locatelli, Pietro (1695–1764), important Italian violinist and composer.

Loeffler, Charles Martin (1861–1935), outstanding Alsatian-born American composer.

Loesser, Arthur (1894–1969), esteemed American pianist, teacher, and writer on music, half-brother of **Frank Loesser.**

Loesser, Frank (1910–1969), talented American composer and lyricist.

Loewe, Carl (1796–1869), outstanding German lieder composer.

Loewe, Frederick (1904–1988), remarkable Austrian-American composer of popular music.

Lomax, Alan (1915–), important American ethnomusicologist.

Lombardo, Guy (b. Gaetano Alberto Lombardo, 1902–1977), popular Canadian-American bandleader.

London, George (1919–1985), esteemed Canadian-born American bass-baritone.

Long, Marguerite (1874–1966), notable French pianist.

Lopatnikoff, Nikolai (1903–1976), outstanding Russian-born American composer.

Lortzing, Albert (1801–1851), celebrated German opera composer.

Löschhorn, Albert (1819–1905), German pianist and composer.

Lucier, Alvin (1931–), important American composer of the experimental school.

Luening, Otto (1900–), multifaceted American composer, teacher, flutist, and conductor.

Lully, Jean-Baptiste (1632–1687), celebrated Italian-born French composer.

Lutoslawski, Witold (1913–1994), outstanding Polish composer.

Lutyens, Elisabeth (1906–1983), important English composer.

M

Ma, Yo-Yo (1955–   ), brilliant Chinese cellist.

Maazel, Lorin (1930–   ), brilliant American conductor.

MacDowell, Edward (1860–1908), greatly significant American composer.

Machaut, Guillaume de (c.1300–1377), important French composer and poet.

Maderna, Bruno (1920–1973), outstanding Italian-born German conductor and composer.

Madonna (b. Madonna Louise Veronica Ciccone, 1958–   ), fabulously popular and audacious American rock singer and actress.

Mahler, Gustav (1860–1911), outstanding Austrian composer and conductor in the late Romantic tradition.

Malipiero, Gian Francesco (1882–1973), eminent Italian composer and conductor.

Mancini, Henry (1924–1994), highly successful American composer, arranger, pianist, and conductor of popular music.

Mantovani (b. Annunzio Paolo Mantovani, 1905–1980), enormously successful Italian-born English conductor of popular music.

Marenzio, Luca (c. 1553–1599), important Italian composer.

Markevitch, Igor (1912–1983), greatly talented Russian-born composer and conductor.

Marley, Bob (b. Robert Nesta Marley, 1945–1981), Jamaican reggae singer and composer.

Marriner, Sir Neville (1924–   ), outstanding English conductor.

Marschner, Heinrich (1795–1861), important German opera composer.

Marshall, Ingram (1942–), innovative American composer.

Martenot, Maurice (1898–1980), French inventor of the electronic instrument "Ondes musicales," also known as "Ondes Martenot."

Martin, Frank (1890–1974), greatly renowned Swiss composer.

Martini, Giovanni Battista (1706–1784), famous Italian pedagogue, writer on music, and composer, known as Padre Martini.

Martinon, Jean (1910–1976), significant French conductor and composer.

Martinu, Bohuslav (1890–1959), remarkable Czech composer.

Martirano, Salvatore (1927–), American composer of the modern school.

Mascagni, Pietro (1863–1945), famous Italian opera composer.

Mason, Daniel Gregory (1873–1953), eminent American composer and educator.

Mason, Lowell (1792–1872), distinguished American organist, conductor, music educator, and composer, father of William Mason.

Mason, William (1829–1908), esteemed American pianist, pedagogue, and composer.

Massenet, Jules (1842–1912), illustrious French composer.

Masur, Kurt (1927–), eminent German conductor.

Matthay, Tobias (1858–1945), eminent English pianist.

Mattheson, Johann (1681–1764), famous German composer, music theorist, and lexicographer.

Maxfield, Richard (1927–1969), American avant-garde composer.

McCartney, Paul (1942–), English rock singer, songwriter, and guitarist; member of the fantastically popular rock group The Beatles.

McCormack, John (1884–1945), famous Irish-born American tenor.

McFerrin, Bobby (1950–), gifted black American popular vocalist, son of baritone Robert McFerrin.

McPartland, Marian (1918–), English jazz pianist and composer.

Mehta, Zubin (1936–), exuberant Indian conductor.

Méhul, Étienne-Nicolas (1763–1817), famous French composer.

Melba, Dame Nellie (1861–1931), famous Australian soprano.

Melchior, Lauritz (1890–1973), celebrated Danish-born American tenor.

Mendelssohn, Felix (1809–1847), famous German composer, pianist, and conductor.

Mengelberg, Willem (1871–1951), celebrated Dutch conductor.

Mennin, Peter (1923–1983), eminent American composer and music educator.

Menotti, Gian Carlo (1911–), remarkable Italian composer and librettist.

Menuhin, Sir Yehudi (1916–), celebrated American violinist.

Mercadente, Saverio (1795–1870), important Italian opera composer.

Merman, Ethel (b. Ethel Agnes Zimmerman, 1908–1984), popular American singer and Broadway star.

Merrill, Robert (1917–), noted American baritone.

Messiaen, Olivier (1908–1992), outstanding French composer.

Mester, Jorge (1935–), talented Mexican-born American conductor.

Metastasio, Pietro (1698–1782), famous Italian poet and opera librettist.

Meyerbeer, Giacomo (1791–1864), famous German composer.

Miaskovsky, Nikolai (1881–1950), prolific Russian composer.

Michael, David Moritz (1751–1825), German violinist, clarinetist, horn player, and composer.

Midler, Bette (1945–), lovable American singer, actress, and comedienne.

Midori (b. Goto Mi Dori, 1971–), prodigious Japanese violinist.

Milhaud, Darius (1892–1974), eminent French composer.

Miller, Glenn (1904–1944), famous American trombonist and bandleader.

Milstein, Nathan (1904–1992), celebrated Russian-born American violinist.

Mingus, Charles (1922–1979), remarkable black American jazz double-bass player, pianist, bandleader, and composer.

Mitropoulos, Dimitri (1896–1960), celebrated Greek-born American conductor and composer.

Monk, Meredith (1942–), noted American composer, singer, dancer, and filmmaker.

Monk, Thelonious (1917–1982), noted black American jazz pianist and composer.

Monroe, Bill (1911–), pioneering bluegrass mandolinist, vocalist, and composer.

Montague, Stephen (1943–), important American composer and pianist.

Monteux, Pierre (1875–1964), celebrated French-born American conductor.

Monteverdi, Claudio (1567–1643), outstanding Italian composer who established the foundations of modern opera.

Moog, Robert (1934–), American designer of electronic musical instruments.

Moore, Douglas (1893–1969), distinguished American composer.

Moore, Gerald (1899–1987), renowned English piano accompanist.

Moran, Robert (1937–), important American composer of the avant-garde.

Morley, Thomas (c.1557–1602), famous English composer.

Morton, "Jelly Roll" (b. Ferdinand Joseph La Menthe, 1885–1941), pioneer black American composer and pianist of ragtime, blues, and jazz.

Moscheles, Ignaz (1794–1870), eminent Czech-born pianist, conductor, pedagogue, and composer.

Mosolov, Alexander (1900–1973), Russian composer.

Moszkowski, Moritz (1854–1925), famous German pianist and composer of Polish descent.

Mozart, Leopold (1719–1787), German-born Austrian composer, violinist, and music theorist, father of **Wolfgang Amadeus Mozart.**

Mozart, Wolfgang Amadeus (1756–1791), supreme and prodigious Austrian composer whose works in every genre are unsurpassed in lyric beauty, rhythmic variety and effortless melodic invention.

Mumma, Gordon (1935–), innovative American composer, performer, and electronic music engineer.

Munch, Charles (1891–1968), eminent Alsatian conductor.

Munz, Mieczyslaw (1900–1976), esteemed Polish-American pianist and pedagogue.

Musgrave, Thea (1928–   ), remarkable Scottish composer.

Mussorgsky, Modest (1839–1881), great Russian composer, one of the "Mighty Five."

Muti, Riccardo (1941–   ), greatly talented Italian conductor.

Mutter, Anne-Sophie (1963–   ), talented German violinist.

N

Nabokov, Nicolas (1903–1978), distinguished Russian-born American composer.

Nancarrow, Conlon (1912–   ), remarkable American-born Mexican composer, innovator in the technique of composing for player piano.

Nelsova, Zara (1918–   ), brilliant Canadian-born American cellist of Russian descent.

Newman, Alfred (1900–1970), American film composer and conductor.

Newman, Ernest (1868–1959), English music critic.

Nielsen, Carl (1865–1931), greatly significant Danish composer.

Nikisch, Arthur (1855–1922), famous Austrian conductor.

Niles, John Jacob (1892–1980), American folksinger, folk-music collector, and composer.

Nilsson, Birgit (1918–   ), greatly renowned Swedish soprano.

Nilsson, Bo (1937–   ), Swedish composer of ultramodern tendencies.

Nin-Culmell, Joaquín (1908–   ), Cuban-American pianist and composer.

Noble, Ray (1903–1978), English bandleader, composer, and arranger.

Nono, Luigi (1924–1990), remarkable and socially conscious Italian composer in the modern tradition.

Nordica, Lillian (1857–1914), distinguished American soprano.

Nörgård, Per (1932–), prominent Danish composer.

Norman, Jessye (1945–), gifted black American soprano.

Norrington, Roger (1934–), scholarly English conductor.

Nyiregyházi, Erwin (1903–1987), remarkable and eccentric Hungarian-American pianist.

O

Obrecht, Jacob (c. 1450–1505), famous Netherlandish composer.

Ockeghem, Johannes (c. 1410–1497), great Flemish composer.

Odetta (b. Odetta Holmes, 1930–), revered black American folksinger and guitarist.

Offenbach, Jacques (1819–1880), famous French composer of German descent.

Ogdon, John (1937–1989), remarkable English pianist.

Oistrakh, David (1908–1974), great Russian violinist.

Oliver, Henry Kimble (1800–1885), American composer.

Oliver, Joe "King" (1885–1938), outstanding black American jazz cornetist and bandleader.

Oliveros, Pauline (1932–), innovative American composer.

Orff, Carl (1895–1982), outstanding German composer.

Ormandy, Eugene (1899–1985), outstanding Hungarian-born American conductor.

Ornstein, Leo (1892–   ), remarkable Russian-born American pianist and composer.

Orrego-Salas, Juan (1919–   ), Chilean composer.

Overton, Hall (1920–1972), American composer.

Ozawa, Seiji (1935–   ), brilliant Japanese conductor.

P

Pachelbel, Johann (1653–1706), celebrated German organist, pedagogue, and composer.

Pachmann, Vladimir de (1848–1933), eccentric Russian-born Italian pianist.

Paderewski, Ignacy (1860–1941), celebrated Polish pianist and composer.

Paganini, Niccolò (1782–1840), legendary Italian violinist.

Paik, Nam June (1932–   ), Korean-American avant-garde composer and experimenter in the visual arts.

Paine, John Knowles (1839–1906), prominent American composer.

Paisiello, Giovanni (1740–1816), famous Italian composer.

Palestrina, Giovanni Pierluigi da (c. 1525–1594), great Italian composer; with Byrd and Lassus, foremost in his age.

Palmgren, Selim (1878–1951), eminent Finnish composer.

Panufnik, Andrzej (1914–1991), eminent Polish-born English conductor and composer.

Parker, Charlie "Bird" (1920–1955), noted black American jazz alto saxophonist in the bebop style.

Parker, Horatio (1863–1919), eminent American composer.

Parry, Sir Hubert (1848–1918), eminent English composer.

Pärt, Arvo (1935–   ), remarkable Estonian composer.

Partch, Harry (1901–1974), innovative American composer, performer, and instrument maker.

Parton, Dolly (1946–), successful American singer, guitarist, and songwriter of country and pop-rock music.

Pasatieri, Thomas (1945–), talented American opera composer.

Patti, Adelina (1843–1919), Italian soprano.

Paulus, Stephen (1949–), American composer.

Pavarotti, Luciano (1935–), greatly renowned Italian tenor.

Pears, Sir Peter (1910–1986), renowned English tenor.

Peerce, Jan (1904–1984), noted American tenor.

Penderecki, Krzystof (1933–), celebrated Polish composer.

Pennario, Leonard (1924–), brilliant American pianist.

Pergolesi, Giovanni Battista (1710–1736), remarkable Italian composer.

Peri, Jacopo (1561–1633), significant Italian composer, called "Il Zazzerino" for his abundant head of hair.

Perlman, Itzhak (1945–), brilliant Israeli-American violinist.

Perotin (c. 1155–c. 1205), celebrated French composer.

Persichetti, Vincent (1915–1987), remarkable American composer of classical modernity.

Peters, Roberta (1930–), outstanding American soprano.

Peterson, Oscar (1925–), noted black Canadian jazz pianist.

Petrassi, Goffredo (1904–), outstanding Italian composer and teacher.

Petrucci, Ottaviano dei (1466–1539), Italian music publisher.

Pfitzner, Hans (1869–1949), eminent German composer and conductor.

Philidor, François-André (1726–1795), noted French composer and chessmaster.

Philipp, Isidor (1863–1958), eminent French pianist and pedagogue.

Piaf, Edith (1915–1963), noted French chanteuse.

Piatigorsky, Gregor (1903–1976), great Russian-born American cellist and pedagogue.

Piccinni, Niccolò (1728–1800), significant Italian composer.

Pjiper, Willem (1894–1947), renowned Dutch composer.

Pinza, Ezio (1892–1957), celebrated Italian bass.

Piston, Walter (1894–1976), outstanding American composer.

Pleyel, Ignaz Joseph (1757–1831), eminent Austrian-French pianist, piano manufacturer, music publisher, and composer.

Plush, Vincent (1950–   ), remarkable Australian composer.

Pollini, Maurizio (1942–   ), famous Italian pianist and conductor.

Ponce, Manuel (1882–1948), distinguished Mexican composer.

Ponchielli, Amilcare (1834–1886), celebrated Italian composer.

Pons, Lily (1898–1976), glamorous French soprano.

Popper, David (1843–1913), famous Czech cellist and composer.

Porter, Cole (1891–1964), remarkable American composer of popular music.

Porter, Quincy (1897–1966), significant American composer.

Poulenc, Francis (1899–1963), brilliant French composer.

Pousseur, Henri (1929–   ), Belgian composer of the ultra-modern school.

Powell, "Bud" (b. Earl Powell, 1924–1966), black American jazz pianist.

Powell, John (1882–1963), American pianist, composer, and ethnomusicologist.

Powell, Mel (1923–   ), remarkable American composer.

Praetorius, Michael (1571–1621), great German composer, organist, and music theorist.

Presley, Elvis (1935–1977), fantastically popular American rock 'n' roll singer.

Previn, André (1929–   ), brilliant German-born American pianist, conductor, and composer.

Prey, Hermann (1929–   ), outstanding German baritone.

Price, Florence B. (1888–1953), black American teacher and composer.

Price, Leontyne (1927–   ), celebrated   black American soprano.

Prince (b. Prince Roger Nelson, 1958–   ), provocative black American rock singer, instrumentalist, and songwriter.

Prokofiev, Sergei (1891–1953), great Russian composer.

Prout, Ebenezer (1835–1909), eminent English music theorist and teacher.

Puccini, Giacomo (1712–1781), superior Italian composer of remarkably enduring operas, including *La Bohème* and *Madama Butterfly*.

Purcell, Henry (1659–1695), great English composer.

Q

Quantz, Johann Joachim (1697–1773), famous German flutist, writer on music, and composer.

R

Rabaud, Henri (1873–1949), noted French conductor and composer.

Rachmaninoff, Sergei (1873–1943), greatly renowned Russian-born American pianist, conductor, and composer.

Raff, Joachim (1822–1882), Swiss composer and pedagogue.

Rainey, Ma (b. Gertrude Pridgett, 1886–1939), prominent black American blues, jazz, and vaudeville singer.

Raitt, Bonnie (1949–), American popular singer and guitarist, daughter of Broadway actor-singer, John Raitt.

Rameau, Jean-Philippe (1683–1764), great French composer, organist, and music theorist.

Ran, Shulamit (1949–), Israeli pianist and composer.

Rands, Bernard (1934–), remarkable English-born American composer.

Rattle, Simon (1955–), brilliant English conductor.

Ravel, Maurice (1875–1937), great French composer whose ballet *Boléro* became a spectacularly successful orchestral piece.

Read, Daniel (1757–1836), important American tunebook compiler and composer.

Read, Gardner (1913–), important American composer.

Rebikov, Vladimir (1866–1920), Russian composer.

Reese, Gustave (1899–1977), eminent American musicologist.

Reger, Max (1873–1916), celebrated German composer.

Reich, Steve (1936–), remarkable American composer, an early proponent of musical Minimalism.

Reicha, Anton (1770–1836), distinguished Czech-born French music theorist, pedagogue, and composer.

Reinagle, Alexander (1756–1809), prominent English-born American pianist, teacher, impresario, and composer.

Reinecke, Carl (1824–1910), renowned German pianist, composer, and conductor.

Reiner, Fritz (1888–1963), eminent Hungarian-born American conductor.

Reinhardt, Django (1910–1953), Belgian jazz guitarist.

Reményi, Ede (1828–1898), prominent Hungarian violinist.

Resnik, Regina (1922–), American soprano, later mezzo-soprano.

Respighi, Ottorino (1879–1963), Italian composer of colorful symphonic scores.

Revueltas, Silvestre (1899–1940), remarkable Mexican composer.

Reynolds, Roger (1934–), important American composer.

Rheinberger, Joseph (1839–1901), eminent German organist, conductor, composer, and pedagogue.

Ricci, Ruggiero (1918–), celebrated American violinist.

Rich, Buddy (b. **Bernard Rich**, 1917–1987), remarkable American jazz drummer and bandleader.

Richter, Hans (1843–1916), eminent German conductor.

Richter, Sviatoslav (1915–), outstanding Russian pianist.

Riegger, Wallingford (1885–1961), outstanding American composer.

Riemann, Hugo (1849–1919), eminent German musicologist.

Ries, Ferdinand (1784–1838), noted German pianist and composer.

Rieti, Vittorio (1898–1994), Italian-born American composer.

Rihm, Wolfgang (1952–), outstanding German composer.

Riisager, Knudåge (1897–1974), prominent Danish composer.

Riley, Terry (1937–), innovative American composer whose composition *In C* launched musical Minimalism.

Rimsky-Korsakov, Nikolai (1844–1908), great Russian composer and master of orchestration, member of the "Mighty Five."

Roach, Max (1924–), remarkable black American jazz drummer and composer.

Robeson, Paul (1898–1976), great black American bass and actor.

Rochberg, George (1918–), significant American composer, first in the 12–tone style and later embracing the precepts of New Romanticism.

Rodgers, Jimmie (1897–1933), pioneering American country-music singer, guitarist, and songwriter.

Rodgers, Richard (1902–1979), celebrated American composer of popular music, most famous for his collaborations with Lorenz Hart and Oscar Hammerstein II.

Rodzinski, Artur (1892–1958), eminent Polish-born conductor.

Roger-Ducasse, Jean (1873–1954), prominent French composer.

Rogers, Bernard (1893–1968), distinguished American composer.

Rogers, Roy (b. **Leonard Slye**, 1911–), popular American country-music singer and actor.

Romberg, Sigmund (1887–1951), famous Hungarian-born American composer.

Ronstadt, Linda (1943–), versatile American pop singer.

Rore, Cipriano de (c. 1515–1565), celebrated Flemish composer.

Rorem, Ned (1923–), brilliant American composer, a masterful melodist, pianist, and writer.

Rosbaud, Hans (1895–1962), eminent Austrian conductor.

Rose, Leonard (1918–1984), eminent American cellist.

Rosen, Charles (1927–), erudite American pianist and musicologist.

Rosenberg, Hilding (1892–1985), important Swedish composer.

Rosenthal, Moriz (1862–1946), famous Austrian pianist.

Ross, Diana (1944–), successful black American pop and soul singer; originally with the Motown group The Supremes.

Rossini, Gioacchino (1792–1868), great Italian opera composer.

Rostropovich, Mstislav (1927–), famous Russian cellist and conductor.

Rouse, Christopher (1949–), imaginative American composer.

Rousseau, Jean-Jacques (1712–1778), great Swiss-born French philosopher and author.

Roussel, Albert (1869–1937), outstanding French composer.

Rózsa, Miklós (1907–), brilliant Hungarian-American composer.

Rubbra, Edmund (1901–1986), notable English composer.

Rubinstein, Anton (1829–1894), renowned Russian pianist, conductor, composer, and pedagogue.

Rubinstein, Arthur (1887–1982), celebrated Polish-born American pianist.

Rudel, Julius (1921–), Austrian-born American conductor.

Rudhyar, Dane (1895–1985), French-born American composer and painter, and renowned mystical philosopher.

Rudolf, Max (1902–1995), eminent German-born American conductor.

Ruggles, Carl (1876–1971), remarkable American composer.

Russolo, Luigi (1885–1947), Italian inventor, painter, and futurist composer.

Rzewski, Frederic (1938–), titanic American pianist, teacher, and composer of the experimental school.

S

Saariaho, Kaija (1952–), important Finnish composer.

Sachs, Hans (1494–1576), famous German poet and Meistersinger.

Sachs, Kurt (1881–1959), noted German-born American ethnomusicologist, author, and teacher, famous for his classification system of musical instruments.

Saint-Georges, Joseph Boulogne, Chevalier de (c. 1739–1799), noted West Indian violinist and composer.

Saint-Saëns, Camille (1835–1921), celebrated French composer.

Salieri, Antonio (1750–1825), famous Italian composer.

Sallinen, Aulis (1935–), prominent Finnish composer.

Salzedo, Carlos (1885–1961), eminent French-born American harpist, pedagogue, and composer.

Salzman, Eric (1933–), American composer, writer on music, and editor.

Sammartini, Giovanni Battista (c. 1700–1775), significant Italian composer and pedagogue.

Sarasate, Pablo de (1844–1908), celebrated Spanish violinist and composer.

Satie, Erik (1866–1925), celebrated French composer, originator of the intentionally unindelible "furniture music."

Sax, Adolphe (1814–1894), Belgian inventor of the saxophone.

Scarlatti, Alessandro (1660–1725), important Italian composer, father of **Domenico Scarlatti.**

Scarlatti, Domenico (1685–1757), famous Italian composer, harpsichordist, and teacher.

Scelsi, Giacinto (1905–1988), remarkable Italian composer.

Schaeffer, Boguslaw (1929–), outstanding Polish composer, pedagogue, writer on music, and playwright.

Schaeffer, Pierre (1910–), French acoustician, composer, and novelist.

Schaefer, R. Murray (1933–), important Canadian composer, active in the creation of outdoor, site-specific works.

Schat, Peter (1935–), significant Dutch composer.

Scheidt, Samuel (1587–1654), important German organist and composer.

Schein, Johann Hermann (1586–1630), important German composer.

Schelling, Ernest (1876–1939), American conductor, composer, and pianist.

Schenker, Heinrich (1868–1935), outstanding and highly influential Austrian music theorist.

Scherchen, Hermann (1891–1966), eminent German conductor, father of **Tona Scherchen.**

Scherchen, Tona (1938–), Swiss-born French composer.

Schickele, Peter (1935–), American composer and musical humorist, creator of the irreverant entertainer P.D.Q. Bach.

Schifrin, Lalo (1932–), Argentine-American pianist, conductor, and composer.

Schillinger, Joseph (1895–1943), Russian-born American music theorist and composer.

Schipa, Tito (1888–1965), famous Italian tenor.

Schippers, Thomas (1930–1977), gifted American conductor.

Schirmer, Gustav (1829–1893), German-American music publisher.

Schmitt, Florent (1870–1958), outstanding French composer.

Schnabel, Artur (1882–1951), celebrated Austrian-born American pianist.

Schnittke, Alfred (1934–   ), prominent Russian composer.

Schoeck, Othmar (1886–1957), eminent Swiss pianist, conductor, and composer.

Schoenberg, Arnold (1874–1951), outstanding Austrian-born American composer and theorist whose intransigent method of organizing music according to twelve equal notes profoundly influenced the direction of 20th-century music.

Scholes, Percy (1877–1958), eminent English writer on music.

Schreker, Franz (1878–1934), eminent Austrian conductor and composer.

Schubert, Franz (1797–1828), great Austrian composer, a supreme melodist and inspired master of lieder.

Schuller, Gunther (1925–   ), significant American composer, conductor, and music educator.

Schuman, William (1910–1992), outstanding American composer, music educator, and administrator.

Schumann, Clara (1819–1896), famous German pianist, teacher, and composer; wife of **Robert Schumann.**

Schumann, Robert (1810–1856), outstanding German composer whose music expressed the deepest spirit of the Romantic era.

Schumann-Heink, Ernestine (1861–1936), famous Austrian-born American contralto and mezzosoprano.

Schütz, Heinrich (1585–1672), great German composer.

Schwantner, Joseph (1943–), prominent American composer.

Schwarzkopf, Elizabeth (1915–), celebrated German soprano.

Schweitzer, Albert (1875–1965), famous Alsatian theologian, philosopher, medical missionary, organist, and music scholar.

Schwertsik, Kurt (1935–), Austrian composer of the avant-garde, horn player, and teacher.

Scott, Cyril (1879–1970), remarkable English composer.

Scotto, Renata (1933–), famous Italian soprano.

Scriabin, Alexander (1872–1915), remarkable Russian composer of harmonically and technically innovative piano and orchestral pieces, often with mystical connotations.

Sculthorpe, Peter (1929–), eminent Australian composer.

Searle, Humphrey (1915–1982), distinguished English composer, teacher, and writer on music.

Seeger, Charles (1886–1979), eminent American musicologist, ethnomusicologist, teacher, and composer, husband of **Ruth Crawford** and father of **Pete Seeger.**

Seeger, Pete (1919–), noted American folksinger, songwriter, and political activist.

Segovia, Andrés (1893–1987), great Spanish guitar virtuoso and teacher.

Seiber, Mátyás (1905–1960), significant Hungarian-born English composer.

Seidl, Anton (1850–1898), famous Hungarian conductor.

Sembrich, Marcella (1858–1935), famous Polish-American soprano.

Serkin, Peter (1947–), outstanding American pianist, son of **Rudolf Serkin.**

Serkin, Rudolf (1903–1991), eminent Austrian-born American pianist and pedagogue.

Serly, Tibor (1901–1978), Hungarian-born American violist, conductor, music theorist, and composer.

Serov, Alexander (1820–1871), important Russian music critic and composer.

Sessions, Roger (1896–1985), eminent American composer.

Shankar, Ravi (1920–), famous Indian sitarist and composer.

Shapero, Harold (1920–), American pianist and composer.

Shapey, Ralph (1921–), American conductor and composer.

Sharp, Cecil (1859–1924), English folk music collector and editor.

Shaw, Artie (1910–), famous American jazz clarinetist, bandleader, composer, and arranger.

Shaw, Robert (1916–), distinguished American choral conductor.

Shchedrin, Rodion (1932–), brilliant Russian composer.

Shearing, George (1919–), prominent blind English-born American jazz pianist.

Sheng, Bright (1955–), remarkable Chinese composer.

Shepherd, Arthur (1880–1958), eminent American composer.

Shostakovich, Dmitri (1906–1975), preeminent Russian composer of the Soviet generation whose style of composition helped define the nature of new Russian music.

Sibelius, Jean (1865–1957), great Finnish composer whose music, infused with the deeply felt modalities of national folk songs, opened a modern era of Northern musical art.

Siegmeister, Elie (1909–1991), significant American composer.

Siepi, Cesare (1923–), admired Italian bass.

Sierra, Roberto (1953–), important Puerto Rican composer.

Sills, Beverly (1929–), celebrated American soprano and opera administrator.

Siloti, Alexander (1863–1945), eminent Russian pianist and conductor.

Simon, Paul (1941–), popular American singer, guitarist, and songwriter.

Sinatra, Frank (b. Francis Albert Sinatra, 1915–), phenomenally popular American singer and actor.

Sinding, Christian (1856–1941), celebrated Norwegian composer.

Skalkottas, Nikos (1904–1949), greatly talented Greek composer.

Slatkin, Leonard (1944–), prominent American conductor.

Slezak, Leo (1873–1946), famous Austrian tenor.

Slonimsky, Nicolas (1894–), legendary Russian-born American musicologist, conductor, and composer, uncle of **Sergei Slonimsky.**

Slonimsky, Sergei (1932–), greatly talented Russian composer.

Smetana, Bedrich (1824–1884), great Bohemian composer.

Smith, Bessie (1894–1937), beloved black American blues, jazz, and vaudeville singer, frequently billed as the ''Empress of the Blues.''

Smith, John Stafford (1750–1836), English music scholar, organist, and composer.

Smith, Kate (1907–1986), beloved American singer of popular music.

Smyth, Dame Ethyl (1858–1944), eminent English composer.

Solomon (b. Solomon Cutner, 1902–1988), outstanding English pianist.

Solti, Sir Georg (1912–), eminent Hungarian-born English conductor.

Sondheim, Stephen (1930–), preeminent American lyricist and composer of works for the Broadway stage, including the Pulitzer Prize-winning *Sunday in the Park with George.*

Sonneck, Oscar (1873–1928), eminent American musicologist.

Sor, Fernando (1778–1839), celebrated Catalan guitarist and composer.

Sousa, John Philip (1854–1932), famous American bandmaster and composer.

Sowerby, Leo (1895–1968), remarkable American composer and organist.

Spohr, Ludwig (1784–1859), celebrated German violinist, composer, and conductor.

Spontini, Gasparo (1774–1851), significant Italian opera composer.

Stamitz, Carl (1745–1801), significant Bohemian violinist, violist, viola d'amorist, and composer, son of **Johann Stamitz.**

Stamitz, Johann (1717–1757), preeminent Bohemian violinist, teacher, and composer.

Starr, Ringo (b. Richard Starkey, 1940–), English rock 'n' roll drummer; member of the fantastically popular rock group The Beatles.

Steber, Eleanor (1914–1990), eminent American soprano.

Steffani, Agostino (1654–1728), eminent Italian composer, churchman, and diplomat.

Steiger, Rand (1957–), important American composer.

Steinberg, William (1899–1978), eminent German-born American conductor.

Steinway (actually **Steinweg**), **Heinrich Engelhard** (1797–1871), German piano manufacturer, founder of Steinway & Sons.

Stern, Isaac (1920–), outstanding Russian-born American violinist.

Steuermann, Eduard (1892–1964), eminent Polish-American pianist, pedagogue, and composer.

Stevens, Halsey (1908–1989), American composer, teacher, and writer on music.

Stevens, Risë (1913–), noted American mezzosoprano.

Still, William Grant (1895–1978), eminent black American composer.

Stockhausen, Karlheinz (1928–), outstanding German composer, a leading proponent of electronic and aleatory composition.

Stokowski, Leopold (1882–1977), spectacularly endowed English-born American conductor.

Stradella, Alessandro (1639–1692), important Italian composer.

Stradivari (Latinized as **Stradivarius**), **Antonio** (1644–1737), celebrated Italian violin maker.

Stratas, Teresa (1938–), outstanding Canadian soprano.

Straus, Oscar (1870–1954), noted Austrian operetta composer.

Strauss, Johann, Jr. (1825–1899), greatly renowned Austrian violinist, conductor, and composer, known as "The Waltz King," son of **Johann Strauss, Sr.**

Strauss, Johann, Sr. (1804–1849), eminent Austrian violinist, conductor, and composer, known as "The Father of the Waltz."

Strauss, Richard (1864–1949), great German composer and distinguished conductor, one of the most inventive music masters of the modern age.

Stravinsky, Igor (1882–1971), great Russian-born French, later American, composer, one of the supreme masters of 20th-century music, whose works exercised profound influence on the direction of 20th-century music.

Strayhorn, Billy (1915–1967), black American jazz pianist, composer, and arranger, associated with Duke Ellington.

Streisand, Barbra (1942–   ), popular American singer and actress.

Styne, Jule (1905–1994), English-born American composer of popular music.

Subotnick, Morton (1933–   ), inventive American composer; husband of **Joan La Barbara.**

Sullivan, Sir Arthur (1842–1900), famous English composer and conductor, famous for his collaborations with the celebrated humorist Sir William Gilbert.

Sun Ra (b. Herman Blount, 1914–1993), innovative black American jazz keyboardist, bandleader, and composer.

Suppé, Franz von (1819–1895), famous Austrian composer.

Süssmayr, Franz Xaver (1766–1803), Austrian composer.

Sutherland, Joan (1926–   ), celebrated Australian soprano.

Suzuki, Shin'ichi (1898–), important Japanese educator and violin teacher, founder of the Suzuki Method of musical instruction through violin playing.

Sweelinck, Jan Pieterszoon (1562–1621), great Dutch organist and composer.

Szell, George (1897–1970), greatly distinguished Hungarian-born American conductor.

Szigeti, Joseph (1892–1973), eminent Hungarian-born American violinist.

Szymanowski, Karol (1882–1937), outstanding Polish composer.

T

Tailleferre, Germaine (1892–1983), significant French composer, the only female member (with Honegger, Milhaud, Poulenc, Auric, and Durey) of "Les Six."

Takahashi, Aki (1944–), innovative Japanese pianist.

Takemitsu, Tōru (1930–), prominent Japanese composer.

Tal, Josef (1910–), prominent German-born Israeli composer.

Tallis, Thomas (c.1505–1585), eminent English organist and composer.

Taneyev, Sergei (1856–1915), significant Russian composer.

Tansman, Alexandre (1897–1986), Polish-born French pianist, conductor, and composer.

Tartini, Giuseppe (1692–1770), famous Italian violinist, music theorist, and composer, noted for his "Devil's Trill."

Tatum, Art (1910–1956), noted black American jazz pianist.

Tausig, Carl (1841–1871), celebrated Polish pianist and composer.

Tavener, John (1944–), important English organist and composer.

Taylor, Cecil (1933–), black American jazz pianist and composer.

Taylor, Deems (1885–1966), greatly popular American composer and writer on music.

Taylor, Raynor (1747–1825), English-American singer, organist, and composer.

Tchaikovsky, Peter Ilyich (1840–1893), outstanding Russian composer, militantly removed from the "Mighty Five," and the most popular composer under the Soviet regime.

Tcherepnin, Alexander (1899–1977), distinguished Russian-born American pianist and composer, son of **Nicolai** and father of **Serge** and **Ivan Tcherepnin.**

Tcherepnin, Ivan (1943–), innovative French-born American composer.

Tcherepnin, Nicolai (1873–1945), noted Russian conductor and composer.

Tcherepnin, Serge (1941–), important French-born American composer and electronic musical instrument inventor.

Tebaldi, Renata (1922–), celebrated Italian soprano.

Te Kanawa, Dame Kiri (1944–), brilliant New Zealand soprano.

Telemann, Georg Philipp (1681–1767), significant German composer.

Tenney, James (1934–), highly influential American pianist, conductor, teacher, and composer.

Terry, Charles Sanford (1864–1936), eminent English music scholar.

Terry, Sonny (b. Saunders Terrell, 1911–1986), innovative black American harmonica virtuoso, singer, and songwriter.

Tertis, Lionel (1876–1975), eminent English violist and teacher.

Tetrazzini, Luisa (1871–1940), celebrated Italian soprano.

Thalberg, Sigismond (1812–1871), celebrated Swiss-born pianist and composer.

Theodorakis, Mikis (1925–   ), important Greek composer.

Theremin, Leon (1896–1994), Russian inventor of the space-controlled electronic instrument that bears his name.

Thibaud, Jacques (1880–1953), celebrated French violinist.

Thomas, Ambroise (1811–1896), noted French composer.

Thomas, Augusta Read (1964–   ), American composer.

Thomas, Michael Tilson (1944–   ), talented American conductor.

Thomas, Theodore (1835–1905), renowned German-American conductor.

Thompson, Oscar (1887–1945), American music critic and editor.

Thompson, Randall (1899–1984), eminent American composer.

Thomson, Virgil (1896–1986), imaginative American composer and singularly brilliant music critic.

Thorne, Francis (1922–   ), noted American composer.

Tibbett, Lawrence (1896–1960), outstanding American baritone.

Tiomkin, Dmitri (1894–1979), Ukrainian-born American film composer.

Tippett, Sir Michael (1905–   ), renowned English composer.

Toch, Ernst (1887–1964), eminent Austrian-born American composer.

Torelli, Giuseppe (1658–1709), famous Italian violinist and composer.

Torke, Michael (1961–), American composer and pianist.

Tormé, Mel (1925–), talented American pop and jazz vocalist, pianist, and composer.

Toscanini, Arturo (1867–1957), great Italian conductor.

Tourel, Jennie (1900–1973), prominent Russian-born American mezzosoprano.

Tournemire, Charles (1870–1939), distinguished French organist and composer.

Tovey, Sir Donald (1875–1940), eminent English music scholar, pianist, and composer.

Tower, Joan (1938–), American composer and pianist.

Trampler, Walter (1915–), eminent German-American violist.

Traubel, Helen (1899–1972), noted American soprano.

Tucker, Richard (1913–1975), brilliant American tenor.

Tucker, Sophie (b. Sophia Abuza, 1884–1966), ribald American entertainer.

Tudor, David (1926–), brilliant American pianist and composer.

Tureck, Rosalyn (1914–), eminent American keyboardist.

Turina, Joaquín (1882–1949), prominent Spanish composer.

U

Uribe-Holguín, Guillermo (1880–1971), eminent Colombian composer.

Ussachevsky, Vladimir (1911–1990), innovative Russian-born American composer.

Ustvolskaya, Galina (1919–   ), important Russian composer.

V

Vaet, Jacobus (c.1529–1567), notable Flemish composer.

Vallee, Rudy (b. Hubert Prior Vallée, 1901–1986), popular American singer, saxophonist, bandleader, and actor.

Van de Vate, Nancy (1930–   ), American composer.

Van Vactor, David (1906–1994), American composer and conductor.

Varèse, Edgard (1883–1965), remarkable French-born American composer who introduced a totally original principle of organizing sound, profoundly influencing the direction of 20th-century music.

Vaughan, Sarah (1924–1990), black American jazz and pop singer and pianist.

Vaughan Williams, Ralph (1872–1958), great English composer whose music is deeply rooted in native folksongs.

Vecchi, Horatio (b. Orazio Tiberio, 1550–1605), significant Italian composer.

Venuti, Joe (1898–1978), Italian-born American jazz violinist.

Verdi, Giuseppe (1813–1901), great Italian opera composer whose genius for dramatic, lyric, and tragic stage music has made him a perennial favorite of opera enthusiasts.

Viardot-García, Pauline (1821–1910), celebrated French mezzosoprano.

Victoria, Tomás Luis de (1548–1611), great Spanish organist and composer.

Vieuxtemps, Henri (1820–1881), celebrated Belgian violinist and composer.

Villa-Lobos, Heitor (1887–1959), remarkable Brazilian composer.

Vincent, John (1902–1977), American composer.

Viotti, Giovanni Battista (1755–1824), famous Italian composer and violinist.

Vitali, Giovanni Battista (1632–1692), significant Italian composer.

Vitry, Philippe de (1291–1361), famous French music theorist, composer, poet, and churchman, also known as Philippus de Vitriaco.

Vivaldi, Antonio (1678–1741), greatly renowned Italian composer, whose works include the perennial favorite of concertos, *The Four Seasons.*

Vladigerov, Pantcho (1899–1978), prominent Bulgarian composer.

Vogel, Wladimir (1896–1984), significant German-Russian-born Swiss composer.

Vogelweide, Walther von der (c. 1170–c. 1230), famous German Minnesinger and poet.

Vogler, Georg Joseph (1749–1814), noted German pianist, organist, music theorist, and composer, also known as Abbé Vogler.

W

Waart, Edo de (1941–   ), noted Dutch conductor.

Wagenaar, Bernard (1894–1971), Dutch-born American violinist, conductor, and composer.

Wagenseil, Georg Christoph (1715–1777), Austrian composer and music theorist.

Wagner, Richard (1813–1883), great German composer whose monumental music dramas, written to his own librettos, radically transformed the concept of stage music.

Waits, Tom (1949–   ), idiosyncratic American songwriter and performer.

Waldstein, Ferdinand Ernst Gabriel (1762–1823), German-Bohemian amateur musician, friend and patron of Beethoven, and dedicatee of Beethoven's *Waldstein Sonata*, op.53.

Waldteufel, Émile (1837–1915), famous French conductor and composer of light music.

Wallenstein, Alfred (1898–1983), American cellist and conductor.

Waller, Thomas "Fats" (1904–1943), noted black American jazz pianist, organist, singer, bandleader, and composer.

Walter, Bruno (1876–1962), eminent German-born American conductor.

Walton, Sir William (1902–1983), eminent English composer.

Ward, Robert (1917–   ), American stage composer.

Warfield, William (1920–   ), noted black American baritone.

Waring, Fred (1900–1984), famous American conductor of popular music and inventor of sundry kitchen appliances.

Waters, Muddy (b. McKinley Morganfield, 1915–1983), black American blues singer, exponent of the Mississippi Delta Blues style.

Watts, André (1946–   ), brilliant American pianist.

Weber, Ben (1916–1979), American composer.

Weber, Carl Maria von (1786–1826), celebrated German pianist, conductor, and composer in the German Romantic tradition.

Webern, Anton von (1883–1945), remarkable Austrian serial composer, innovator of *Klangfarmelodie* and pupil of Arnold Schoenberg.

Weelkes, Thomas (c.1575–1623), important English organist and composer.

Weill, Kurt (1900–1950), remarkable German-born American composer, husband of **Lotte Lenya.**

Weinberger, Jaromir (1896–1967), notable Czech composer.

Weingartner, Felix, Edler von Münzberg (1863–1942), illustrious Austrian conductor.

Weir, Judith (1954–), important Scottish composer.

Weisgall, Hugo (1912–), distinguished Moravian-born American composer.

Weiss, Adolph (1891–1971), influential American composer.

Welk, Lawrence (1903–1992), popular American bandleader and accordionist.

Wellesz, Egon (1885–1974), eminent Austrian-born English composer, musicologist, and pedagogue.

Whiteman, Paul (1890–1967), celebrated American conductor of popular music.

Widor, Charles-Marie (1844–1937), distinguished French organist, pedagogue, and composer.

Wieniawski, Henryk (1835–1880), famous Polish violinist and composer.

Wilbye, John (1574–1638), important English composer.

Wilder, Alec (1907–1980), remarkably gifted American composer, distinguished in both popular and serious music.

Wilhemj, August (1845–1908), famous German violinist.

Willaert, Adrian (c. 1490–1562), important Flemish composer.

Williams, Alberto (1862–1952), prolific Argentine composer.

Williams, Hank (b. Hiram Williams, 1923–1953), American country-music singer, guitarist, and songwriter.

Williams, John (1932–   ), enormously successful American film composer and conductor.

Wilson, Brian (1942–   ), American singer, composer, and producer, founder of the rock group, The Beach Boys.

Wilson, Olly (1937–   ), black American composer.

Winner, Septimus (1827–1902), American composer of popular music.

Wittgenstein, Paul (1887–1961), one-armed Austrian-born American pianist who commissioned concertos for left hand alone from Ravel, Strauss, Prokofiev, and others.

Wolf, Hugo (1860–1903), famous Austrian composer, master of the German lied.

Wolf-Ferrari, Ermanno (1876–1948), famous Italian opera composer.

Wolff, Christian (1934–   ), brilliant French-born American composer of the experimental school.

Wolpe, Stefan (1902–1972), significant German-American composer.

Wonder, Stevie (b. Steveland Judkins Hardaway, 1950–   ), phenomenally successful and enduring black American soul singer, keyboardist, and songwriter.

Wood, Sir Henry (1869–1944), eminent English conductor.

Wuorinen, Charles (1938–   ), respected American composer.

X

Xenakis, Iannis (1922–), eminent Greek-born French composer and music theorist whose training in engineering and architecture led him to derive a "stochastic" method of composition from scientific principles.

Y

Yannay, Yehuda (1937–), Rumanian-born Israeli-American composer.

Yepes, Narciso (1927–), talented Spanish guitarist.

Youmans, Victor (1898–1946), American composer of popular music, including the perennial favorite of songs, "Tea for Two."

Young, La Monte (1935–), American composer of the extreme avant-garde and early proponent of musical Minimalism.

Ysaÿe, Eugène (1858–1931), famous Belgian violinist, conductor, and composer.

Yun, Isang (1917–), important Korean-born German composer.

Z

Zador, Eugene (1894–1977), Hungarian-American composer.

Zappa, Frank (1940–1993), outspoken American rock artist, whose compositions in both popular and serious forms, the latter influenced by the works of Varèse, teem with artfully dissonant counterpoint.

Zarlino, Gioseffo (1517–1590), important Italian music theorist and composer.

Zelter, Carl Friedrich (1758–1832), eminent German composer.

Zemlinsky, Alexander von (1871–1942), important Austrian composer and conductor.

Zender, Hans (1936–   ), German conductor and composer.

Zimbalist, Efrem (1889–1985), eminent Russian-born American violinist and pedagogue.

Zimmermann, Bernd-Alois (1918–1970), important German composer.

Zukerman, Pinchas (1948–   ), outstanding Israeli violinist and conductor.

Zukofsky, Paul (1943–   ), remarkable American violinist and conductor.

Zwillich, Ellen Taaffe (1939–   ), remarkable American composer.